THE COMPLETE
BIRD OWNER'S
HANDBOOK

THE COMPLETE
BIRD OWNER'S
HANDBOOK

Gary A. Gallerstein, D.V.M.

with

Heather Acker, A.H.T.

HOWELL BOOK HOUSE

New York

Macmillan General Reference
A Simon & Schuster Macmillan Company
1633 Broadway
New York, NY 10019-6785

Macmillan Publishing Company is part of the Maxwell Communication Group of Companies.

Library of Congress Cataloging-in-Publication Data
Gallerstein, Gary A., D.V.M.
   The complete bird owner's handbook/by Gary A. Gallerstein with
Heather Acker.
      p. cm.
   Includes bibliographical references and index.
   ISBN 0-87605-903-5
   1. Cage birds. 2. Cage birds—Diseases. I. Acker, Heather.
II. Title.
SF461.G35   1994
636.6'8—dc20   93-2621

10 9

Printed in the United States of America

Dedicated, with love,
to
my wife, Laura,
&
my children, Laura, Eric, and Mitchell

Contents

Contents

MEDICINE

REFERENCES

Dr. Gary Gallerstein and his umbrella cockatoo, Crash.

About the Authors

Gary A. Gallerstein, D.V.M.

Dr. Gallerstein is a practicing veterinarian and owner of Acacia Animal Hospital in Escondido, California. At Acacia, he and his associates take care of over 10,000 patients of all species, including birds, dog, cats, small mammals, reptiles and other exotic pets. Dr. Gallerstein's primary interest is birds, their medical and surgical needs as well as the education of their owners.

Graduating from the School of Veterinary Medicine at the University of California, Davis, in 1978, Dr. Gallerstein began developing his avian medical expertise at a large group practice in San Francisco. He has never looked back. His dedication to avian medicine has been a source of inspiration to many young students. He is an active member of many professional organizations, bird clubs and other animal-related groups. A widely requested speaker at both local and national seminars, as well as all levels of public schools, Dr. Gallerstein stays very involved in his profession.

Dr. Gallerstein realized very early that many bird owners lacked informative, educational material about their birds. He took their needs very seriously, and that concern led to his becoming an author. His first book, *Bird Owner's Home Health and Care Handbook*, published in 1984, has been considered the standard in the bird care field since it first appeared. The goal he had of creating a practical, easy to read, complete guide for bird owners had been met.

Rapid advancements in the field of avian medicine, nutrition and husbandry dictated the need for a more current reference source. Dr. Gallerstein's second book, *The Complete Bird Owner's Handbook*, is even more complete, yet remains as practical and ''user friendly'' as the first.

In his spare time, he and his family enjoy the numerous outdoor activities available in southern California.

Heather Acker, A.H.T., and her yellow-nape
Amazon, Green Thing.

Heather Acker, A.H.T.

Heather was only seven years old when she decided her life's work would involve animals. Childhood dreams do come true! In addition to working in the veterinary medical field since 1974, she is a registered Animal Health Technician (A.H.T.) and has earned her community college teaching credential in animal health. Since 1982, she has been working with Dr. Gallerstein at the Acacia Animal Hospital. Her interest in birds has involved both breeding and medical aspects. In addition, her diverse background also includes working at the San Diego Wild Animal Park in the veterinary department. Heather lives with all her animals (and husband, Bob) on the Renegade Ranch in Ramona, California.

Betty Byers Schmidt

Betty cannot remember a time in her life when she was without a bird. She has been actively involved in breeding birds since 1968. She has owned as many as 300 birds and has handfed as many as eighty to ninety baby birds at one time. Betty believes the success of the captive-bred pet bird population is dependent upon cooperation among breeders. Sharing successes, failures and genetic information is vital to the future of pet birds. A long-term member of the Hookbill Hobbyists, a large San Diego bird club, she is currently on the board of directors. In addition, the new role of "grandma" is keeping her very busy!

Christine Davis

Christine has been an avian behavior consultant since 1974. She works primarily by telephone from her southern California office. The number of worldwide clientele she serves attests to the fact that bird owners are eager to understand their "feathered friends" and are willing to put both time and effort into doing so. Christine feels that the key to raising young birds properly and humanely changing undesirable behaviors of adult birds is to understand the bird's needs and motivations. She urges all animal people to truly appreciate and enjoy their special companions. Most importantly, always love them for what they are— not for what we want them to be.

Mike and Deb Morrison

Mike and Deb Morrison are the owners of D & M Bird Farm in San Diego, California. They are the innovators of "Aquabrood," a baby bird brooder or animal intensive care unit. They both feel the future of aviculture lies in the hands of hobbyists and professional bird breeders. In order to sustain the survival of all currently available species, breeders should specialize in at least one species for aviculture, as well as familiar "pet trade" varieties. Most importantly, breeders should strive to keep complete, accurate records, share experiences and expand their knowledge. They also need to work cooperatively with other breeders to trade offsping to help maintain viable genetic diversity.

Nicole Perretta and her red-tailed hawk, Jamaica.

ILLUSTRATOR/ARTIST

Nicole Perretta

Nicole is an accomplished illustrator at the ripe ''old'' age of twenty-one. She has studied and drawn birds since early childhood. Nicole is a falconer and also rehabilitates injured wild birds. She is working to attain a master's degree, both in fine art and ornithology. Many of her own birds were used as models for this project.

Acknowledgments

THE FIRST EDITION of *The Bird Owner's Home Health and Care Handbook* began as a series of simple informational handouts for our clients and finally evolved into a "real" book. It has been very well received and widely read. An updated revision has long been overdue. Up until recently, however, there hasn't been enough time in my life to undertake the demanding task of rewriting. However, in this edition, there have been others involved in its conception and development. Once again, what began as a simple revision has evolved into an entirely new book.

Heather Acker has helped make this edition a reality. She has greatly assisted with the general health care chapters. Heather, thanks for your hard work and dedication to this project. The rewrite whould have been much more difficult without you!

Thanks are also due to:

Nicole Perretta, artist extraordinaire, for her magnificient drawings. I was indeed fortunate to have found such a young and talented artist with masterful skills far beyond her years.

Betty Byers, aviculturist, for once again giving unselfishly of her time. Her valuable writing contributions and enthusiastic support have been greatly appreciated.

Chris Davis, avian behaviorist, for her much-appreciated contribution on the challenging subject of improving our bird's behavior and for assisting with the section on treatment of feather pickers.

Mike and Deb Morrison, aviculturists, for their much-needed information on baby birds. They have come to realize that writing, even when one is well versed in the subject, requires a lot of effort.

Acknowledgments

Pat Gilman, A.H.T., for assisting with the references, bibilography and numerous other book-related tasks. Thank you for you willingness to take on any task to help get the job done!

Lea Burrell for contributing the home recipes and Jeanne Bennett for cooking and "tasting" them.

Drs. Jeff Glass and Bob Irmiger for reading and making many valuable suggestions for the emergency and disease chapters.

Sally Gallerstein, Susan Gallerstein and Wayne Zucker for their help and encouragement.

The Association of Avian Veterinarians and many fellow avian veterinarians for their numerous contributions to the advancement of avian medicine and surgery. I have indeed been priviledged to learn from, work with and develop friendships with so many dedicated individuals.

Computers and word processing for their astonishing technological capacities. My first book was written in longhand—not even with the benefit of a typewriter! The very demanding task of writing has been made so much easier and even fun!

Mr. Sean Frawley and Mr. Seymour Weiss of Howell Book House. Thank you for being my partners on these writing adventures.

Lastly and very importantly, my wife, Laura. Thank you for sharing me with the computer. Relationships require time, and this past year there has not been much of it to go around. Your support and encouragement has helped make this book possible.

To the Reader

YOUR BIRD should *thank you* for taking the time to read this book. It will help him or her live a longer and healthier life.

The general care recommendations are those most commonly agreed upon by avian health care professionals, and the first aid recommendations provide safe and simple guidelines to follow when your bird is sick. These recommendations have been reviewed and agreed upon by several avian veterinarians. However, they will *not* work in every case. *Your veterinarian should always be consulted first, before any home treatment is attempted and at the earliest signs of disease.*

If the advice of your veterinarian is contrary to that found in this book, be sure to follow his or her prescription for the care of your bird. Veterinarians know best because they will have the benefit of a thorough history and a hands-on examination.

Introduction

WELCOME TO THE WONDERFUL WORLD OF BIRDS! As pet bird ownership reaches staggering proportions, the need for complete, easy-to-understand health care information has become increasingly important. Here are a few interesting statistics: Pet birds now number over 12.9 million, and are found in 5.7 percent of all households; 65 percent of bird owners own a dog, and 47 percent of them own a cat!* Birds are second *only* to cats (dogs are third) in overall pet popularity. These are amazing statistics, and truly support the contention that "birdmania" is sweeping the United States.

Thirsty for knowledge, bird owners have more to learn now than ever before. So much has been learned in the ten years since the first edition of this book was written, we decided to change its name. The new name was chosen for good reason. This second edition is intended to be the *most* complete book available on pet bird care. It has been completely rewritten and contains much more information. Many new chapters have been added, and an abundance of new, updated information has been included in every section. It reflects the advances in nutrition, reproduction and medicine over the past decade.

This rapidly increasing knowledge on the care of pet birds is truly an information explosion. The credit goes to the many dedicated individuals so very willing to share all their knowledge they have learned. In addition, to help spread this new information, many new bird clubs, associations and magazines have been formed. More avicultural conventions and meetings are being held nationwide than ever before. These are all designed to provide a forum for the exchange of information. The wonderful world of pet birds continues to really involve

*From data prepared for the American Veterinary Medical Association, 1988.

people working together toward two very ambitious goals—the advancement of avian care and the survival of rare and endangered species.

This book has been written and designed to help guide the pet bird enthusiast through much of this new information. The format has been specially developed to make this information available in a very "user-friendly" fashion. It is hoped that the book will become a frequently used reference in the care of all pet birds.

From the decision-making process when selecting a bird, to coping with the grief of its loss, every subject in between has been covered. The book has been divided into four new sections, Getting Started, Health Care, Medicine and References. This allows for quicker and easier access to the subjects of the reader's choice.

Getting Started covers two chapters that guide you through selecting the *right* bird and the first few weeks of ownership.

Health Care includes everything readers need to know to keep a bird happy and healthy. Safety in the home, caging, nutrition, baby bird care, grooming and behavior are just a few of the many subjects covered in these six chapters.

Medicine encompasses seven chapters. From basic anatomy and physiology, physicals, diseases, emergencies, veterinarians, home care and pet loss, it's all there. The emergency and disease chapters, along with the Index of Signs, have been designed to help find required information fast when a bird is sick or injured.

References is a wonderful "hodgepodge" of information the reader should find useful. A species guide, (Everything you Always Wanted to Know About . . .) an introduction to bird breeding, bird organizations and publications, environmentally-friendly birdkeeping, and avian research are only some of the valuable lore contained within.

All in all, I'm hoping you find this book the most informative and helpful publication of its type. A word of caution however—this book is *not* intended as a substitute for veterinary care. It is designed to educate the reader about pet birds in sickness and in health. Too often, bird owners don't recognize the early warning signs of illness in their birds. This can allow the disease process to go unnoticed until the bird becomes very sick. My hope it to educate readers on all aspects of birds' health. By so doing, birds will remain healthier and many problems will be avoided. However, like all living creatures, birds will become sick sometime during their lifetime. When this does happen, learn to recognize the very earliest warning signs of disease and get the care your bird needs *before* its condition becomes life threatening. The pet bird of the nineties will continue to be a much healthier and happier bird than ever before.

GARY A. GALLERSTEIN, D.V.M.

BIRD KEEPING: A
Brief History

BIRD KEEPING HAS a long history dating back thousands of years. Evidence suggests birds were probably the first animals kept strictly for pleasure.

Historians believe the Chinese were first to develop an appreciation for the very colorful variety of birds. Birds have been found depicted in earliest Chinese silk paintings and porcelains, objects that date back to almost 4,000 B.C. The sport of falconry first began in China around 2,000 B.C. and by 600 B.C. the Chinese were also using cormorants to fish for them. The Egyptians however, appear to have been the earliest bird keepers; there is an account of Queen Hathepsut collecting hawks and falcons for display in the royal zoo during 1,500 B.C The pigeon, it is believed, was first domesticated by the Egyptians, and their appreciation of birds in general is well documented in their artwork. Second only to the cat, birds are probably the next most popular art image used by the ancient Egyptians.

Alexander the Great has been credited as modern history's founder of aviculture. He abolished the killing of beautiful peacocks for their meat, and had them shipped home to his native Greece. It is said he discovered the ring-necked parakeet, now called Alexander's parakeet. Birds were even taken into battle with the warriors during their conquest of foreign lands.

Aristotle authored many works on the fascinating world of birds. These were based on descriptions of birds brought back by Alexander the Great. *Psittace,* a pet bird Aristotle frequently wrote about, formed the basis of the scientific name for the parrot family—Psittacine.

Bird Keeping: A Brief History

During the Roman Empire, many homes had large aviaries built to house pigeons, and raucous magpies were kept to announce the arrival of visitors. The Romans introduced bird keeping to most of Europe, and are condidered to have been the first bird traders. The Portuguese, however, with their large sailing fleets, are credited with the introduction of the canary to Europe. Thus began a love affair of Europeans with bird keeping. And breeding the canary to produce its distinctive yellow color has formed the basis for much of the avian genetic information we have today.

The eighteenth century marked the beginning of the bird fancy as we know it today. Almost any stately home in Europe could boast an aviary filled with beautiful birds. With the introduction of the budgerigar (common parakeet, or "budgie"), serious bird fanciers were on their way. England was a true pioneer in the field of aviculture, and the English influence on bird breeding and husbandry over the years has been remarkable.

The Avicultural Society of America, the first American bird club, was founded in 1927, and was a sister club to the Avicultural Society of England. During the 1950s the United States experienced a dramatic increase in ownership in pet birds, primarily the "budgie." This marked the beginning of a literal explosion of pet bird keeping in America. The 1970s saw the beginning of the introduction of wild-caught parrots as pets. In the 1980s and 1990s we've seen and continue to see the amazing success of domestically produced birds for the pet trade. Bird clubs and societies, bird magazines and bird specialty stores continue to grow in popularity. "Birdmania" continues to sweep our country and the world!

Getting Started

Scarlet Macaw
Loving
$ (May Bite)

Cockatiel
Good
$ Whistler

Blue-fronted
Amazon
Good
$ Talker

1

Buying Your Bird

Suggestions for Selecting the Right Bird for You

BIRDS can be found in a magnificent assortment of colors, sizes, personalities and prices! *Prior* to acquiring a new bird, plan to spend some time researching the type of bird best suited to your particular life-style. Remember, your new feathered friend is going to become a member of your family and could even live to be a hundred years old or more. This could be truly a lifetime investment!

Birds are more than beautiful, animated, (in some cases) talking creatures. Most of us have not grown up with pet birds and therefore don't realize that they have their own individual personalities and unique characteristics, and that each species has certain predictable qualities and requirements. These factors *must* be considered during the decision-making process to help ensure the best possible match between owner and pet.

Before you invest, use the following guidelines to help match your needs with some of the more important considerations involved in selecting the perfect bird for you. Above all, the more informed you are, the better chance you have of living happily ever after with the bird of your dreams.

EVERYTHING YOU ALWAYS WANTED TO KNOW ABOUT SELECTING PET BIRDS*

What is your purpose or reason for wanting a bird? Companionship? Hobby? Aviculture (bird breeding)? Child's pet? Cagemate (companion for an-

*but never thought to ask!

other bird)? Home decoration? Identifying the purpose or reason begins the selection process and helps to narrow down the possible choices.

How much time do you have to spend with your bird? On a daily basis, consider food preparation, cleaning, training and playtime, Certain species in general, and certain birds in particular, will simply demand more of your time. A good rule of thumb is, the larger and more tame the bird, the more time its care will require.

How much space do you have in your home to keep a bird? Cage size may be an important consideration. In general, cage size is directly proportional to the size of the bird (see Appendix A).

What personality traits are most important to you? Some birds are playful, some cuddly and very loving. Some sing or talk, some are aggressive, and some just prefer to be left alone. Remember the character traits you would like when interviewing prospective candidates. Begin your selection process by identifying the species that most represents the qualities you desire in a pet bird. In addition, with love and proper training, most birds become wonderful additions to the family.

General behavorial characteristics of the various species have been omitted from this section. The species guide (Appendix A) page provides information on basic personality traits.

Do you want a talker? Remember birds don't actually talk, they simply mimic sounds they hear. Talking ability can be difficult to evaluate. In a strange or stressful environment, birds are usually more quiet. Even when brought home, many birds will not begin to talk until they feel more secure in their new surroundings. Unfortunately, there are *no* guarantees a bird will talk. A young bird, even from a species well known for talking ability, may not "grow up" to be a good talker. The best bet is to obtain a bird with an already established vocabulary. For information on teaching your bird to talk, refer to Chapter 6.

What can you afford to pay for a bird? The cost is important, but over the years the original price paid will become increasingly less important if your bird provides the happiness and rewards that you were anticipating. Many factors determine cost. These include availability, imported vs. domestically raised, age and personality. Remember to include the cost of housing (cage, playpen, etc), food and health care in your proposed budget.

What about cleanliness? Birds can be messy. Although this fact is often forgotten with the excitement of purchasing a new bird, it nevertheless needs to be remembered. The larger the bird and the more time spent out of its cage, the more there will be to clean up. Expect to vacuum more frequently to clean up spilled food, feathers and droppings.

Is the destructiveness of a bird a concern? Parrots, if given the opportunity, will often damage personal property. They often love to chew, scratch and play with all sorts of different things. The larger the bird, the more potential for damage. When birds are out of their cage, they should always be supervised.

How much noise, if any, is tolerable? Do you have close neighbors that might object? Some birds and some species in general tend to be more noisy than others. Most birds vocalize at sunup, sundown, when they want attention and often when the mood just simply suits them.

What age bird would you like? There are both advantages and disadvantages to a young versus adult bird. Young birds are usually more easily tamed and trained. They will more readily accept a variety of foods, and this will help insure better long-term health. But, like a young puppy, they demand more time. On the other hand, adult birds are usually more calm and sedate and their personalities are more predictable. However, their previous history is unknown, and they can be more set in their ways. Determining age in mature birds is very difficult and *usually* impossible.

What is the source of the bird? Imported? Domestically raised?

Imported birds, once the mainstay of the pet bird trade, are increasingly becoming more difficult to obtain. Although these birds are generally less expensive than their domestically raised counterparts, initially they are usually more stressed, frightened and defensive. However, although unpredictable, these birds over time and with proper taming techniques may become loving pets.

Domestically raised birds are quickly becoming the more common and certainly the preferred type of pet bird. These birds have been raised around humans and are simply more accepting of the home environment.

Author's Note: Smuggled birds are unfortunately a reality, especially in states bordering Mexico. They are less expensive, but speaking as an experienced avian veterinarian, let me assure you they are often plagued with serious health problems. They are often sold at swap meets, street corners and directly from cars and vans. Such birds should never be purchased, and those selling them should be reported to the proper authorities.

PARROT CONSERVATION

Protecting all birds, especially endangered ones, is the responsibility of all bird fanciers.

> . . . Where is man without the beasts?
> If the beasts were gone, men would die
>   from a great loneliness of spirit
> For whatever happens to the beasts
>   soon happens to man . . .
> —*Indian Chief Seattle, 1854*

Where do pet parrots come from? This is difficult to imagine when visiting your local pet shop. Many parrots are now facing extinction due to mass exportation from their countries of origin. In addition, lush rain forests have been destroyed due in part to capturing parrots for the pet bird trade.

The long-term survival of *all* birds is dependent on preserving their natural habitats and maintaining a stable population in the wild. This is essential for their reproduction and subsequent survival.

Many new laws and regulations have been or are being written to prevent wild birds from entering the pet bird trade. Fortunately, there is no more importation of wild-caught birds for the pet bird trade.

Parrot conservation is in its infancy. The combined efforts of both aviculturists and recently formed organizations to protect endangered parrot species will help insure the survival of these magnificent creatures.

What can you do?

- Buy only domestically raised birds.
- Become an aviculturist.
- Support a parrot conservation organization (see Appendix D).

HEALTH: THE *MOST* IMPORTANT CONCERN

You've given much time and thought to the type of bird that best fits your life-style. You've looked at lots of birds, shopped around and are ready to buy. PROCEED WITH CAUTION . . . ! Is the bird healthy? For many soon-to-be new pet bird owners this notion is simply never considered.

Fortunately, *most* newly purchased birds *are* healthy, especially those acquired from a reputable bird seller. It is very difficult to imagine that this new

Do your part to help ensure the long-term survival of all of our magnificent birds. This umbrella cockatoo has been domestically bred and raised. It was never a part of any natural environment. *(Bonnie Jay)*

bird you are about to buy might be sick. However, all living creatures can become ill.

What can be done to minimize the chances of acquiring a sick bird?

- Read and reread Chapter 10 and any other related information you may have.
- Observe your prospective new bird, and others nearby, very closely for any signs of disease.
- Look at the cleanliness and overall appearance of the facility housing the birds.
- Ask the seller about a health guarantee and make every effort to get it in writing.
- Either before you buy or immediately afterward have your new bird examined by an avian veterinarian.

There are costs involved with a veterinary examination. Is it worth it? Your bird is going to be a member of the family for many years to come. An exam is similar to insurance—it will help protect against the possibility of unplanned medical expenses in the future. If a health guarantee is offered, it's usually valid for only a few days after the sale. Since there are often substantial costs involved

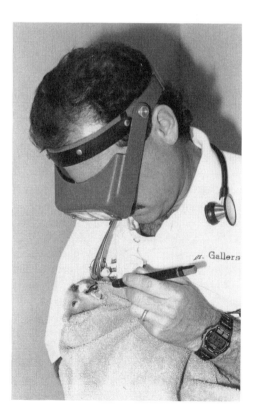

All newly acquired birds should be examined by an avian veterinarian as soon as possible.

with purchasing a new bird, it would be money well spent to protect your investment. Last but not least, there is the possibility of birds transmitting disease to other birds and even to humans. To help protect you and your family, a checkup is a wise choice.

For information on health exams and locating an avian veterinarian in your area, refer to Chapter 13.

WHERE TO BUY . . .

Birds can be purchased from pet stores, bird stores, commercial breeders, auctions or individuals (swap meets, garage sales, newspaper ads). For the inexperienced buyer, it is best to purchase a bird from a pet store knowledgeable about birds or an experienced breeder. These people have a reputation to protect. They should offer a health guarantee and, ideally, an exchange policy should you later decide the bird is not the one for you.

Buying from an individual is more risky. If the bird is a previously owned pet, it may have an unfavorable aggressive or noisy personality, be destructive or have a hidden illness. However, there are always going to be exceptions. Sometimes a loved family pet will need a new home. Just be extra cautious, to ensure the bird has the qualities you most desire. Auctions are also risky—in this fast-paced environment there is little time to properly evaluate all the criteria discussed in this chapter.

For good recommendations ask your bird-owning friends, bird club members and avian veterinarians. Look at lots of birds, listen to what the seller has to say and ask questions. Take your time and don't be in a hurry. Remember, you'll be living with your decision!

LEG BANDS: WHAT ARE THEY FOR?

Most birds commercially sold will have a metal band around the lower part of one of their legs. This is a leg band, and it's found in a variety of shapes, sizes and colors. It's a very simple identification system.

Closed bands ("seamless" bands) form a continuous circle, like a ring, and denote a domestically bred bird. These bands are placed on the legs of very young birds. The numbers, letters or design engraved on the band indicates, in code, the breeder and sometimes the birth date of the bird. For parakeets, the law requires they all be banded. Also, some states now require *all* birds domestically raised to be closed banded. In addition, these same states require that *all* birds for sale be closed banded.

Open bands have a small break in the circle. All legally imported birds must pass through federal quarantine procedures, and during this time a band is placed on one of the legs. Each quarantine station has it own identifying marks, and this is noted on the band.

Leg bands serve a useful purpose. However, they can also cause problems (see Chapter 11).

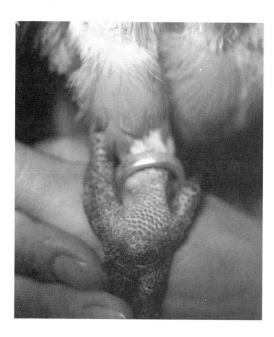

Closed leg bands, such as this one, are used to indicate a bird that has been domestically bred.

IN CONCLUSION . . .

Birds make wonderful pets, but during the selection process much time and thought must be given. If it's the *right* bird for you, it will bring many years of happiness. Be especially careful when buying a so-called "bargain bird." The best bargain is a healthy bird with a good temperament.

Open leg bands identify a bird that has been legally imported into the United States.

9

"How much is that birdie in the box?"

2

Your New Bird

The Do's and Don't's

"An ounce of prevention is worth a pound of cure"
—Old proverb

CONGRATULATIONS! You have a new bird! Please think about all the changes your new friend has just gone through. In addition, combine these with all the changes its new life will bring. Adapting to all these stresses is a lot to ask of any living creature.

Introducing a bird into a new environment means new sights, sounds and smells. A whole new world of sensory perceptions opens up. Each bird will react differently to its new surroundings, and it will take time to adjust to these changes. Some birds will adapt very quickly, while others require more time.

During this adjustment period, allow time for your bird to just be itself. When first bringing your bird home, do everything possible to minimize changes in its environment. Allow the normal behavior to develop. Take the time to first become familiar with your own bird's personality.

Remember to be very careful moving around your new bird. During this very early adjustment time, a loud noise or quick hand movement could startle your pet and delay the confidence building you must now establish. Also, if frightened or startled, the bird could bite. You can see how important these early contacts are to the future of the relationship.

A common mistake new bird owners make is expecting too much of their new pet too soon. It takes time to get to know your new friend, and vice versa: birds tend to be conservative. On average you can expect this adjustment period to take about one month.

STRESS

Stress, as defined by *Webster's Dictionary*, is "a physical, chemical or emotional factor that causes bodily or mental tension and may be a factor in disease causation." It's important to understand that all new birds are stressed to some degree. This is highly dependent on the individual bird. Age, captive vs. domestic status, breeding cycle, and health all play a significant role in the amount of stress an individual bird will be under at any given time. Let's look at what stress does to the body.

Nature has given all animals, including birds and humans, a fight or flight response. This allows them to cope with stress and avoid danger. When confronted with a stressor (something that causes stress), certain changes occur in the chemical makeup of the body. This assists the animal in running faster to get away from the stress, or helps protects the body if a fight ensues. Thus, "fight or flight"! This is truly a phenomenal occurrence. Providing the stressor goes away, the body can return to normal. In animals, if the stressors never go away, they will have to live with these chemical, physical and emotional changes.

Just how do these changes affect a bird? Stress causes decreased resistance to disease. This is due to their immune system being supressed during periods of stress. It can also lead to other problems throughout the body.

Minimizing your bird's exposure to stress will play an important part in its overall health. Stress is a part of everyday life; however, the key is to lessen it. Let's look at some of the most common causes of stress in a pet bird and see which ones we can work to eliminate or at least keep to a minimum.

CAUSES OF STRESS

- New home/new owners
- Separation anxiety from cagemate or previous owner
- Temperature extremes
- Overcrowding
- Daylight/darkness excesses (greater than fifteen hours per day of either)
- Inadequate caging
- Loud noises
- Harassment from other animals (including man)
- Poor nutrition, changes in diet
- Molting
- Breeding
- Disease

MINIMIZING STRESS: GUIDELINES FOR THE FIRST MONTH OR SO OF OWNERSHIP

Do buy your bird from a reliable source. This is one of the most important things you can do to combat stress. It will greatly reduce the problems encountered.

Do obtain as much basic information on your new bird as possible. For example, what is the normal diet, what type of cage has it been in, what toys does it like or dislike? These questions will help you to create an environment that is as similar as possible to your new bird's past. This is not to say those circumstances cannot be changed, but remember change is stressful, and during these first few weeks, minimizing stress is an important priority. (Of course, if the conditions the bird was being kept in before you acquired it were unhealthy or dangerous, immediate change is for the better. Remember, there are no set rules—every situation is different.)

Do get a health checkup for your bird. Detecting any physical problems early will help minimize the long-term effects of illness. Many health guarantees require a new bird exam by a veterinarian.

Do allow time for the bird to acclimate to its new environment. This varies with each individual bird. If your new bird has been well socialized and likes attention, then continue to give it. This is where a good history can help ("He likes to be scratched here, but hates to be touched there"). Knowing what type of attention the bird likes will help minimize stress. If your bird is not accustomed to people and not well socialized, give it "space." During this period, keep handling and interruptions to a minimum.

Do ensure plenty of rest and relaxation. Quiet time is very important. Allow maximum time for sleeping, and realize that total darkness is important for sleep. Cage covers can be used if needed, but only if your bird is accustomed to one. Otherwise, you may be adding a new stress.

Do isolate the new bird for a thirty-day period from any other birds you might have. Keep the newcomer in a separate room and avoid cross-contamination of food and water bowls. This will help to prevent the spread of disease if there is a hidden problem.

Do provide the ideal cage environment (see the section on caging in Chapter 3). Introduce new cage toys and other accessories slowly over time.

Do keep the new bird's diet similar to what has been fed. Try to introduce new foods slowly, but always keep an adequate supply of the previous diet available unless it is very deficient.

Do keep the cage area warm. Birds can expend tremendous amounts of energy trying to stay warm. Provide warmth and the bird can conserve energy for other essential life functions. An ambient temperature of 75° to 80°F is ideal, and avoid cold drafts and the consequences they can bring.

Do consider having the wings trimmed if the bird will be allowed out of its cage on a playpen or with you. This will prevent flying away or flying accidents that frequently happen.

SAFETY CHECKLIST

- Poisonous plants
- Paint fumes, insecticides and other poisons
- Windows—closed, opened or conducting direct sunlight on the cage causing overheating

- Mirrors
- Ceiling fans, cold drafts
- Smoke
- Kitchen—open pots on stove, hot dishwater
- Teflon pan burning, causing toxic fumes
- Lead—paint, drapery and fishing weights, stained-glass caulking, toys
- Spoiled foods, moldy grains, unwashed fruits, vegetables
- Long toe nails, beaks
- Cages—sharp edges, bars too wide, broken bars
- Other household pets, inquisitive children

THE DON'T'S

Don't expect too much too soon. New bird owners are frequently unrealistic in their expectations of their new bird. Untamed birds cannot be "broken" overnight, and birds cannot always adjust quickly to new foods overnight. Birds also can't be trained to talk overnight. These desired behaviors require time, effort and trust. Once again, have patience. Create a lasting relationship based on trust, not fear.

Don't create too many changes at once. Remember, everyone is a stranger to your new bird. Avoid parading your friends and neighbors in front of its cage for now. Wait until the adjustment period is well under way and then slowly introduce the bird to new people.

SPECIAL CONSIDERATIONS

Baby birds are most sensitive to changes in temperature, food and environment. Therefore, learn as much as possible about baby bird care *prior* to purchase (see Chapter 5).

Health Care

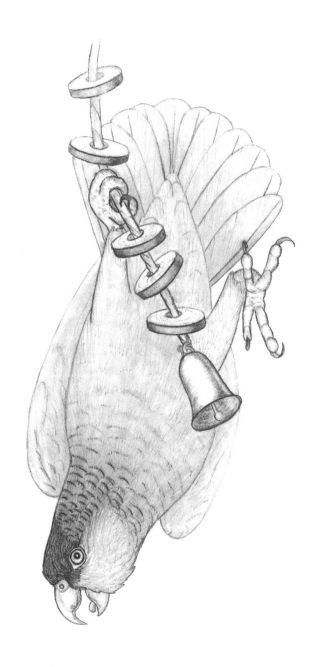

Health Care

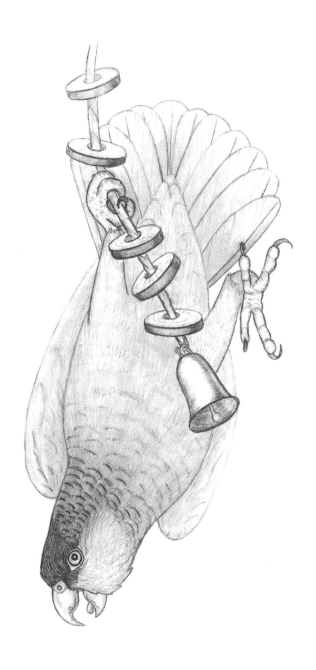

3

Creating a Happy Environment

Home Safety, Proper Caging and Travel Tips

CREATING a happy environment involves providing a place your bird can call home, where it has all the basic necessities of life. Foremost in these necessities is security, feeling safe from danger. Food, water and entertainment are very high on the list as well. Successfully providing this "home sweet home" for your bird requires considerable thought and planning.

This chapter will cover all the essentials that make up a happy environment for your bird. Safety, proper caging, toys and safe, responsible travel tips are discussed.

INTRODUCING YOUR BIRD TO OTHER FAMILY MEMBERS: CHILDREN AND ANIMALS

Bringing a new bird into your home is a very exciting event for the entire family. However, this is also the most dangerous time for all involved. "Bird-proofing" your home may not yet have been done. Precautions must be taken to ensure that injury will not occur to your new pet or other family members during this getting-acquainted period.

Children

Safety and intelligent guidance are the keys to allowing children to interact with pet birds. Not only can beaks and claws cause injuries, but loud squawks can frighten youngsters. On the other hand, children can also pose a danger to the well-being and happiness of our pet birds.

Age of the child is not so much an issue as is an understanding of living things, and the respect that they *must* be accorded. Children must be taught not to put fingers, hands or faces into or up against the cage. Teasing must be avoided. Children don't always know what constitutes teasing, and the concept must be taught. They must learn not to feed anything to the bird without permission. Older children must be cautioned on the use of cleaning products, chemicals and aerosols around birds. Above all, supervision is the key. Keep your eyes and ears tuned to potential problems. Remember also that kids are constantly going outside, opening and closing doors. Make sure the bird is secure in its cage and the possibility of escape has been eliminated.

Birds and children together are a wonderful sight to behold. The opportunity for your child to grow up with a bird as a companion is a treasured gift that must be treated accordingly. The future of aviculture is in the hands of our children. Encourage their interest and teach them well.

Dogs And Cats

Contrary to popular belief, birds, cats, and dogs can mix well in the same household, but it takes planning and extra thought. Remember that cats and dogs

Birds and children can share wonderful friendships. Before introducing the two, consider both the temperament of the bird and the maturity of the children.

are hunters by nature, and a bird's quick movements are attractive to them. The damage caused by dogs and cats to pet birds is most often very serious or even fatal. It is paramount to understand the possible dangers involved when different species are kept under the same roof.

Small birds such as "budgies," canaries and lovebirds move about very quickly in their cages, and this stimulates a cat's attention. Cats are very attracted to brightly colored objects that move quickly. It is therefore essential to keep your smaller birds protected from the curious and agile cat. Remember that cats can jump, climb and reach many places never thought possible. Not all cats will be interested in birds, but for those that are, constant vigilance is imperative.

Larger species such as Amazons and macaws are intimidating to cats and are in less danger. Dogs pose the greatest risk to larger birds. Birds on the floor or outside their cages are most susceptible. Even the most mellow dog may snap if bitten or teased by a bird. Always be close by when birds and dogs are in the same room. Prevent a tragedy before it happens.

Other Birds

Once the pet bird "bug" has struck, acquiring more birds is the next step. When introducing a new bird to a home with other birds, there are some important points to consider. First, keep the new bird completely separated from your existing birds for thirty days. This will help to minimize the potential for disease spread.

Begin by only keeping the same species together, "budgies" with "budgies," cockatiels with cockatiels and so on. Larger birds may not "mix" as well. When trying to get birds acquainted with each other, first keep them in their own cages, in the same room, at a safe distance. Next, gradually move the cages closer. Try leaving both cage doors open with the cages facing each other, and let the birds meet when they are ready. The first actual meeting should be outside of either cage, on neutral ground if possible, especially with the larger birds. Make sure they are well supervised and have emergency plans at the ready, if the need arises, to separate them in a hurry. *Never* leave the area until you are convinced the birds will be completely compatible.

Many serious injuries can result when strange birds are left together unsupervised. "An ounce of prevention is worth a pound of cure" cannot be emphasized enough. More than once bird owners have sadly admitted, "I never thought this would happen." But it could! Don't let it happen to you. Use common sense and proceed cautiously when first introducing your beloved pet bird to other animals.

SAFETY AROUND THE HOME

Creating a happy environment means keeping your bird safe from the dangers found in today's modern homes. Birds, because of their small size and delicate respiratory system, are especially susceptible to household hazards. Common household items never considered dangerous to humans, dogs and cats could quickly become life threatening to birds. Becoming aware of these potential perils will help prevent some common disasters with your bird.

Wings and Toenails

Surprising to most people, the easiest way to *prevent* a host of emergencies is to keep your bird's wings and nails trimmed (see Chapter 8). Some of the most common tragedies involve birds flying into objects such as ceiling fans. Also, they can mistakenly land in boiling water, hot oil or even a bowl of soup. By keeping the wings trimmed, you can prevent these accidents from ever happening. Also, long toenails can easily get snagged in carpet, cages and toys, increasing the chance of injury to your bird.

Open Windows and Doors

Birds can escape through open windows and doors. Some birds like perching on top of doors and have been injured when the door is closed. Also, while following an owner out of a room, they could be caught in a closing door. Birds have also been known to fly into sliding glass doors, windows and mirrors, perhaps not realizing they are solid objects. Cover mirrors and place stickers on sliding glass doors if birds are allowed to fly free in the home.

Kitchen Hazards

Kitchens are the most dangerous room in the home for your bird. Hot stoves, boiling water and oil, cooking fumes, dishwater and a battery of small kitchen appliances could all prove deadly to your bird. Birds' natural curiosity can get them into trouble they might not get out of. Therefore, birds should *not* be allowed into this room. However, many bird owners will continue to allow their pets into the kitchen. If this is going to be the case with you, become aware of these dangers and use good common sense.

Caution!! The fumes from overheated nonstick cooking surfaces can be deadly to birds (see Chapter 11). These kinds of cooking surfaces should not be used in a home with birds. Be sure to read labels before buying and examine those items already in the home. If any of these products have nonstick surfaces, consider giving them to a ''birdless'' friend. Replace them with other types of cookware not dangerous to birds.

These utensils *could* have non-stick surfaces:

- Pots and pans
- Cookie sheets
- Waffle irons and other appliances
- Drip pans for your stove
- Irons and ironing board covers

Examples of products that are or can be Teflon coated.   *(Bonnie Jay)*

Fumes

Due to the nature of the respiratory tract of birds, they are extremely sensitive to chemical fumes, smoke and environmental toxins. In addition to kitchen-produced odors, paint fumes, pesticides and smoke are the most common problem areas. For a more complete list of these potential poisons, refer to *Common Household Poisons* in Chapter 11.

Whenever any odor-producing chemicals are used in the home, birds should be removed for at least twenty-four to forty-eight hours, or until all detectable smells have disappeared. For everyday household odors, air filters can be helpful.

Drowning

Toilets, partially empty beverage glasses, and dishwater are all potential dangers to a curious bird. Some birds may try to drink from a toilet and fall in. Birds might also try to drink from a partially empty beverage glass and fall in. They can actually drown in as little as half an inch of fluid. If this could be your bird, take the necessary precautions.

Lead

Lead poisoning is a real threat to birds. A bird's natural curiosity and strong beak makes peeling and swallowing this soft metal very easy. Unfortunately, there are still sources of lead in our home environment. It is extremely toxic to

This innocent-looking scene of a bird drinking from a glass of water could actually result in a dangerous situation. Any open containers of water or other liquid can lead to drowning, burns or poisoning.

birds and care should be taken to identify and remove any potential sources. See Chapter 11 for more information.

Poisonous Plants

Many people do not realize some of their favorite plants could be poisonous. Once again, the natural curiosity of birds, their ability to fly and their need to chew, makes any plant a possible target. Plants serve a very special function in our homes. They are very pleasing to the eye and in addition help to filter environmental toxins out of the air. Experts frequently recommend one plant for every one hundred square feet of space in your home.

In selecting plants for your home, make sure they are nonpoisonous. If needed, a nursery can identify plants already in the home. See Chapter 11, for a complete listing of poisonous plants.

Safe Plants for the Home

Acacia	Figs: creeping, rubber,	Pittosporum
African violet	fiddle leaf, laurel	Pothos
Aloe	leaf, weeping	Prayer plant
Baby's tears	Monkey plant	Purple passion
Bamboo	Mother-in-law's tongue	Schefflera (umbrella)
Begonia	Nasturtium	Sensitive plant
Bougainvillea	Natal plum	Spider plant
Chickweed	Norfolk island pine	Swedish ivy
Christmas cactus	Palms: areca, date, fan,	Thistle
Cissus (Kangaroo vine)	lady, parlour,	Wandering jew
Dracaena varieties	howeia, kentia,	White clover
Ferns: asparagus, birds	Phoenix, sago	Zebra plant
nest, maidenhair,	Peperomia	
Boston	Petunia	

HOW TO PREVENT POISONING IN YOUR BIRD

- Make sure food and water is always fresh
- Wash all fruits and vegetables prior to feeding
- Many household products are potentially poisonous; keep out of bird's reach
- Do not use any products with strong fumes such as cleaning products around your bird
- Do not use any fungicides, herbicides, insecticides or rodenticides around your bird. If you must use them, consult your avian veterinarian first as to which are the safest products and what is the safest way to use them.
- Do not let your bird near house plants. Both of you will be grateful.
- Do not leave cigarettes or other tobacco products around where your bird can get to them.
- The kitchen area presents special problems especially for free-flying birds. Use caution!
- Consult your avian veterinarian if any potential problems with your bird are noticed.

TEMPERATURE AND HUMIDITY

Most birds are from tropical environments where the temperature is always warm and the humidity is high. Few areas in the Northern Hemisphere can duplicate these conditions. Fortunately for us, most birds will still thrive in conditions different from their natural habitats.

Many birds are kept in outdoor aviaries year round without any noticeable problems. Most pet birds are kept indoors with relatively little temperature variation. Birds should be kept warm—68° to 75° F is ideal. However, most will still do fine in the 60° to 90° F range. Any greater temperature extremes may be

Birds are curious creatures. When given the opportunity, they will often chew on many potentially harmful objects. Birds should not be left unsupervised at liberty in the home.

dangerous. It is *very* important that any temperature changes be made *gradually*. Rapid temperature changes can cause problems for birds maintained in a controlled environment.

Heating your bird's environment is a necessity in many areas of the country, and doing it safely is as important for the humans involved as it is for the birds. Fire hazards must be avoided, as well as the potential for carbon dioxide poisoning.

The sun's rays can be used for heating. Be careful, though, of the magnifying effects windows can have. On a hot day, birds can become overheated in a cage sitting too close to a window.

Electric space heaters can be used, but be careful of the fire hazard. Use them only in areas free of clutter and falling bird dust and feathers.

Infrared heat lamps are commonly used to provide accessory heat for birds. Use the 250-watt amber bulbs. This color is more relaxing and allows the bird to sleep at night. These lamps get very hot, so the light fixture must be properly rated to accept these high-wattage bulbs. Do not allow anything to come in contact with the bulb or fixture. Also, make sure the fixture is securely attached and will not fall over.

Heating pads must be used with extreme caution. Birds can chew on them or be burned. They are not designed for use with birds, so extra thought and fire precautions must be taken. Make sure the pad cannot be reached by the bird's beak. Birds must be allowed room to move away from a heat source if they become too warm. Therefore, pads should be placed near the sides of the cage and not beneath it.

Wood-burning stoves and kerosene heaters require oxygen to burn. Therefore, always keep a window slightly open when using this type of heating for you and your birds. Smoke and fumes may also pose a risk.

A thermometer can be located near the cage to accurately monitor the temperature. Also, during the winter, an air filter can be used, since windows are usually kept closed. In areas with long periods of extended darkness, a special ultraviolet light available at pet stores can provide benefits similar to sunlight.

Humidity is very important—the higher the better. In a dry environment, spraying and bathing your bird frequently is highly recommended.

FIRE/DISASTER PREPAREDNESS

No one likes to thinks about calamities. However, birds are more susceptible to smoke from a fire than any other animal. Quick response is essential in an emergency if birds are to be saved. As with your family's emergency plans, create one for your birds.

Can the cage be picked up and carried to safety? Does it have wheels that work? Is there clear access out of the house for a large cage? Can the bird be removed from its cage if disaster strikes? If so, where would it be put for safekeeping?

Here are some ideas to consider. Have an emergency kit for your bird. It will be different from a standard first-aid kit. There would be supplies in it for coping with a natural disaster. Nonperishable food and water, cups and a towel for restraint should all be available. These can be stored in a small carrier that can house your bird and be used for emergency transport.

Quick response is necessary during a disaster. Practice your family's plan on a regular basis. Everyone in the family should know what to do with your feathered friend and other pets in the event of a fire, earthquake, hurricane, tornado or other natural disaster.

STOLEN AND LOST BIRDS

With a little luck and careful planning, you will never experience the heartache of losing a bird. Never forget, it can happen to even the most conscientious owner.

To keep from losing your bird, the wings should always be properly trimmed. However, if your bird does manage to escape, keep calm and use its personality to your full advantage. First, always try and keep your bird in sight, or at least note the direction in which it's traveling. Use a favorite food, toy, companion bird, whistle, song or anything else you can think of to attract its attention. If your escaped bird is in a tree, slowly and calmly try coaxing it down. If that's not possible, sometimes wetting its feathers with a hose will prevent it from being able to fly. Be careful, however; this effort could also cause the bird to become frightened and fly away.

Put the bird's cage outside where the bird might see it. If there is another bird in the house, put it outside also. The sight and sound of its friend may entice your bird home. Immediately notify neighbors of the loss. Post signs and contact the newspaper. Don't give up.

Theft of a bird usually occurs without warning. This is more of a problem for bird breeders than for the single bird owner. It is also most likely to occur with more expensive birds, such as macaws and cockatoos. If starting a breeding program or amassing a large collection of birds is a consideration, keep these safeguards in mind:

- Never "brag" about your birds to strangers. Make sure the background noise on your answering machine doesn't "advertise" your birds.
- When purchasing bird supplies from strangers, consider paying cash. Checks have names and addresses on them.
- Never leave your bird unattended. This includes the backyard, car or anywhere else. It only takes seconds for a thief to strike.
- Take pictures of your bird, and record its voice and any words or sayings it knows.

Bird Identification

There are a couple of ways to positively identify your bird if it is lost or stolen. One is to have a small microchip implanted under the skin. This microchip

For positive identification a tiny microchip is being implanted beneath the skin of this Amazon parrot.

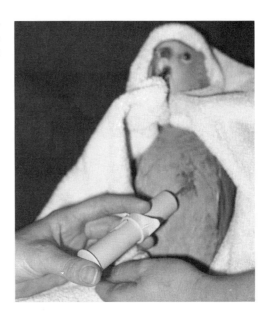

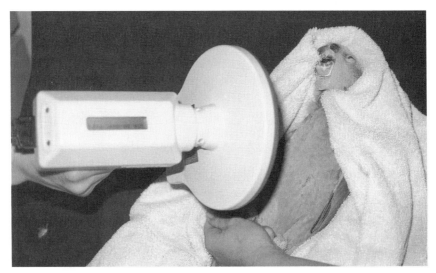

An electronic reading device quickly scans the bird for its microchip, which contains the one-of-a-kind identification number.

A close-up of the reading device displays this bird's personal ID number.

remains with your bird for life. Each bird will have its own identification code. If the bird is ever lost or stolen, positive identification can be easily and quickly made. These systems are rapidly becoming more generally available.

Another method of positive identification involves chromosome mapping of a bird's own blood. This process is most commonly used for sex identification. However, your bird's unique "map" can be stored and kept in a registry. If your bird becomes lost and there is question of ownership, a drop of blood can be taken, a new "map" made and compared to the one on file. No two birds will ever have the same "map." Therefore, ownership can be proven by identical "maps." This appears to be a foolproof method of identification.

The disadvantages of both systems are that they require time and some small expense to have them done, demand cooperation from at least one other party, and are not visible. However, either system can help and both are recommended. Remember, these must both be done *before* the need might arise. Contact your veterinarian for additional information.

CAGING (HOME SWEET HOME)

"Home is where the heart is." Whether for animals or humans, the home should be a place of security and a safe sanctuary where peace and happiness exists. These thoughts should be remembered for your bird when selecting caging. In addition, convenience and cleanliness are two very important factors in selecting a cage. It is not as easy as one may think to provide housing that meets all these requirements.

Size

The dimensions of the cage must be adequate for the size of the bird. For instance, a macaw wingspan can be thirty-six inches. In order to provide enough space to live, a macaw cage should have opposing sides that are greater than thirty-six inches apart. An ideal rule of thumb is that the cage should allow the bird to maximally extend its wings in all directions.

Smaller birds such as "budgies," canaries and lovebirds are more flight oriented, and their cages should be designed to allow for this. In general, the bigger cage is preferable. However, the larger the cage the more cleaning will be involved.

Bar Spacing

The spaces between the bars of the cage present a major safety concern for the occupant. While your goal is to provide the largest cage practical, be very aware of the bar spacing. With the larger cages, the bar spacing is generally wider. *No bird should be able to fit its head through the bars of its cage.* If it can, it is in a potentially life-threatening situation.

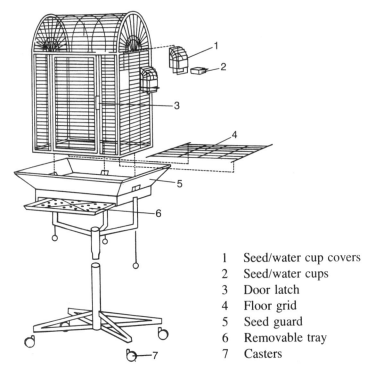

1   Seed/water cup covers
2   Seed/water cups
3   Door latch
4   Floor grid
5   Seed guard
6   Removable tray
7   Casters

The well-designed cage.

This Hyacinth macaw should not be able to squeeze its head through the cage bars.

Many of the newer cages come in a variety of bar spacing to accommodate the owner who wants a large cage for a small bird. These are also generally the better made and more expensive ones. Bird specialty stores and bird magazines will have information on these cages.

Cage Material

The material used to manufacture the cage should also be a major consideration when purchasing this important piece of equipment. Metal is the most common material used to make bird cages.

Wrought iron is commonly used, and these cages are frequently manufactured in Mexico. Because these are generally the least expensive, they have traditionally been the cage of choice for larger birds. They are usually painted with a flat black paint; unfortunately, the color can rub off and soil the bird. Contrary to past beliefs, these cages are no longer painted with lead-based paints. A popular option is to have the cage sandblasted and powder-coated for durability and ease of cleaning.

Stainless-steel cages are also very popular as they are very durable and easy to keep clean. Make sure the welds are not accessible to the bird's beak. Some of the larger birds will enjoy gnawing until a weld breaks.

Cold-rolled steel is a relative newcomer to the field of bird cages. It is extremely durable and usually comes powder coated. The finish is easy to clean and virtually indestructible.

Wood cages are also available, but are not recommended. They cannot be adequately cleaned and disinfected. They can also be chewed up and destroyed by your fine feathered friend. A wood cage is not a good choice for any bird—regardless of its size.

Design

Cage design should be both pleasing to the eye and functional. There are several important reasons for this.

Cages can be fashioned in squares, rectangles, rounds, triangles and other exotic shapes. Make sure the cage being considered has parallel bar spacing in all areas accessible to the bird. Bars with spaces that narrow at the ends, such as some on the top of a dome-shaped cage, can catch wings, feet and toes and lead to serious injury.

Cage designs have been developed to allow maximum enjoyment for both owner and pet. They should also provide maximum convenience for cleaning, feeding and access to your bird. Newer models can be found with a skirt or extension around the base to catch food and droppings before they reach the floor. Playpens that attach to the top of the cage are another option. In addition, many have special feeder-cup designs to make feeding birds more convenient and with less possible contamination from the droppings.

Remember, no matter what the shape chosen, newspaper or other similar

Well-designed cages should provide maximum enjoyment for the bird as well as convenience and eye appeal for owners. Just as birds come in an assortment of sizes, so do their "homes"! *(Animal Environments)*

paper will be used on the cage floor. The easier the paper is to change, the more often it is likely to be changed. Make sure the basic cage design will use the standard newspaper shape without having to cut the paper up.

Mobility

Wheels, or casters, on the bottom of the bigger cages can be of real value. Larger cages often need to be moved for cleaning, and when a change of scenery for your bird is desired.

Doors

The size of the cage door, its location on the cage and the type of latch are factors to consider. The larger the door, the easier the cage is to clean, but it also increases the chance of a bird escaping. The latch should be human friendly as well as birdproof. Remember, larger birds can be masters of figuring out how to open all different kinds of latches. It is not uncommon to see padlocks on larger cages, not as a deterrent to theft, but to prevent the bird from escaping! However, if this is necessary, make sure the cage can be opened quickly in the event of an emergency.

Flooring

The design of the cage floor is important for ease of cleaning, decreasing contamination and helping to keep the bird clean. The easier the floor is to clean, the more frequently it will probably be cleaned. Many cages come with a pull-out cage floor designed for quick cleaning and paper changing.

Birds love to spend time working on their cage locks. Make certain the latch or lock is "birdproof."

Ideal flooring includes a removable tray, paper and a grate.
(Animal Environments)

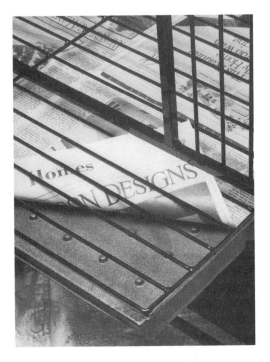

Grates along the bottom of the cage will allow food and droppings to fall through to the pan below. A grate will also prevent the bird from being able to track through its droppings or pick up spoiled and contaminated food. Use of a grate helps decrease the potential for spread of disease and will keep your bird cleaner. Remember, in the wild birds never come into contact with their own droppings.

Newspaper, computer paper and butcher paper are the *best* and least expensive floor liners. Multiple layers of paper can be placed on the floor and removed a few layers at a time when they become soiled. The appearance of your bird's droppings is an excellent indicator of its health. These can be best evaluated on paper. If chewed on, the ink in newspaper will *not* cause problems.

Other products, such as dried corn cobs, crushed walnut shells, pelletized grasses, sawdust, cat litter or artificial grass are *not* recommended for cage floor liners. Some of the disadvantages of these materials are poor visualization of droppings and digestive problems if eaten.

Feeders

The arrangement of feeders has also been taken into account on newer cage designs. Some cages have the food cups outside the cage to maximize indoor space, while others have a separate door to access the food cups, which is especially useful with an aggressive or untamed bird. This type of feeder design will make it easier for "bird-sitters" to feed your bird.

CAGE ACCESSORIES

In addition to the cage itself, there are many accessories needed to round out your pet's environment. Each part of the cage must be customized for your bird's size, strength and activity level. Not every bird needs every accessory mentioned, just as a child doesn't need every toy on the market.

Perches

Perches are not normally included with new cages. Therefore, they will need to be purchased separately. Birds spend most of their lives standing on two feet. They eat with their feet, and even use them for play. Birds should have a variety of places to sit in the cage without having to hang on the bars.

An important factor when selecting perches is to vary their thickness and shape. For this reason, natural wood branches work best. Natural hardwood perches are best for large birds and ideal for any birds that like to chew. For smaller birds, softer wood branches from fruit and eucalyptus trees work well. Of course, branches treated with pesticides should never be used.

A word of caution: Sandpaper perch covers are not recommended. They can injure a bird's feet. Concrete perches, six to eight inches long, have recently been introduced and may help keep beak and nails short. They should be used along with conventional wood perches. There are also many other unique ideas for perches, and these are limited only by one's imagination.

Perches can easily become soiled and must be frequently cleaned. Also, perches should not be placed over food areas, to prevent droppings from falling into food or water.

Braided, colorful rope perches provide an option to the traditional wood perch.

Feed Cups

Feed cups are available in a variety of sizes, shapes, textures and colors. Most importantly, they must be easy to clean and withstand the ravages of being chewed on. Some cups will have a cover to help prevent food from being tossed out. However, they are also more difficult to clean. For large birds, metal and heavy-duty plastic cups are recommended; pottery crocks are also frequently used. Unfortunately, these can develop small cracks, which will harbor disease-producing organisms. Discard them if they become cracked.

Most feeder cups can be washed in a dishwasher. Again, make sure the cups are placed in use in areas that are not as likely to become contaminated with droppings.

Swings

Swings provide a wonderful source of entertainment for many birds. There are a large variety of different shapes and sizes available. These range from the very simple plastic swing for canaries and budgies to the elaborate ''activity centers'' for larger birds.

Toys

Toys will help turn a house into a home. They bring fun and exercise into a bird's environment and can help to minimize boredom. However, they must be safe in order not to risk possible injury. The size, shape and durability of toys selected must be based on the type of bird; very simply, larger birds need tougher toys.

For instance, plastic beads can be lots of fun for a ''budgie,'' but can spell disaster for a parrot. Be careful of toys hung by chains and ''jingle-bell'' type bells. Toes and beaks could get stuck in them. Mirrors are fun for small birds, but larger birds could break them. Pieces of leather, rawhide dog chews, metal rings and small lava rocks are some of the favorite toys for large birds.

Cage Covers

Birds seem to prefer darkness when sleeping. Cage covers can provide this in a dimly lit room. They can also serve to protect birds from drafts during the night. The cover should be washable.

Playpens

Playpens are activity centers outside of the cage. They help keep the bird in one area while providing a variety of fun and games. They can be located on top of the cage or be a freestanding ''gym.'' Playpens usually consist of perches, ladders and swings with food and water cups on a flat base designed for total

This is only a small sampling of the wide variety of toys available for birds.

Toys can be made from a variety of materials, including metal, plastic, wood, rock, leather and even food items such as nuts. Remember, larger birds require stronger toys! *(Animal Environments)*

A playpen such as this one can sit on top of the cage or be lifted off and moved to another location in the home. *(Animal Environments)*

enjoyment. Toys can also be added to the playpen for more pleasure still. Quality workmanship is important. Sharp edges, protruding nails or flimsy construction can injure birds. An untamed bird may not be able to enjoy its playpen for a while, so this is one accessory that can be purchased later.

T-Stands

T-stands are another type of activity center for birds away from the cage. The T-stand usually consists of a single perch that stands six inches to three feet off the ground, with food and water cups attached. Toys can be hung from T-stands for additional entertainment. The T-stand is an ideal place to begin training your bird. As the T-stand is mobile and can be easily moved from room to room, it allows birds to participate in more family activities. A bird that frequently flies off the T-stand can get into trouble. Therefore, birds using a T-stand must learn to stay on it until taken off.

CLEANING AND DISINFECTING

Keeping your feathered friend's home environment clean and sanitary is an area often overlooked. Remember, organisms found in a dirty environment cause the majority of health problems. Therefore, the health of both owner and bird benefit from a clean and sanitary home for your bird.

Birds in the wild are accustomed to living in a clean, fresh environment.

T-stands can be either elaborate or very simple; both work well.
(Animal Environments)

For example, as they move around in the trees, their waste material immediately falls to the ground, well below where they are perched. They rarely, if ever, come in contact with their own wastes. When pets are kept in a caged environment, they are exposed to potential health problems arising from their small, confined living arrangement and forced proximity to their own wastes. Since bird droppings have no odor, they can be easily overlooked when general housecleaning chores are done. Therefore, it is essential to remember to clean and disinfect their "home sweet home."

What does disinfecting mean? It is the act of destroying infective agents, namely bacteria, viruses, and fungi. These are the "germs" that cause disease.

Metal, plastic, tile and cement are easiest to disinfect. Wood, bamboo and wicker caging should not be used because they allow germs to penetrate their surfaces and cannot be adequately disinfected. Wooden perches and toys can be used but require frequent, thorough cleaning.

An ideal cleaning schedule is outlined below:

Daily

Change the food and water.
Soak the water dish in dilute bleach solution (1 part chlorine bleach to 30 parts water) or hot water and dish soap.
Wash the food dish.
Change the cage paper.

Weekly

Clean the cage.
Clean all accessories.

Every Two Weeks

Thoroughly disinfect the cage and accessories.

Cleaning

Cleaning can be done with mild soap and lots of hot water. Use a scrub brush (or nonabrasive cleansing pad) and a lot of elbow grease! Perches can be soaked in hot water and scrubbed with an abrasive brush or wire-bristle brush. Rinse all items well, and if possible allow the cage and all accessories to dry in the sun. The sun's rays also act to disinfect. Wooden items should be completely dry before putting them back in the cage. Two sets of cups, perches and accessories are ideal. This allows one set to be drying while the other is in use.

Disinfecting

Disinfecting is an important part of maintaining a clean, sanitary environment. There are many different types of disinfectants available, each having their own unique characteristics. It is important to realize that a degree in chemistry is not necessary to do a good job. Two basic requirements are important for a good disinfectant. First, it must be effective against most of the common "germs" found in a bird's environment. Second, it must be able to be used safely around both humans and birds.

There are many good disinfectants available that fit these requirements. Consult a pet bird professional for a current recommendation covering conditions in your local area.

Many disinfectants are rendered *useless* in the presence of organic debris (dirt)! Therefore, thorough cleaning of all surfaces with soap and water is essential *prior* to disinfecting. Once all the surface debris has been removed, the disinfectant can go to work killing "germs."

Safety is critical when using disinfectants. Birds are especially sensitive to chemicals and fumes, so use caution when disinfecting. Rinse all items well and let them air dry. Additional safety tips are provided below:

SAFETY TIPS FOR DISINFECTING

- Use gloves and protective eye wear when mixing solutions.
- Follow all manufacturer's recommendations *carefully*. Exact dilutions must be used—more is *not* better!
- Always add water first, chemicals last, to avoid splashing chemicals into your face.

TRAVEL TIPS

Having pet birds is such a wonderful experience, many owners have not stopped to consider what would be done with their bird when a trip out of town becomes necessary. This section will discuss the options available when traveling with or without your bird.

"The Decision": To Travel with or without Your Bird

While many people would not consider leaving their pet in someone else's care, others would not consider taking their bird out into the real world. Many factors enter into the decision-making process. Below are many of the points to consider:

- Is your bird in good health? Do not travel with a sick bird.
- Is your bird acclimated to travel? If not, start with short trips in the car to help with confinement and motion problems.
- Do you have a travel cage or carrier for your bird? Airlines have special requirements. Call them for details.
- Does your destination allow birds? Some resorts and foreign countries do not allow pet birds to be brought in.
- Are the changes in travel and destination temperatures safe?

- Is a health certificate required? When leaving the state or country or traveling by air, an exam by a veterinarian is required to certify your bird's health. These exams are usually required seven to ten days prior to departure. Check with airlines, embassies or any other governmental agency. This is *very* important because regulations frequently change.
- Check with your destination's agricultural laws. Some types of birds are actually legally banned from some areas because of possible agricultural damage in the event of escape.

As can readily be seen above, traveling with a bird can be very complicated. Unfortunately, most owners are not even aware that many travel restrictions apply. Frequently, these details are never addressed until the last minute or when a personal emergency arises. Remember, everyone who owns birds will at some time or another have to leave home. Will your bird stay at home or travel with you? Regardless of your decision, advanced planning is *essential*!

LEAVING "BIRDIE" HOME

Many owners feel very comfortable leaving their birds in the hands of someone competent while they are away. They can choose to have someone come into the home to care for the bird, or the bird can be taken to a facility that cares for birds while owners are away.

In-Home Care

In-home care can be provided by friends, relatives, neighbors or a professional pet-sitting service. Most importantly, the "bird-sitter" must be responsible and trustworthy, and any knowledge of birds is an added bonus. Remaining at home provides your bird with the security of being in familiar surroundings. Everything basically stays the same, i.e., the cage, room, sights, and smells. However, the routine will change a little, since there will be a "new" person feeding, cleaning and entertaining your feathered friend. Your bird will also not be exposed to other birds. Another advantage of "bird-sitters" is not having to leave your home vacant while traveling. A vacant house is a target for burglars. "Bird-sitters" can live full-time in your home or stop by once or twice daily to feed, clean and play with your bird.

1. Make sure to leave explicit written directions:
   - Feeding, cleaning, and entertainment guidelines
   - Special likes and dislikes of your bird
   - Phone number of avian veterinarian, bird store and trusted, knowledgeable bird person
   - Phone number, if possible, where owner can be reached
2. Stock up on all necessary supplies.
3. Consider leaving the cage locked, but be sure to leave the key and maybe a spare one, too!

4. Introduce the "bird-sitter" to bird, home and general routines *prior* to leaving.

Bird Boarding

Boarding your bird can be a way of getting expert care. Most importantly, there should be people knowledgeable about birds on staff. Boarding options include in-home care, boarding kennels, veterinary hospitals, bird pet stores, and specialized bird boarding and training facilities.

Many birds are stimulated by seeing other birds in the same environment. Listening to other birds may help with their talking ability. Many owners think their birds are happier getting out of the house a couple of times a year.

- A veterinary health check-up may be required *prior* to boarding.
- Ask about caging availability—your own? or theirs?
- Make sure to leave explicit written directions.
- Bring the bird's regular food.
- What about things like toys, cage cover?

Remember, it is a major responsibility for someone to care for your bird. Choose carefully.

TRAVELING WITH "BIRDIE"

In general, birds travel very well. However, some advance planning and preparation are necessary. For flying or driving across state lines or international borders with your bird, a veterinary-signed health certificate is usually required.

By Car

This is certainly the least complicated way to travel. It's safest to keep the bird caged during the drive—either in its regular cage, if it fits, or in a travel carrier. The bird should be able to stand up, turn around and, ideally extend its wings. Remove any hanging toys or swings that could injure the bird when moving. Seat-belt the carrier to the seat. Bring along adequate food and a container of water for the journey. Fruit is also a good water source when traveling.

Be prepared for weather changes. A squirt bottle filled with water can help to cool a bird on a hot day. Hotel reservations should be made in advance, and be sure to ask if birds are welcome. Please be courteous and clean so other pets will be welcome in the future. Try to avoid leaving birds unattended in cars. Remember, they can easily be stolen.

Some birds may experience signs of car sickness, such as regurgitation of food. While medications are not recommended to prevent this problem, withholding food before a short trip may help. Also, try covering the carrier or cage. Remember, too, that birds will travel better in a smooth-riding motor home.

Transport carriers are needed if the bird's cage is too large to be easily moved. Many different types of carriers can be used, as shown here and at the top of the opposite page. Remember, cardboard and soft woods may not be practical for larger parrots.

Do not keep birds on the floor of the car. Toxic fumes and increased heat from the engine will be more concentrated in this confined area. In addition, smoking in the close confines of a car should be avoided.

By Train or Bus

Pets are not allowed.

By Air

While this may be the easiest way for people to travel, unfortunately it is the most complicated for pets. Advance planning is absolutely essential. Airlines must first be contacted to find out their policy on transporting birds. Believe it or not, airline policies can even vary depending upon the person providing the information. Therefore, keep a record of the date and employee you spoke with.

Limitations and restrictions vary with the airline. Some allow under-the-seat carriers, while others only allow baggage compartment travel. There are specific requirements for the size of the carrier. In addition, expect an extra charge for pets. Airlines also have different requirements for written health certificates.

One major obstacle of transporting birds by air is the temperature requirements. Some airlines will not accept pets in the baggage compartment if the outside temperature at any stopover or final destination is higher than 80°F or lower than 40°F. Unless pets can travel in the passenger cabin, this weather policy can be a problem. However, remember, these policies are for the pet's benefit.

The carrier should contain food, but no water. Oranges, apples or other fruit can help provide needed fluids during the flight. Consider lining the carrier with indoor/outdoor carpeting for insulation and padding. A perch should be positioned close to the floor and prevented from moving. Screws placed through outside walls into the perch will hold it in place.

This type of transport carrier has been designed for "under-the-seat" airline travel.

FOREIGN TRAVEL

If at all possible, avoid foreign travel with your bird. The obstacles to overcome can be overwhelming. First of all, each country has its own specific requirements. To make matters worse, this information can be very difficult to obtain. Considerable paperwork, government involvement and a number of different "fees" are just some of the problems associated with overseas travel. If traveling to a foreign country with a bird is essential, start up to seven months in advance to make all the arrangements.

First, contact the foreign embassy of the country or countries of your destination. Ask how to obtain the information on the requirements for bringing pet birds into the country. This will often require numerous phone calls or letters. The information can be difficult to obtain and often varies from one person to another. And due to the frequently changing rules of all the different countries, the U.S. Department of Agriculture cannot even provide much current information. They will, however, try to help when requested.

Once familiar with the country's regulations, the airlines involved must be contacted for their specific requirements. Arrangements must also be made with a veterinarian specially licensed to issue foreign health certificates. The certificate must be sent to a district office of the USDA for an official United States Government seal of approval. Another difficulty arises because airlines require health certificates to be issued only up to seven to ten days in advance. All paperwork must go smoothly and quickly or problems could arise.

Immediately before returning to the United States, call the USDA to get all the current requirements. Another health certificate will need to be issued and a leg band applied. There are also only certain ports of entry, and all birds entering the country will need to be quarantined.

GENERAL ADVICE FOR TRAVELING

- Plan ahead!!
- Travel with a health certificate.
- Get wings and nails trimmed prior to leaving.
- Remove toys from the cage to prevent injury.
- By car, use a seat belt to secure the cage.
- Never leave the bird unattended.
- Play the bird's favorite music if possible.
- Carry a spray bottle of water during hot weather.
- Keep fresh foods in a cooler with ice.
- Carry a container of water.
- Start months in advance for international travel.
- Obtain a recommendation for an avian veterinarian in your destination area.

ADDRESSES AND PHONE NUMBERS YOU MAY FIND HELPFUL

Port Veterinarian—Animal and Plant Health Inspection Service—U.S. Department of Agriculture

Arizona: Nogales 85628	(602) 364-5681
Alaska: Anchorage 99645	(907) 376-9376
California: Inglewood 90301	(213) 215-2352
California: San Ysidro 92073	(619) 428-7308
Colorado: Denver 80211	(303) 837-3481
Florida: Miami 33166	(305) 536-6920
Hawaii: Honolulu 96850	(808) 541-2803
Idaho: East Port 83826	(208) 267-2396
Illinois: Rosemont 60018	(312) 353-5715
Maryland: Annapolis 21401	(410) 962-7726
Massachusetts: Boston 01590	(508) 865-1421
Michigan: Detroit 48216	(313) 226-3139
Montana: Sweetgrass 59484	(406) 335-2142
New York: Buffalo 14305	(716) 846-4026
North Dakota: Dunseith 58329	(701) 263-3364
Texas: El Paso 79901	(915) 534-6218
Vermont: Derby Line 05478	(802) 873-3161
Washington: Olympia 98502	(206) 753-9430

U.S. Fish and Wildlife

California: Los Angeles	(213) 297-0063
Hawaii: Honolulu	(808) 541-2862
New York: New York	(718) 917-1767
Florida: Miami	(305) 536-4788

4

Nutrition

Feeding for Health, Vitality and Longevity

GOOD NUTRITION is the *most* important element in the health, vitality and longevity of our pet birds.

"Your bird is what it eats!" Most people now understand the importance of a good diet for themselves. Birds are no different. Unfortunately, the actual nutritional requirements necessary to create a good, well-balanced diet for pet birds are not yet known. This is complicated by the fact that to some degree each species has its own unique set of essential nutrients. Eventually these requirements will all be known. Until then, diets will continue to evolve based on years of experience and trial and error.

Historically, birds have been classified into two groups—seed eaters and meat eaters. This has formed the basis for parrots originally being fed mostly seeds. As time passed, fruits and vegetables were added to better "round out" the diet. Today, the combination of commercial diets, home cooking, fresh fruits and vegetables and possibly some seeds have proved to produce the happiest and healthiest pet birds.

In birds, the rate at which life-sustaining chemical reactions occur in the body is the fastest of all animals. The energy needed to generate these vital activities is known as metabolism. Based on their body size, birds require relatively large amounts of food to generate this energy. In fact, if a 175-pound human, pound for pound (or gram for gram), were to eat the same amount of food each day as a hummingbird, he/she would have to eat 175 pounds of potatoes, 28 eggs, 100 slices of bread, 50 cups of milk and 17 pounds of hamburger! Remember, this is compared to a hummingbird. Larger parrots have a considerably slower metabolism. However, it still illustrates the incredibly high energy requirements needed to sustain birds' daily activities. Any lack of proper nutrients, including a decreased food intake, will affect them very quickly.

One further comment: Malnutrition needs to be mentioned. This is the result of an improper balance between what a living creature eats and what is required to maintain optimal health. Malnutrition is usually associated with eating too little (undernutrition), but don't forget it can also be associated with an incorrect balance of basic foods and by dietary excess (overnutrition). In many instances, in an attempt to provide pet birds with the best diet possible, they have been "oversupplemented" with "too much of a good thing." This too will cause health problems.

Remember, just provide a variety of good wholesome foods to eat. Commercially formulated pet bird food is now available and is highly recommended. In addition, throw in some freshly cooked foods as described in this chapter, a few fruits and vegetables and, of course, include fresh water. Now, *if* all bird owners had the time to prepare this wonderful food on a daily basis, and *if* all birds would eat everything offered, life would be very easy. This chapter will explain in much more detail all the factors involved in providing the very best diet for pet birds.

A nutritious, well-balanced diet will help to ensure a healthy, happy bird with beautiful feathering and proper body weight.

NATURAL FEEDING BEHAVIORS

Habitat

The native habitat for each species of bird is usually not taken into account when selecting a proper diet. Also, the seasonal changes in the native habitat will affect the availability of the various foods. What a parrot eats in the Amazon jungle is different from what a cockatoo eats in Australia. Even though this chapter does not distinguish between the native diets of the various species, it attempts to meet the general nutritional needs of all parrots.

For those interested in finding out more about the diets of birds in their native habitat, additional research will be needed. For information on a bird's country of origin, see the species guide in Appendix A. Next, consider finding answers to some of these questions:

- What seed-or fruit-producing plants would likely be the primary food source?
- What foods available locally most closely match those in the wild?
- What kinds of trees are used for nesting? Knowing the tree types would help to determine food availability.
- When are their seasons? Climate changes? Countries of origin below the equator have seasons opposite those above the equator. Seasonal molting, reproduction and food availability can all be affected

Foraging

In the wild, it is common for birds to spend the morning foraging for food. They move from place to place seeking, probing, tearing and discovering edible foods. In other words, they work for their food. They must also always be on the lookout for predators during their food searches. To minimize exposure to danger, birds have evolved a food-holding sac called a crop. This allows them to ingest large amounts of food in a short time and move on to a safe haven to digest it. The day is left for other activities, but the food search begins again in the afternoon.

What is usually done with pet birds is to provide food for them all day long. Foraging and twice-daily feeding behaviors are eliminated. What can result is boredom, lack of natural curiosity and "fussy" feeding preferences.

To help ensure a pet bird's emotional and physical well-being, an attempt should be made to modify the environment to stimulate natural feeding behaviors. It may require time for birds to adjust to new routines and toys. Remember, persistence pays off!

The list below provides some ideas to eliminate feeding boredom and stimulate interest. These are only some suggestions—creativity and imagination can supply the rest.

- Hang vegetables/fruits on a rod-type feeder. Birds must hold the feeder to keep it from moving while they eat.

Food/toy combinations can be used to stimulate natural foraging behaviors. These are just a few of the many possibilities.
(Animal Environments)

- Weave foods into the bars of the cage. The bird must climb to the spot and "unweave" them.
- Provide cooked chicken leg bones for larger parrots. It will require considerable effort to strip the meat and crack the bone to reach the rich marrow.
- Stuff food in the "nooks and crannies" of pine cones. This encourages food seeking and probing behaviors. "Goodies" will reward the bird for its efforts.
- Commercially prepared or homemade food-toy combinations can combine nuts, dried fruits and vegetables. This combines playtime with food gathering activities.
- Put your bird on twice-a-day feedings. Remove food after twenty or thirty minutes. This stimulates active feeding twice a day, and provides the thrill of anticipation.

"LIFE STAGES" AND NUTRITION

Age, reproductive status, environmental changes (stress) and sickness will all affect dietary needs. Therefore, during these times, diets should be modified to reflect the body's new demands.

Following is a chart indicating the types of changes that occur, and how the diet must be modified to adjust to the body's changing needs.

LIFE CHANGES REQUIRING DIETARY MODIFICATIONS

Growth	⇑ calories from all food sources, ⇑ protein
Temperature extremes	⇑fats, carbohydrates for cold; ⇑fruits, water for heat
Exercise increase	⇑calories from carbohydrates and other food sources
Reproduction	⇑calories, ⇑ protein, ⇑ calcium intake, ⇑ fruits and vegetables
Stress	⇑carbohydrates and fruits
Disease	keep bird eating, feed favorite foods, ⇑ calories, ⇑ protein and follow veterinarian's advice

THE BASIC NUTRIENTS

A complete diet consists of a balance of certain key food elements. These are the nutritional building blocks that sustain life.

Water

The body is composed of approximately 80 percent water! Every cell is dependent on water for its very existence. It is necessary for energy production, transportation of nutrients and to help regulate body temperature. It is well-known a body can survive longer without food than without water. Under extreme conditions, it is possible to lose 50 percent of muscle mass and almost 100 percent of fat stores, but a 15 percent fluid loss could lead to death!

AVERAGE DAILY WATER INTAKE*

Finch/canary	½ teaspoon
"Budgie"	1 teaspoon
Cockatiel	2–3 teaspoons
Amazon parrot	5–8 teaspoons
Macaw/cockatoo	10–15 teaspoons

Proteins

Proteins are essential for the health and maintenance of all body tissues. They play a key role in normal growth, reproduction and resistance to infection. Proteins are made up of small subunits called amino acids. Every species has its own requirements for certain amino acids. These essential amino acids cannot be manufactured by the body and must be supplied in the diet.

*These amounts are only guidelines, since diet and other environmental factors will greatly influence water intake.

Common sources of protein include beans, nuts, eggs, meat and dairy products.

Carbohydrates

Carbohydrates are the body's primary fuel. They are found in plants and include starches and simple sugars. Carbohydrates not immediately needed by the body are stored in the liver and muscles. Fiber, often found in carbohydrates, helps to maintain normal intestinal function and prevent constipation.

Common sources of carbohydrates include fruits, vegetables and cereal grains.

Fats

Fats are the most concentrated energy source. They provide more than twice as much energy per unit than either protein or carbohydrates. Fats insulate and store energy for the body and are also required for the normal absorption of fat-soluble vitamins A, D, E and K.

Common sources of fats include nuts, seeds and many dairy products.

Minerals

Minerals play a crucial role in the maintenance and strength of bone, normal cell function, nerve conduction and muscle contraction. They are also important in maintaining the proper balance of body fluids.

Minerals are required in only minute amounts, but the balance between different minerals is critical. If this balance is disrupted it can lead to serious problems. Therefore, supplementation, if needed at all, is usually best done with a complete, balanced mineral supplement.

Common sources of minerals include egg shell, cuttlebone, oyster shells, fish and bone meal, mineral blocks and commercial vitamin/mineral supplements.

Vitamins

Vitamins promote and regulate a wide variety of body functions. They are essential for normal development, growth and maintenance of good health. Without them, the utilization of protein, carbohydrates and fat would be impossible.

Birds require approximately thirteen essential vitamins. They appear to be able to only partially manufacture three of them—vitamins C, D_3, and niacin. Vitamins are found naturally in the food supply.

Common sources of vitamins include a good diet and commercial vitamin/mineral supplements.

WHAT TO FEED

There is *no* such thing as a "perfect diet." To come closest, feed a fresh, balanced variety of foods. On the surface, this seems easy to accomplish. However, birds are not always cooperative. They may not be willing to taste new foods. Therefore, first learn what constitutes good nutrition. There are many ways to achieve an optimal diet. It is most important that birds eat something from each of the food groups rather than multiple items from a single group.

Water

A constant source of water is essential. Be sure the container is clean and the water is changed at least daily. More frequent changes are needed if the bird "dunks" its food in it, since food will quickly contaminate the water. Also, place food and water cups in areas where droppings will not fall into them. For example, keep them out from under perches.

Commercially Formulated Diets

Commercially formulated diets are highly recommended as part of a balanced nutrition program. They provide a combination of nutrients from all the food groups and have been developed from research and years of field observations. Formulated bird foods have eliminated much of the guesswork bird owners face when trying to provide a balanced, nutritious diet.

The many formulated diets commercially available are manufactured in a variety of forms such as pellets, crumbles, and cakes; ask your avian veterinarian

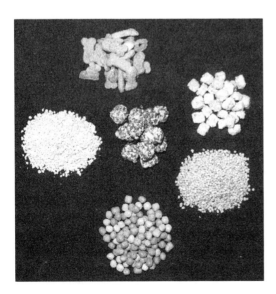

This is a small sampling of the variety of commercially formulated bird diets available. Note the different sizes, shapes and textures. Birds, like people, have food preferences. Remember, one brand may be preferred over another.

Some birds like to pick up food with their feet. Larger pieces allow for easier "self-service." *(Lafeber Company)*

or local bird shop for a recommendation. Switching birds to this type of diet may present some challenges; see the discussion later in this chapter.

Note that while commercially formulated diets can be fed as the sole source of nutrition, to stimulate natural feeding behaviors, consider adding a small percentage of foods from the other categories.

Home-Cooked Diets

Home-cooked diets can be visually appealing, provide a good variety of food sources and are usually well-accepted by birds. Most commonly foods such as beans, rice, corn, pasta and whole grains are cooked and combined to form a fresh, healthy diet. It's important to remember variety. Be sure to include an assortment of beans, grains, vegetables and possibly a good vitamin and mineral supplement.

Most bird owners cook up a large amount, divide it into small quantities and freeze the portions. This allows the food to be fed fresh. It is commonly fed twice daily, in the morning and evening. Cooked foods spoil quickly, so it is recommended to remove them from the cage after thirty minutes.

Later in this chapter is an assortment of fun recipes your bird will enjoy.

Note: Home-cooked diets should *not* be fed as the sole source of nutrition. They need to be supplemented with foods from the other categories.

Rule #1   (30-Minute Rule)
Never leave cooked foods, fruits and most vegetables in the cage longer than 30 minutes. Bacterial, fungal and mold contamination can begin this quickly.

Seeds

Seeds can satisfy a bird's natural feeding behavior. However, through the years birds have been fed far too many seeds and not enough other important foods. If the diet plan is well thought out, adding seeds can be an intelligent option. Bird species native to more arid grassland regions, such as cockatiels and cockatoos, fare better on a higher-percentage seed diet. Amazons and macaws from the New World tropical rain forests have limited access to seeds in their natural habitat.

The problem with seeds is they are high in fat (up to 50 percent), deficient in some important nutrients and can cause finicky eating habits.

*NUTRITIONAL DEFICIENCIES OF A SEED DIET**

Protein (Amino Acids)

Lysine, methionine

Vitamins

Vitamin A, vitamin D, riboflavin, vitamin B_{12},
Possibly vitamins E and K, pantothenic acid, niacin, biotin, choline

Minerals

Calcium, possible sodium

Trace Minerals

Possibly iron, copper, zinc, manganese, iodine and selenium

The fresher the seeds, the higher the nutritional value. Because seeds are high in fat, they can become rancid. Freshness can be checked by sprouting the seeds. Fresh, nutritious seeds will spout in only one to two days of soaking. Try to purchase seeds from a high volume dealer. The turnover will be faster and the seeds should be fresher.

During certain times of the year, especially in the warmer climates, some seeds will be "buggy." Some insects will hatch among seeds, regardless of how well they are handled and stored during processing. A few moths or grain beetles will not hurt birds; however, the nutrient composition of the diet will be changed. Therefore, it would be better not to feed them. Freeze the seed mix for twenty-four hours after purchase. This will kill the bugs. Afterward, refrigerate seeds to maintain their freshness.

Note: Seeds should not form more than 25 percent of the total diet. In addition, there should be a good variety of seeds. Make sure your bird continues to eat the other foods provided.

---

*Dr. Randal N. Brue, Director of Nutritional Research, Kaytee Products, Inc., Chilton, Wisconsin.

Vegetables

Vegetables are a marvelous source of carbohydrates and vitamins. However, they are not a complete diet. There is a tremendous variety of vegetables and all are safe for birds. They do, however, vary in their nutritional content. In general, light-colored vegetables with a high water content, such as iceberg lettuce and celery, are low in nutrients but take up a lot of room in the stomach. A good source of information regarding the nutritional content of 470 vegetables is the U.S. Government book *Composition of Foods: Vegetables and Vegetable Products*. This book is available from the U.S. Government Printing Office, Washington DC, 20402.

Most vegetables can be offered uncooked. However, for a change of pace, and perhaps greater acceptability, try cooking them first. Remember the Thirty-Minute Rule for cooked foods given earlier in the chapter. The size of the pieces offered may affect whether the bird will eat it or not. Some birds prefer diced foods, while others prefer to tear up the pieces themselves. Uncooked corn on the cob, carrots and other firm vegetables can be hung from the cage as an edible toy.

Note: Vegetables could form between 30 and 50 percent of the diet. Be sure to vary the selection of vegetables to maximize their benefits.

COMMONLY FED VEGETABLES (AND LEGUMES)

Artichokes	Collards	Potatoes
Asparagus	Corn	Pumpkin
Beans (all types)	Cucumbers	Radishes
Beet greens	Dandelion greens	Spinach
Beets	Endive	Sprouts (all types)
Broccoli	Green beans	Squash
Brussels sprouts	Green/red peppers	Sweet potatoes
Cabbage	Jicama	Swiss chard
Carrots	Kale	Turnips
Cauliflower	Mushrooms	Turnip greens
Celery	Mustard greens	Watercress
Chicory greens	Okra	Yams
Chili peppers	Peas	Zucchini
Cilantro		

Fruits

Fruits are a valuable addition to the diet and provide a quick energy source. Virtually all pet birds eat fruit in the wild. Most fruits are safe; however, avocados and the pits from certain fruits should not be fed (see the list of foods to avoid, later in the chapter). There is also a government publication about fruits and their nutritional content. Order a copy of *Agriculture Handbook No. 8–9* from the United States Government Printing Office, Washington, DC 20402.

Fruit is high in sugar, making it very palatable. This also makes it attractive to ants and other insects, and it is very subject to bacterial contamination. Therefore, remove uneaten fruit *within 30 minutes* to avoid these problems. Fruits can also form a "sticky" mess in the cage. Be sure to keep the cage clean.

Note: Approximately 10 percent of the diet can be fruit. Use seasonal varieties to your best advantage. Make sure all fruit is fresh and washed.

COMMONLY FED FRUITS

Apples	Guava	Pears
Apricots	Honeydew	Persimmons
Bananas	Kiwis	Pineapple
Berries	Kumquats	Plums
Cantaloupe	Mangoes	Pomegranates
Figs	Oranges	Raisins
Grapefruit	Papayas	Tangerines
Grapes	Peaches	Watermelon

Meat and Dairy Products

Surprisingly, meat and dairy products are enjoyed by pet birds. In small amounts, all types of these foods are safe and nutritious. Common choices include eggs, cheese, yogurt, chicken, ground beef, dog food and monkey biscuits. Remember the Thirty-Minute Rule.

Birds are deficient in the enzyme lactase necessary to digest dairy products. Therefore, most birds can tolerate only small amounts. Yogurt is especially good because the cooking process makes it easier to digest.

Note: Up to 5 percent of the diet can be meat and dairy. Consider using leftovers from the family meal.

SUPPLEMENTS

Vitamins/Minerals: Vitamin/mineral supplements are usually not necessary when feeding a commercially formulated diet. For any other diet plans these are a good idea to use. Use only a balanced supplement made exclusively for pet birds and follow manufacturer-recommended amounts. "Too much of a good thing" can also cause problems.

Use powdered vitamin/mineral supplements sprinkled on soft foods or mixed in with home-cooked diets. Parrots have dry tongues, and powdered supplements on seeds mostly fall to the ground rather than in the mouth. Do not use supplements that are added to water. It will increase the rate at which bacteria contaminate the water.

Note: There are many brands of vitamin and mineral supplements for birds. Consult your avian veterinarian or bird pet shop for a recommendation.

Grit: Grit consists of small pieces of sand and stones once thought to be crucial for digestion of food in the bird's gizzard. The notion of feeding grit to pet birds was "borrowed" from poultry. Chickens and turkeys eat whole seeds and require small bits of sand to grind off the coating of the seed in order to digest it. Parrots, on the other hand, crack their seeds before they eat them. This eliminates the need for "grinding stones" in the gizzard. Smaller softbill species, such as canaries and finches, do require extremely small amounts of grit. Two pieces per week is probably adequate for these birds.

There is a danger in overfeeding grit to birds. From boredom or sickness, birds sometimes eat too much grit and can develop an impaction in the digestive tract. Sand-covered cage liners should not be used. Birds can eat this sand as well even if it's not called "grit."

Note: Grit is *not* necessary for parrots.

FOODS TO AVOID

Birds can eat almost every thing we humans can. If it's healthy for us, it should be perfectly safe for pet birds. Except for avocados, common sense would indicate the foods below are *not* ideal foods for birds.

Avocados

Surprisingly, avocados have caused severe digestive problems, even death, in a few birds. Even though many parrots seem to tolerate this fruit well, it is not recommended.

Alcohol

Alcohol can obviously cause problems in birds. Even in small amounts it can result in sickness, shock and even death. During a party, watch that guests do not playfully offer alcohol to your bird.

"Junk Food"

"Junk food" is not healthy for humans, and certainly should be avoided in your bird's diet. Potato chips, cookies, candy, salted popcorn and other, similar items with excess salt, sugar and fat fall into this category.

Chocolate

In large amounts, chocolate is poisonous to dogs. It may also cause serious problems in birds. Therefore, don't take any chances and do *not* feed chocolate.

Pesticides and Herbicides

Obviously no one would choose to feed these to a bird. However, in today's hectic life it is important to remember to take time to thoroughly wash all fruits and vegetables. Parrots are especially sensitive to environmental toxins. Consider organically-grown produce.

FINICKY EATERS: GETTING THEM TO ACCEPT NEW FOODS

The best food in the world won't help if it's not eaten! What is fed is *not* as important as what the bird actually eats! If your bird is finicky about its diet, spend the time and exert the effort to increase the variety of accepted foods. Your reward will be a happier, healthier bird. Young birds should be offered an assortment of foods from the very beginning. This will help to eliminate the fussy eater problem.

Adult birds are usually resistant to dietary change, especially those who are "seed junkies." This section is written for them. On the other hand, there will also be those few birds who will readily accept new foods. These are the exception and not the rule. Remember, a bird's food preferences have probably evolved over many years. Don't expect change to occur immediately. Above all else, have patience and be persistent. Most birds can be successfully converted to a new and healthier diet over time.

With any of the suggested methods, there will be food wasted. It will either become spoiled sitting around uneaten in the cage or playfully tossed to the floor. During the conversion process, offer only small amounts and learn to recognize the bird's food preferences. In this way, less food will need to be discarded.

Regardless of the method used, the bird's weight should be monitored. If weight loss exceeds about 10 percent, a veterinarian should be consulted.

Introducing New Foods: Commercially Formulated and Home-Cooked Diets

"One Step at a Time": The new diet is slowly increased while seeds are gradually decreased. This continues until the new food has been accepted. It may take a week or even months for this to occur. Be sure there are *never* enough seeds in the cup to satisfy the bird's hunger. This helps "force" them to try the new food. Monitor weight every few days.

"Cold Turkey": As the name implies, simply remove the seeds and immediately replace them with the new diet. This method is not recommended for novice bird owners, since pet birds will sometimes go without eating for a few days. Monitor weight daily. If weight loss becomes a problem, the old diet will have to be put back in the cage.

"Cold Turkey in the Morning": Remove the seeds at night, before bedtime. In the morning, offer only the new food. A few seeds could even be sprinkled over the new diet. In the evening, allow the bird to go back to eating its regular diet. Continue this "on again, off again" adventure until the bird is eating its new food with no resistance.

"Search and Recovery": Continue to use the regular diet, but mix in the

new foods. The bird will have to pick around this food to get to its seeds. In this way, some of the new food will get eaten or at least tasted. This method works especially well with home-cooked foods.

"Change Is Good": There are many commercially formulated diets available. They come in different shapes, colors, smells and textures. Perhaps a "change of scenery" might help. This method can be tried with or without the presence of the old diet in the cage.

Introducing New Foods: Fruits and Vegetables

"Copycat": Let your bird watch you eat. At mealtime, bring the cage or perch alongside the dinner table. If allowed, let the bird sample food directly from the plate. Also, to help show the bird just how good the food really is, try expressing your pleasure with phrases such as "Mmmm, good!" As discussed, birds have a natural curiosity and desire to mimic, so sometimes this method works well.

"Birds of a Different Feather": Try feeding new foods in different forms: chopped vs. whole, cooked vs. uncooked, cold vs. warm, but *always* fresh. Also, try placing foods in different locations—attached to the cage wall, placed at the end of the perch or in favorite areas outside of the cage.

Rule #2   If a Bird Is Sick, Do Not Try Changing Its Diet
Sick birds are usually eating less at a time when they really need the most nutrition. This is not the time to stress them even more by "forcing" them to make new food choices. However, even sick birds need a complete, balanced diet.

Rule #3   Where There's a Will, There's a Way
Who's training whom? We humans are suppose to be smarter than birds! Be imaginative in the way new foods are presented. Also, ask experienced bird people for suggestions. Persistence pays off. Even having the bird accept one or two new foods is a big accomplishment.

TIME AND NUTRITION

If everyone had unlimited time, there would be no need for this discussion. In the real world this just is not the case. Even people who are passionate about their birds may not always have the time to prepare the very best of diets. This section has been written to provide suggestions on how to combine foods for a well-balanced diet, regardless of the amount of time available.

"LOTS OF TIME"

Commercially formulated diet
Home cooked diets
Fresh vegetables
Fresh fruit
Possibly, small amount of seeds
Fresh water

"SOME TIME"

Commercially formulated diet
Home cooking when time permits (or consider leftovers)
Fresh vegetables and fruits
Small amount of seeds
Fresh water

"NO TIME"

Commercially formulated diet*
Leftovers (including fruits and vegetables)
Small amount of seeds
Fresh water

RECIPES YOU CAN MAKE AT HOME FOR YOUR BIRD

Vegetable Medley

¼ cup paddy rice† or long-grain brown rice
¼ cup hulled millet
¼ cup red lentils
¼ cup small-type pasta (optional)
1¼ cups water
1 cup frozen mixed vegetables

Combine rice, millet, lentils (and pasta), if using, with water and cook in microwave on high for 15 minutes, or until soft. Drain off any excess water and mix in vegetables. Stir to thaw vegetables and cool rice mixture.

Refrigerate leftovers or freeze. This recipe is also good for softbills by adding chunks of apple, banana, papaya or other fruit.

---

*Unless the diet is primarily commercially formulated, consider adding a vitamin and mineral supplement.
†Paddy rice can be found in Oriental markets and some natural food stores. It has a nutty aroma and flavor that is enjoyed by all birds. Finches, canaries and small parrots are especially fond of this rice.

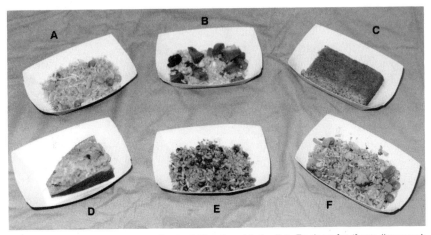

Home-cooked foods are an excellent addition to a bird's diet. Recipes for these "gourmet meals" can be found in this chapter: (A) Luv That Stuffing, (B) Vegetable Medley, (C) Nutri-Birdie Bar, (D) Parrot Tater Melt, (E) Mini Chili, (F) Birdie "Power" Lunch.

Mini Chili

¼ cup adzuki beans*
½ cup long-grain brown rice
¼ cup quinoa†
2¼ cups water
3 whole green chilies
1 bay leaf
Pinch of dried oregano

Place all ingredients in 1½-quart microwave casserole (or 11 × 7 × 2-inch ovenproof-glass dish) and stir to distribute evenly. Cover with wax paper and cook in microwave on high for 35 minutes. Let cool before serving. One-fourth cup is an average serving for a medium-size parrot.

Refrigerate or freeze leftovers. This is very good recipe for small birds.

Luv That Stuffing

¼ cup commercial stuffing mix (try cornbread)
¼ cup defrosted mixed vegetables or either grated carrots, chopped broccoli or diced
    bell pepper
1 tablespoon almonds (slivered, chopped or whole)
1 tablespoon shredded mozzarella cheese
¼ cup cooked pasta (optional)

---

*Adzuki beans can be found in natural food stores. They are an easily digestible protein source and also contain iron, thiamin and phosphorus.

†Quinoa (KEEN-wah) is a grain available in health food stores in bulk or prepackaged. It is easily digested and high in protein.

Place all ingredients in microwave dish. Add just enough water to make slightly moist and stir. Heat in microwave on high until warm, about 30 seconds. Be sure cheese is not too hot before serving. This provides 2 servings for medium-size parrots.

Refrigerate leftovers or freeze.

PARROT TATER MELT

½ baked potato—sweet, white or yam
3 tablespoons chopped raw broccoli
2 tablespoons shredded mozzarella cheese

Scoop out potato and mix with broccoli and cheese in microwave dish. Cook in microwave on high until broccoli is bright green and cheese has melted, about 1 minute. Place mixture back into potato skin. Cool before serving, as is or cut up into pieces. Be sure cheese is not too hot before serving.

Refrigerate or freeze leftovers.

BIRDIE "POWER" LUNCH

1 cup long-grain brown rice
½ cup quinoa
½ cup hulled millet
½ cup almonds (slivered, chopped or whole)
1 tablespoon dried oregano
1 tablespoon dried basil
3 cups water
1 teaspoon chicken bouillon

Place all ingredients in 8 × 8 × 2-inch ovenproof glass dish or 1½-quart glass bowl and stir to mix. Cover with waxed paper and cook in microwave on high for 25 minutes. Add to this fresh cut-up vegetables such as tomato, celery, bell pepper, peas, beans, squash, or brussels sprouts, or defrosted mixed vegetables. Serve warm. One-fourth cup is an average serving for an average size parrot.

Refrigerate or freeze leftovers. This recipe is also enjoyed by smaller birds.

NUTRI-BIRDIE BAR

2 eggs (shells optional)
¼ cup walnuts
¼ cup raisins
18½-ounce box cornbread mix
⅓ cup apple juice
¼ cup applesauce
½ cup defrosted mixed vegetables
½ cup chopped kale leaves or broccoli or shredded carrot

Put eggs, walnuts and raisins in blender and blend a few seconds until egg shells are chopped very fine. Place this mix into bowl with remaining ingredients. Stir until well blended.

Put into a greased 8 × 8 × 2-inch pan and bake at 400°F for 20 minutes. Cool 10 minutes on rack, loosen edges with a knife or spatula and turn out to finish cooling.

This bread can be left in cage all day. Afterward it is best to discard any uneaten portion.

DIETS FOR SOFTBILLS: LORIES, LORIKEETS, MYNAHS, TOUCANS AND PEKIN ROBINS

Up to this point, the nutritional information contained in this chapter has been concerned with the diet of seed-eating birds. "Softbills," on the other hand, eat *only* soft foods. Their special dietary needs make them unique in the bird kingdom. In the wild, fruit makes up the majority of their diet, along with some insects. Depending on which softbills are owned, the dietary recommendations will be slightly different. Before deciding on one of these types of birds as a pet, be aware they do require a little extra time for food preparation and cleanup. Since the bulk of the diet is either soft or liquid-type foods, their droppings will be also be similar!

Lories and Lorikeets

Lories and lorikeets can make wonderful and loving companions. In the wild, these birds feed on fruit, flowers, nectar, pollen and an occasional insect. They have a brushlike tongue, ideally suited for eating these types of foods. Protein needs appear lower than in other birds. Health problems could occur if the level is too high in the diet.

Lories' and lorikeets' food should consist of a commercial lory diet, fresh fruit, nectar and fresh water.

Commercial lory diet: These special diets have been formulated to supply a balanced and nutritious food source. They are available in a wet form, where water needs to be added, and a dry form, fed as a powder. Both are good; however, with the dry diet, their droppings will be a little less watery.

Fruit: All fruits are good to feed. Feed them diced, or at least sliced. Fruits should be fresh. However, canned fruit with no sugar added makes an acceptable alternative.

Nectar: Even if your birds are on a commercial lory diet, consider adding a little nectar to the diet every day.

Mynah Birds, Toucans and Pekin Robins

A mynah bird, toucan and Pekin robin diet should consist of mostly fruit, a few vegetables, a good protein souce and fresh water.

Fruit: Most any food will do, but feed citrus sparingly. Fruits such as pears, apples, grapes and papaya are good choices. They should be offered diced, since they are usually swallowed whole.

Vegetables: Some of these birds also enjoy vegetables. Raw mixed vegetables can be added to the fruit mix.

Protein: Since fruit and vegetables are low in protein, a good source needs to be added to the diet. Commercial mynah bird pellets are recommended and can be soaked in water or fruit juice. A few insects, such as mealworms and crickets, can also be offered.

Fruits, vegetables, and the protein source can all be blended together in a food processor. Even tofu, carrots and some cheese can be added. Mynah bird pellets can be used to control the texture of this formula, which should be moist and still a little crumbly. Pound cake soaked in fruit juice or some type of nectar is often a much-enjoyed treat.

Some of these birds have a tendency to store abnormally high amounts of iron in their livers (iron storage disease). Therefore a good protein source with special attention paid to a low iron content is important. The iron content of the food should be less than 150 parts per million (150 ppm). Dog and cat foods and monkey chow should *not* be fed. Also, dried fruits, raisins and spinach should not be fed for the same reasons.

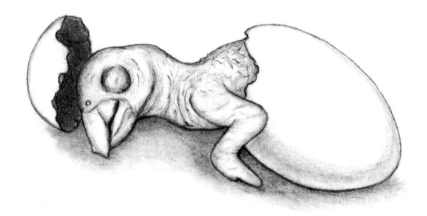

5

Baby Birds

Housing, Feeding and Weaning

by Mike and Deb Morrison

HAND-REARING young birds is challenging, rewarding and, at times, stressful. However, these birds are worth the effort and usually make the best companions. Proper nutrition and care during this growth period are essential for a long and healthy life.

For the first time "baby raiser," start out with a chick that is at least six weeks old. These birds are easier to rear, require less time and let the owner avoid the need for expensive brooding equipment.

The seller should provide written instructions for rearing your new baby bird. This chapter will help further explain the hand-rearing process. Once these "basics" are mastered, common sense will help guide the reader through this new experience. Remember, the effort spent will soon result in a trusting and loving new family member.

REASONS FOR HAND-FEEDING

- Hand-raised birds make the most affectionate and trusting pets.
- Parents fail to feed their young.
- Parents mistreat their young.

SUPPLIES FOR HAND FEEDING

- Brooder
  Heat and humidity source
  Thermometer

Bedding material
Cleaning and disinfecting supplies
• Food and feeding equipment
Spoon or syringe
Thermometer for food
• Weighing scale (optional)

BROODERS

A brooder is a heated and humidified enclosure for housing young chicks. It provides an environment for optimum growth and health. Brooders can be as simple as an aquarium or a cardboard box with a bowl of water inside and a heating pad underneath. They can also be very elaborate, with automatic temperature and humidity controls. For the new bird owner raising a chick over six weeks old, a simple brooder should be sufficient. An additional consideration in the selection of brooding equipment should be ease of cleaning and disinfecting.

Temperature Requirements

Chicks recently hatched and up to four weeks of age require environmental temperatures of 92 to 96°F. These very young birds should also be housed in a brooder with thermostatically controlled settings.

Chicks over four weeks of age require environmental temperatures around 85°F. These chicks usually do well in a simple or basic brooder as described

Brooders are important to the health and growth of baby birds. This is an example of a brooder that provides automatic heat and humidity. By keeping babies in smaller individual containers within the brooder, contamination is minimized and cleaning made easier. *(Mike Morrison)*

above. An aquarium thermometer placed on or near the floor of the brooder is very helpful for monitoring temperatures.

Temperatures that are too cold or too warm can be harmful to the young bird. A change in a chick's behavior can indicate a problem. If the bird is too cold it will shiver, develop slow responses or may suffer crop-emptying problems (see pages 190–191). A chick that is too warm may pant, develop reddening of the skin, or hold the wings out and away from the body.

COMMON BROODING TEMPERATURES

Newly hatched	92–96°F
1–3 weeks	90–92°F
4 weeks through weaning	85°F

Humidity Requirements

Proper humidity is very important for optimal growth, digestion and resistance to disease. Humidity of 40 to 55 percent in the brooder is best for young birds.

For simple brooders with the proper temperature, adding a container of water with holes punched in the lid should be adequate to sustain proper humidity level. The brooder must also be covered with a towel or other suitable material to maintain the proper humidified environment.

Bedding Materials

Absorbent bedding materials are necessary to keep the chick clean and dry. Chicks under three weeks old are usually kept on facial tissue, paper towels, hand towels and diapers. Chicks over three weeks old can be kept on commercially available products. These vary from pelletized grasses to recycled paper products. These products are preferable for older chicks because they have greater absorbency. If ingested, the bedding material should be able to pass through the digestive tract without problems.

Bedding materials should be changed whenever soiled or at least after each feeding. If any of the bedding materials become frayed at the edges, they should be trimmed to avoid injuring a chick's toes or feet. Wood shavings, dried corncobs or walnut shells are *not* recommended as suitable bedding materials. These products can be mistakenly ingested and cause serious digestive tract problems.

Cleaning and Disinfecting

Good sanitation is absolutely essential for the prevention of health problems. Hands should always be clean and washed prior to handling the bird. Brooders and equipment must be cleaned and disinfected whenever dirty.

There are many good disinfectants available. Bleach (properly diluted), antibacterial soaps or Lysol can be used. However, other commercially available disinfectants can be found from bird equipment suppliers (see Chapter 3).

FOOD AND FEEDING EQUIPMENT

Diet

As with all young animals, good nutrition is essential. The optimal diet should promote growth, development and resistance to disease. Chicks require a liquid diet prior to weaning. Solid foods should not be fed until close to weaning time. For the novice baby bird raiser, commercially prepared diets are preferable to homemade formulas.

When first bringing the chick home, it's usually best to continue feeding the same diet the bird has been receiving. If the formula needs to be changed, do so gradually over several feedings. The formulas should be mixed together, increasing the proportion of new formula at each feeding. The gradual changeover will reduce stress and increase the acceptance of the new food.

Hand-feeding formulas should be prepared fresh with each feeding. The food should be fed at a temperature between 100° and 110°F. A human thermometer can be used to test the food. If a microwave is used for warming, heat only the water and then add formula. This method avoids dangerous "hot spots" in the food, which can burn the digestive tract.

A healthy chick on a good diet will appear bright, alert and responsive. Daily weighings are very helpful. In addition, the feet and toes are a good indicator of health and weight. They should appear plump and round, not long, slender and dried out. Feathers should be clean, shiny and in neat order. "Stress lines" (see Chapter 12) should not be present.

As mentioned above, commercial hand feeding formulas are recommended. However, if not available, a home-made formula can be substituted until a commercial one can be found.

RECIPE FOR HOMEMADE FORMULA

¼ cup Gerber's High Protein Baby Cereal
1 jar Gerber's Strained Mixed Vegetables
¼ cup high-quality dry dog food
Avian vitamins and minerals (follow label instructions)
Peanut butter, applesauce, or hard boiled egg (optional)

Mix ingredients in blender. Add enough water to form soupy consistency.

Note: This recipe should only be used until a commercial formula can be obtained. It is *NOT* recommended for long-term use.

Feeding

There are two common utensils used for hand-feeding parrots, a spoon that has been bent into a funnel shape or a feeding syringe, proportionate to the size of the chick's beak. The smaller the beak, the smaller the syringe necessary for feeding. A plastic eye dropper for small birds and even a turkey baster for larger birds can also be used. For the beginner, the spoon method usually works best.

Chicks should be hungry at every feeding. A chick that does not seem interested in food should *not* be forced to eat. A hungry chick will respond by bobbing its head and/or make a chirping sound. These actions decrease the chance of aspirating food and choking.

If there is no feeding response, it may be necessary to actually touch the sides of the beak to initiate a feeding response. This action mimics the joining of the parent's and chick's beaks. If the chick still does not respond, look for some underlying reason. This might include food that is too cold or too hot, a chick that is too cold or feeding schedules too close together. There may also be a medical reason for the loss of appetite (see later in this chapter).

FEEDING FREQUENCY

The frequency of feeding depends on age, species, and "thickness" of the food. A good rule of thumb is feeding every two to three hours for the first week

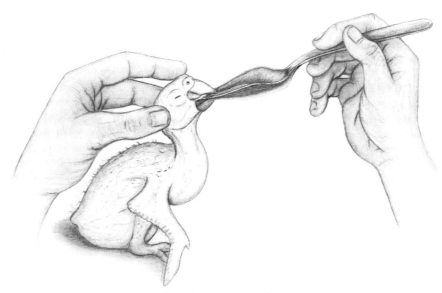

Spoonfeeding a baby bird.

Proper technique for spoon-feed-
ing an eight-week-old Blue and
Gold macaw. *(Mike Morrison)*

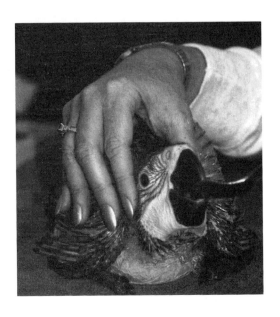

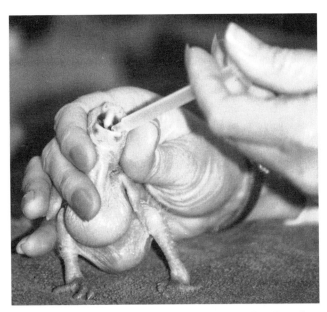

Proper technique for syringe-feeding a one-week-old Blue Front Amazon. *(Mike Morrison)*

Frequency of Feedings per Day: *general guidelines*

SPECIES	0–7 DAYS	7–21 DAYS	21 DAYS–WEANING
Budgerigar	5–8	4–6	3–4
Cockatiel	5–8	4–6	3–4
Conure	5–8	4–6	3–4
Senegal	5–8	4–6	3–4
Amazons	5–8	4–6	3–4
African Grey	5–8	4–6	3–4
Cockatoo	5–8	4–6	3–4
Small macaw	5–8	4–6	3–4
Large macaw	5–8	4–6	3–4

after hatching. Chicks over six weeks of age require two to four feedings each day. Maintaining a regular feeding schedule is very important.

There is some controversy over the need for late-night feedings with very young chicks. A six-to seven-hour break allows the crop to empty completely and may lessen the chance for medical problems to occur. The decision to feed or not to feed in the middle of the night should be made on an individual basis. Some newly hatched chicks require a late-night feeding, while others do not. However, this decision depends on many factors, including strength and alertness of chick, ease of hatching and if the yolk remains in the chick's abdomen. If the yolk is not completely absorbed, there will be a yellow coloration of the abdomen. In this case, the initial two to three feedings should consist of only sterile water, Pedialyte (human rehydration supplement available at grocery stores) or Ensure (human geriatric supplement available at drug stores). This will allow the newly hatched chick to completely absorb the remaining yolk.

As the chick develops, feedings gradually become less frequent while the amount of food accepted increases. After three weeks of age, the feeding schedule decreases to three to four times daily or about every six hours. The crop should be empty between feedings. If the chick is fed prior to complete crop emptying, there is an increased risk of infection. The frequency of feedings can be reduced to one or two daily as the chick nears weaning age.

Feeding Technique

Practice makes perfect. Hand-feeding is really a very simple technique that will quickly be learned. In addition, the time spent will begin the bonding process. Therefore, proceed slowly and be gentle.

First, sit facing the chick. Food should be offered from the left side of its beak. During the feeding process, try to direct the food toward the right side of the mouth. Food should be offered in bite-size amounts and allowed to be swallowed before more is given. Stop feeding when the crop is full. Watch for the crop to become well rounded and taut.

Quantity of Food per Feeding: *general guidelines*

SPECIES	0–7 DAYS	7–21 DAYS	21–28 DAYS	28–35 DAYS	35–48 DAYS	48 DAYS– WEANING
Budgerigar	.25–2 cc*	2–4 cc	5cc	5 cc	5 cc	weaned
Cockatiel	.5–4 cc	4–10cc	10cc	10 cc	10–15 cc	weaned
Conure	.5–4 cc	4–10cc	10–15cc	15–20 cc	15–25 cc	15 25 cc
Senegal	.5–5 cc	5–10cc	10–15cc	15–20 cc	15–20 cc	20 cc
Amazons	1–10cc	10–35cc	25–45cc	40–50 cc	45–60 cc	60 cc
African Grey	1–6 cc	6–30cc	30–40cc	40–45 cc	40–50 cc	50–60 cc
Cockatoo	.5–10cc	10–35cc	35–60cc	50–70 cc	50–80 cc	60–80 cc
Small macaw	.5–6 cc	6–20cc	20–30cc	25–35 cc	35–50 cc	40–50 cc
Large macaw	1–10cc	10–50cc	50–80cc	80–100cc	80–100cc	100–120cc

*1cc is equal to 1/5 teaspoon.

Although uncommon, problems associated with feeding sometimes occur. coughing and/or "violent" head shaking could suggest choking on food. If this is suspected, contact your veterinarian immediately.

In addition, the chick should be thoroughly cleaned after each feeding. Any food or droppings seen on the beak, feathers or legs should be removed. This is easily done with a little warm water applied with a facial tissue, paper towel, Q-tip, or cotton ball.

QUANTITY OF FOOD

The amount of food fed at each feeding depends on the age and species of the chick. The best rule of thumb is to continue feeding until the crop appears well rounded and taut. As the chick grows, the volume of food is increased.

Don't overfeed. A crop that is frequently overfilled and overstretched could lead to medical problems.

WEIGHT MONITORING

If possible, chicks should be weighed first thing every morning *before* feeding. This is valuable information used to monitor growth and health status. There should be a constant and steady weight gain throughout the hand-rearing period. Weight should be carefully charted every day. Weight loss could indicate a problem.

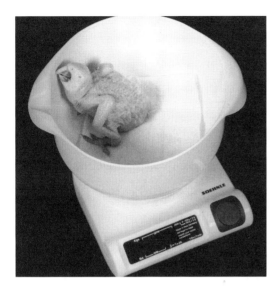

Baby birds should be weighed on a gram scale every day.
(Bonnie Jay)

Weights measured in grams are much more accurate than those measured in ounces.

WEANING

Weaning is the transition period when the chick begins to eat solid foods on its own. It is also a *very* stressful time for both the chick and its owner. The weaning time varies by species.

A chick ready to be weaned usually refuses to eat its formula and instead prefers solid foods. Most birds will naturally wean themselves. However, some birds may need to have their hand-feedings reduced to stimulate the weaning

Weaning Ages: *general guidelines*

SPECIES	WEANING AGE
Budgerigar	5–6 weeks
Cockatiel	6–8 weeks
Conure	6–9 weeks
Senegal/Meyers	7–9 weeks
Amazons	10–12 weeks
African Grey	12–15 weeks
Cockatoo	12–15 weeks
Small macaw	8–10 weeks
Large macaw	12–15 weeks

77

process. Chicks should not be allowed to go to bed hungry. When handfeeding only once daily, make this the last meal before bedtime. In the morning, always provide a fresh supply of transition food.

It's very common to expect a weight loss during the weaning period. Losses of 5 percent are normal. If weight losses become excessive, contact your avian veterinarian immediately.

TRANSITION FOODS FOR WEANING

Moistened commercial bird foods
Cereals (e.g., Cheerios, Rice Krispies)
Cooked vegetables or fresh fruits*
Cooked pastas*
Seeds and spray millet

DROPPINGS

A chick on formula will have droppings containing more liquid than those seen in adult birds. The more watery the formula, the wetter the droppings. The feces are normally brown or brownish-green in color. The droppings should also be essentially odorless.

MEDICAL PROBLEMS ASSOCIATED WITH HAND-REARING

Signs to Watch For

- Change in behavior: less active and depressed
- Appetite loss
- Slow crop-emptying time
- Weight loss or slow weight gains
- Regurgitation
- Change in droppings
- Moistness or matting of feathers at base of neck

Possible Causes

Infections: Bacterial and yeast are most common. Infections often involve the digestive tract. Slow crop-emptying times are common. In young chicks, the crop should empty in two to three hours; in older chicks, six hours.

"Crop Burns": Formula that is too hot and sitting in the crop can actually burn its way through the outer layer of skin. Look for moistness or matting of feathers at the base of the neck. As noted earlier in this chapter, check the temperature of food before feeding. Also, mix the formula well.

---

*Remove cooked and fresh foods after 2 hours.

78

All domestically raised baby birds should be banded. Bands are available in different sizes depending on the type of bird. Bands are placed on the babies when they are very young so they can "grow into" them. *(Mike Morrison)*

First Aid for Baby Bird Problems

There are no safe and effective home treatments. Baby birds can develop life-threatening problems quickly. Contact your avian veterinarian at the *first* sign of problems.

SUMMARY

This chapter provides basic hand-rearing guidelines and suggestions. If good results are not seen in your new baby, *don't* hesitate to seek advice. It is better to be safe than sorry.

By providing proper housing, bedding, sanitation, nutrition and care during this critical period, you will greatly enhance your bird's chances for a long, happy, healthy life. Yearly checkups with an avian veterinarian will help ensure that proper conditions of care and nutrition are maintained.

A hand-fed bird will be more than a pet, it will be part of the family.

6

The Well-Mannered Parrot

by Christine Davis

IDEALLY, THE RELATIONSHIP between you and your bird should be a wonderful loving experience. A "well-mannered" parrot that can harmonize with its environment helps to achieve this lasting partnership. In other words, these birds interact well with people, are pleasant to be around, display minimal screaming and aggression and can entertain themselves when left alone.

While pet birds can be as intelligent and different as children, on some levels they are still wild animals. However, once we understand the world from a bird's perspective, it will be much easier to marvel at the perfection of all birds. Remember, they are perfect in their natural surroundings. It is only our unrealistic expectations for their behavior in our strange, artifical environment that causes problems in our relationships with them. After all, we would make terrible birds in the wild if the situation were reversed.

As with all creatures, understanding, compassion and respect are the keys to the growth of a long and mutually beneficial relationship. In this chapter, concepts to help understand and explore the behaviors of our well mannered parrot "to be" are explained. In addition, the concepts involved with teaching and correcting undesirable behaviors, and tips for training and talking are discussed.

A mentally well-adjusted bird will enjoy human companionship and will also be able to play by itself on a perch or in a cage. *(Bonnie Jay)*

UNDERSTANDING OUR WILD FRIENDS

Traditionally, humans have expected their animal friends to be loyal and affectionate, always happy and very forgiving of their owners' shortcomings. Unfortunately, this describes the "perfect" dog! Unlike birds, dogs have been "programmed" for 10,000 to 15,000 years to be companions for humans.

Most of our birds are only one or two generations away from the jungle and have an entirely different set of "rules and regulations." Because of this, your little parrot friend has no concept of the traditional owner/pet relationship and can only treat humans as they would other members of their flock. In fact, human behavior can be rather mystifying to most birds. Our actions are frequently not understood by our logical little feathered friends.

They're Bright

Emotionally, most of the larger parrots have the development of a two- to three-year-old human child. One of the similar characteristics they have is a short attention span. This must be understood and kept in mind at all times while working with them.

Intellectually, parrots are at the top of the class! In a scientific study, Dr. Irene Pepperberg has been working with Alex, an African Grey. He is extremely intelligent and can identify colors, shapes, objects and even people. This suggests that parrots can perform some visual behaviors at approximately the level of a four-year-old child. It has also been recently theorized, if properly trained, some birds are capable of understanding and using the human language at basic levels.

With this in mind, it is easy to see how a parrot, if forced to sit in one boring place for long periods of time, may begin to "misbehave." How can this be prevented?

1. Offer Variety: Provide a variety of toys and different locations for the bird. If it is becoming bored, noisy or rowdy, lovingly return it to its cage for fifteen to twenty minutes. This allows time for the bird to eat, rest and experience a change of scenery. It can then be returned to the original location.

2. Anticipate and Avoid Potential Problems: Birds are flock creatures and need to feel like members of *your* flock. Every ten or fifteen minutes, interact with the bird by talking to, looking at, tickling or picking it up for a few seconds to show that you remember it is part of the family. Reward your bird *before* it feels the need to misbehave for your attention.

3. Do Not Reward Unwanted Behaviors: If your bird is misbehaving, do not reward such behavior by looking at it, picking it up or talking to it. Birds are intelligent and will quickly learn to perform the undesired behavior, "training" you to interact with them!

4. Respect: Respect the bird's intelligence. Like any other intelligent creature, your bird will respond in the manner in which it is treated. Remember this and your relationship with your bird will always be strong and gratifying.

WILD-CAUGHT VERSUS HAND-RAISED

Wild-Caught Birds

Occasionally, a wild bird will be acquired as a pet. Although it may seem aggressive, it must be understood the wild-caught parrot is terrified of predators and sees humans in this category. They *know* you are going to "kill 'em and eat 'em." This is their point of reference!

In order to modify this natural tendency, it will take extra time to build a friendship. Do not expect instant results. The wild individual needs to be treated with *love* and *compassion*, and not "broken" into submission. Remember, this bird did not *ask* to be here; and, it is up to you to prove *your* good intentions— not the other way around! Here are some simple tips for building a friendship:

1. Provide a Quiet Environment: Cage the new bird in a quiet room, preferably in a corner, where it will feel protected and can observe activity without being in the center of it.

2. Slowly Gain Trust: Several times a day, walk up to the bird, speaking softly and slowly. After the bird becomes relaxed and its favorite foods are evident, treats can be offered through the cage bars. The wild-caught bird should have access to food at all times. Withhold only its very favorites for hand-feeding. If the bird is too frightened to take the treat, slowly place it in the food cup and back away to a distance where the bird will feel comfortable. You may even have to leave the room when the bird eats for the first few days.

3. Let the Bird Establish Its Own Pace: As the bird becomes confident, gradually stand closer to the cage, until the food can be offered from your hand. Allow the bird to "come around" at its own pace, even if it takes a few months. Remember, a wild bird will feel threatened by your attentions until you can convince it that you mean no harm.

Treats can be offered to frightened birds through the safety of the cage bars. *(Bonnie Jay)*

4. Have Realistic Expectations for the Bird and for Yourself: Remember the wild-caught bird *is* a wild animal, and you may need a trainer or behaviorist to assist in further taming. Contact a local avian veterinarian for a reliable referral in your area.

Hand-Fed Birds

A domestically bred bird is still, genetically, a wild animal. It is essential that it learn how to interact socially with members of its human ''flock.''

1. Socialize Your Friend: Pay attention to the bird's likes and dislikes and play games with it. Collect a variety of toys and place or roll them on a flat surface such as the floor, table, bed or sofa. Let the bird chase or nibble on them.

2. Understand the Bird's Fears: Sometimes, a bird will be afraid of new objects, even toys. This is because the fear of strange things is a very useful survival trait in the wild. Any new object could be a predator or a trap. Respect the bird's fears and let it see the new toy resting in a place far enough away for the bird to feel safe. Play with the toy yourself in the bird's sight, while talking in a pleasant voice. Often, a little patience will be all it takes for your feathered friend to enjoy all the wonderful things that have been collected for it!

3. Talk to the Bird: Always look into the bird's eyes when talking to it, speaking in a cheerful, animated voice. Not only will the bird enjoy the exchange,

Your bird will be able to enjoy new toys if you play with them first and then offer them to your little friend.
(Bonnie Jay)

but it duplicates the way birds communicate in the wild. This approach will also have a comforting effect.

DOMINANCE: "WHO'S THE BOSS?"

Just as everyone appreciates a well-mannered child, the same is equally true for our pet birds. Children learn manners from their parents, much the same as birds must learn from their owners what is expected of them.

Birds do not see humans as their masters, but as other members of their flock. Therefore, even though humans make up part of the "flock," their natural tendency is to try to achieve the most dominant position! Unfortunately, without knowing it, people allow their birds to become the dominant member of the family. Pet owners often will even *encourage* this behavior without realizing they are doing so. This can create problems. Teach your little companion a few handy tips to keep it in the proper "pecking order" within your family.

The Proper "Pecking Order"

1. Keep Birds Perched at/or Below the Level of Your Heart: Dominance in the flock is conveyed by the bird perching in a position higher than that of their companions. Owners mistakenly "tell" their birds that they are dominant by allowing them to perch at shoulder level or higher. There are obviously exceptions, but in general birds will begin to take advantage of this higher stature. In these instances, they will become "little rascals" and could get out of hand.

Keep birds on the wrist or forearm. Prevent them from perching on shoulders. When they are not being held, they should also be kept on perches in which the top of their head comes to the owner's heart level. Interestingly, the heartbeat will also have a soothing effect on the bird and will help to prevent the desire to dominate.

2. Birds Must Be Supervised When Out of Their Cages: When a bird is

 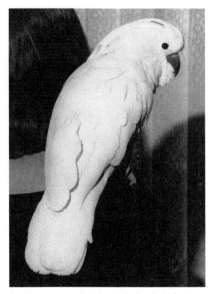

Keep your bird on the wrist, hand or forearm, keeping the top of its head at the level of your heart. *(Bonnie Jay)*

To discourage dominant behavior, do not allow your bird to perch on your shoulder. *(Bonnie Jay)*

outside of its cage and not being handled, it should have a play "gym" or perch to play on. Birds that are allowed to run loose in the house can damage property, and even worse, they can harm themselves.

If taught to stay in a play area, birds learn to entertain themselves. When other members of the family are occupied, they will not demand constant attention. A secure, well-behaved bird will want to be with its owner, but will also be able to play by itself.

Simple Commands to Establish Dominance

Another effective way to show your bird "who's the boss" is to begin teaching it a few simple behaviors. Since you establish these behaviors, they will provide the beginnings of the control necessary to create the proper family pecking order.

1. Getting onto the Hand: The well-mannered parrot will step onto a hand when asked. It is easier to teach a bird while it is on a perch. Simply present your hand in front of the bird, keeping it as stable as possible. In a pleasant voice, ask the bird to get on (try "Come here"). Gently forcing your hand against one of its legs will sometimes be needed for encouragement.

Remember, most birds prefer to step slightly forward and upward. Hold your hand in front of, and slightly higher than, the perch the bird is on. Some birds feel more comfortable getting onto a stick or hand-held perch. In these situations, their feelings should be respected.

86

Most birds prefer to step forward and slightly upward when perching on a hand or arm.*(Bonnie Jay)*

If the bird is a clumsy baby, try cupping your hands gently around the body and gently lift it from the perch. Do not make a bird step onto your hand until it is capable of doing so comfortably. Remember, you are the bird's friend and caretaker and need to both build a trusting relationship and make your pet feel safe.

2. Returning to the Cage: Reverse the process to return the bird to its cage or perch. Remember, birds usually prefer stepping up and forward. The command of "Go back," or "Time to go back," can be used. Remove your hand *only* when the bird is securely perched.

Even though a large bird appears full grown, it can still be a little clumsy. Be sensitive to the bird's capabilities. Also, whenever giving a command, use a sweet voice. Remember, the bird is your friend—*invite* it to come to you, don't demand. Eventually, the sight of your hand being presented to your bird will be the visual "cue" to come to you. No verbal cue will be required.

TALKING

Almost every owner of parrot or Mynah wants to know if the bird is going to talk. Remember each one is an individual. Even among the more talkative species, *your* particular bird may not *want* to talk, or may not be *able* to talk, for some physical or environmental reason.

There are many ways to try to teach a bird to talk. The following suggestions have been very helpful.

1. Speak Clearly and Naturally: Vocalizing is a natural part of a bird's life in the wild. Your pet bird will enjoy any type of verbal exchange with you. Speak clearly. If your speech is mumbled or distorted, the talking bird will make the same type of sounds and will not be a clear talker.

Some birds are physically incapable of duplicating sounds. Often, they will "speak" in chirps and whistles. Answer their attempts in a friendly manner, exactly as you would another person who has a foreign accent! This will encourage them to keep interacting with you on a vocal level.

The voice should be pitched a little higher than normal. This will make it clearer for the bird to understand and easier for it to copy.

2. Try Teaching with Audio Tapes: Homemade and commercial tapes can be used to teach a bird to talk. They should be played for about ten minutes at a time, two or three times a day.

Remember, a bird will only mimic taped sounds, without understanding their meaning. However, recent scientific studies are showing that birds can understand and consciously use many words and phrases. However, words and sentences must be used in context if the bird is expected to truly understand them.

In conclusion, if a bird is to be a good friend, remember it is okay if it turns out to be the "silent type." It can still be a wonderful companion. Most of all, if owners become angry about what they consider to be a shortcoming, they will not be able to appreciate all of their birds' other wonderful attributes!

"TRICKS" OR TRAINED BEHAVIORS

Everyone has been charmed, at one time or another, by the sight of a bird riding a bicycle or playing basketball. Although some people do not approve of teaching birds to perform, many birds *enjoy* learning a few behaviors. In addition, training can be a wonderful way to interact with a bird who does enjoys being a ham. There are several books available that can teach owners how to train their bird. The titles are included in the Bibliography. Here are only a few brief suggestions:

1. Respect the Bird's Likes and Dislikes: Remember, the bird is your friend. It is important for it to enjoy life with you. If your bird likes little props, toys, balls, bells and similar items, it will probably enjoy learning behaviors that use similar objects. If the bird enjoys lying on its back, dancing to music or running in circles on the floor, it will probably prefer learning behaviors that incorporate these types of activities.

2. Keep Sessions Short: Like a small child, a bird has a short attention span. It can become cranky and disagreeable if forced to interact for too long a period of time. It is up to the owner to realistically anticipate and respect his/her bird's needs.

3. Keep Sessions Fun for Both of You: Remember, your bird is a companion. Most professionally-trained birds appearing in shows have been chosen for their performing capabilities and are often not pets.

To train your friend, withhold a favorite food and use it for a reward. Combine this with a verbal cue, or command. Pine nuts, or shelled, broken-up peanuts make nice, small treats. However, most birds who have a good relationship with their owners will only require praise, love and affection as the reward! Do not keep your feathered friend hungry. This is unnecessary and can negatively affect your relationship.

4. Love Them for What They Are: If your bird is a lovable little "lump" that does not do much of anything, it should be loved just for the way it is. Appreciate your bird's unique personality. If you do, it will always, without fail, and to its best ability, reflect a secure, happy attitude in everything it does. Don't forget, *your bird is your friend.* Developing and perfecting this friendship needs to be your main objective, and anything in addition is the proverbial icing on the cake.

UNDESIRABLE BEHAVIORS

Sometimes your bird will begin to "misbehave." Usually the bird is not "bad," but is behaving normally for the way in which you have interacted with it. Unfortunately, *we* are often the direct cause of the very behaviors we dislike! If we understand the world from the bird's perspective, everything it does will make more sense.

The two most common behavior problems in pet birds are biting and screaming.

Biting

Birds use their beaks for a variety of reasons. Often, people will misunderstand their bird's natural use of its beak as an aggressive behavior. The bird may only be trying to convey a message in the same way in which it would "talk" to another bird. Another bird would naturally understand the situation and avoid being bitten. Unfortunately, humans are not as observant as their avian friends and will unintentionally provoke biting behavior in their birds!

1. Respect the Bird's Needs: If a bird is sleeping and is awakened because a person wants to play, the bird may strike out as a warning. This is not aggression. The bird is merely surprised someone would be so inconsiderate! If the bird is napping, eating or playing with a toy, allow it to finish, or verbally alert it before removing it from the activity.

If the bird has always been a good friend and begins to bite, examine the conditions within the environment. Has the owner's working hours become longer? Is the owner distracted or worried about various things? Have there been new people or unusual events occurring in the home? Did strangers try to hold or touch the bird? Birds always reflect even the most subtle changes within their "flock."

As a wild animal, a bird's instincts signal when conditions in the environment do not seem right. Unfortunately, this can be interpreted as being life threatening. If an owner does not pay attention to warning behaviors, which vary with different species, the bird may be "forced" to nip or bite. Educate your friends. Help them understand the bird is a wild animal and unpredictable or unusual situations are extremely stressful to them. You need to be your bird's best friend and protector.

2. *Determine the Cause:* If the bird becomes more and more aggressive, it may be because it is being allowed to perch too high in the environment some of the time, i.e., sitting on your shoulder, on top of their cage or on a tall play gym. Once again, this "tells" the bird it is dominant. Biting can be caused because the bird will feel the need to defend its superior position.

Simply placing your bird on a stand or gym with the top of its head at heart level is often all that's needed to do to put the bird in the submissive "child" role and stop the dominant biting behavior!

If the bird tries to bite while on an arm, make sure you are not doing anything to make it feel insecure. The bird may only be trying to "tell" you, in the only way it knows, it is frightened. It is your responsibility, as the bird's friend and protector, to be aware of its comfort and security.

3. *Try a Few Simple Corrections:* Sometimes, a bird will try to dominate its owner by pinching an arm or hand while being held. To correct this, try gently jiggling or sharply jerking the arm downward three to six inches, giving the bird an "earthquake." Never move so violently that the bird can fall; also, do not scold it. Make your bird believe that, if it bites humans, an earthquake will happen! This technique also works well to correct chewing on clothing and jewelry.

Another simple technique, if the bird is very sociable by nature, is to return it to its cage for ten minutes and ignore it before letting it out again. Birds cannot stand being separated from other flock members and will usually begin to behave in an acceptable manner after being "banished" a few times.

AN IMPORTANT NOTE TO AFRICAN GREY PARROT OWNERS

African Grey parrots are clumsy, especially when they are young. They will often bite because their human friends are actually frightening them by throwing them off balance when they are being petted. This can be alleviated by holding the bird on your arm in so that its beak lightly touches your chest. This "tripod" effect will make the bird feel secure and more willing to accept loving snuggles!

Caution: Please note *it is never necessary to strike a bird*! In addition to the moral issue of striking an animal, birds are fragile creatures and can easily be killed or permanently crippled by a relatively light blow.

Screaming

People will often say they would never share their lives with a bird because they are too noisy, although what we define as noise is a normal part of birds' existence in the wild. Most birds, when well-mannered, will not be excessively loud. It is up to us to teach them what the proper levels of vocalization are in our particular environment.

1. Determine the Cause: Sometimes birds will scream because their human companions leave the room. This is natural and is called separation anxiety. Even some dogs exhibit this behavior when left alone. If a bird begins to scream when the owner leaves the room, the owner should not immediately run back in. If this is done, the owner will be reinforcing the bird's "bad" behavior. The bird will then continue to scream to get the owner to return.

Merely offer a few brief words of comfort from the other room, returning after the bird quiets down. Your bird will then learn to be quiet so you, its human, will return faster.

2. Try These Simple Corrective Techniques: If you are standing near the bird in its cage and it begins to scream for attention, the cage can be completely covered for ten minutes. Do not cover it longer. If this is done, the object of the lesson will be lost and the correction will be useless.

Covering the cage can be tricky. For example, if you are in another room and the bird begins to scream for attention, it is better to be quiet and stay out of the room until the noise stops. If you return to the room to cover the cage, the behavior has just been reinforced. This is what your bird originally wanted, for you to return!

Sometimes, a loud noise from another room, such as banging sharply on a door, smacking a rolled-up newspaper, or slamming a book on a tabletop can stop the behavior for a few moments. If it does, it is important to enter the room where the bird is located, while it is still quiet. This will be reinforcing the silence, instead of the screaming!

If birds are scolded when they scream, they are getting attention and the behavior is being reinforced and rewarded. This will create more problems than before! Amazon parrots and macaws, especially, enjoy the sound of being scolded, and many of them will yell and proceed to enthusiastically tell themselves to "be quiet" or call themselves "bad birds." Although this is amusing, it does not solve the problem and your bird will still continue to scream loudly.

Always reward any desirable sounds the bird makes, even if they are just quiet little chirps or clicks. If this is done, the bird will think of it as a game and a form of communication. It will gradually choose to make acceptable noises to get you to tell it what a good little bird it is. A little praise goes a long way toward creating a wonderfully behaved friend!

REINFORCING OR REWARDING DESIRABLE BEHAVIORS

We often think a great deal about correcting undesirable behaviors, but lose sight of the more important issue of rewarding a bird when it behaves well! Of all the behaviors they will be taught, this will be the most important. Like small children, birds need to be lovingly taught exactly what constitutes "good" and "bad" behavior.

Since birds are similar to two- or three-year-old children emotionally, they need to be taught in the same way. Reinforce good behaviors by "tickling," or other favorite rewards, and offer lots of verbal praise. Remember good behavior does not always consist of doing a "trick" that pleases you. It *does* consist of the bird not indulging in destructive or annoying behaviors. If the bird just sits quietly and plays, or even does *nothing*, it is being a *wonderful* bird. Your special pet needs verbal, visual and physical rewards directly from you to clearly understand this.

Sometimes, just looking at your bird and smiling when it is behaving well is a very strong reward. Kisses and strategically placed scratches rate very high on the "birdie" popularity scale, as does the offering of an occasional food goodie. Have fun with your friend! Your bird will love you for it!

COMPASSION IS THE KEY

Marvel at the birds' perfection. Remember, they *are* perfect in their natural surroundings. Avoid unrealistic expectations of your bird. How would you feel if birds heaped unrealistic expectations upon us and wanted us to behave in a way *they* dictated? Would you be happy? What if birds merely loved us for what we are, humans? How would you feel then? Isn't it time we treated our animal friends in the same ways in which *we* would like to be treated?

Once again, remember, compassion, respect and understanding are the keys to the growth of a long and mutually beneficial relationship. We need to learn to "live" these qualities and get rid of our old programming, which makes us expect unrealistic behaviors from our animal friends. Only then can we find ourselves educated by the experience and enriched by it, as well.

7

Restraint

Catching and Holding Safely

CATCHING or holding a bird will probably become necessary. The reasons for physical restraint include grooming, medicating and some emergencies. Avoiding injury to the holder and the bird are the primary concerns with restraint.

TIPS TO REMEMBER WHEN RESTRAINING

- Work quickly to minimize handling time. Stress and overheating problems will be reduced.
- Plan ahead. Have all tools, equipment, medications or whatever ready *prior to restraint.*
- For small birds especially, a net would be helpful to catch the bird if it escapes.
- Towel selection is based on size of the bird. It will be chewed on, so choose an old one!
- In pet birds, the beak causes injuries. Respect it and protect yourself. (Hawks and other raptors inflict injuries with their feet.)
- Birds have very fragile bones. Their legs and wings are most susceptible to injury.
- Don't put any pressure on the chest while holding a bird. It will interfere with breathing.
- It may help to darken a room just prior to catching birds. The darkness temporarily "freezes" them.

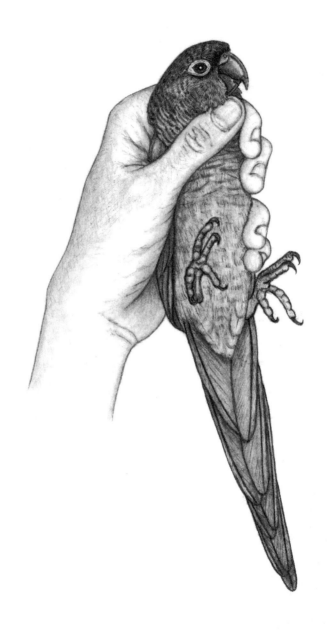

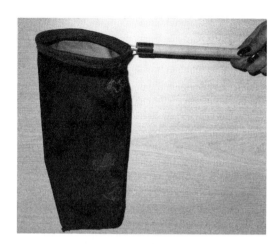

For small birds especially, a net would be helpful to catch the bird if it escapes.

SUPPLIES FOR RESTRAINT

Towels are best to catch and hold birds. Use small washcloths for canaries, parakeets and lovebirds, and kitchen or hand towels for medium-size birds, bath towels for larger birds. Towels work best for two reasons. First, they protect and hide the hands. The bird does not see a human hand approaching, only a towel. The thicker the towel, the more finger protection available. Secondly, the towel allows the bird's body to be wrapped up once it is caught. Wing flapping is avoided.

Contrary to popular belief, gloves are not a good way to catch and hold birds. They imitate the shape of the human hand and don't provide any "wrapping material."

"THE CATCH"

Catching a bird should always be done quickly to minimize stress.

If there is an option, smaller birds are best caught inside the cage or if "finger tame" directly from the hand. Tamed larger birds are usually best captured outside the cage in a confined area such as a corner of a small room. In a large area, it's easier for birds to get away. Untamed larger birds usually need to be caught in their cages.

Inside the Cage

A darkened room makes it much easier to catch smaller birds; the sudden darkness temporarily "freezes" them. If needed, the cage can be carried to a room that can be easily darkened, and a small flashlight used to identify the bird's location so it can be quickly grabbed. If using this technique with larger parrots, be *very* careful. The restrainer also has limited vision, and even friendly parrots will bite when frightened.

"The Catch": (A) Position hands beneath the towel and coax the bird into the corner of a room. (B) Begin to position one hand above and behind the bird. (C) Quickly grasp the head from behind; the other hand then works to control the body. (D) A well-restrained "happy" parrot!

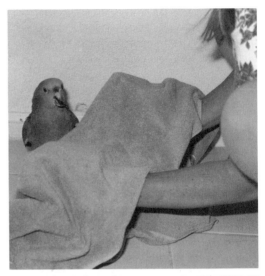

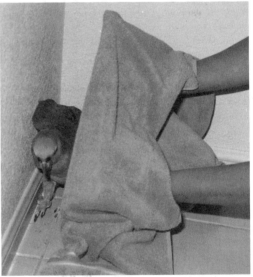

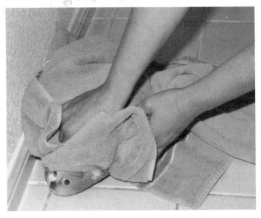

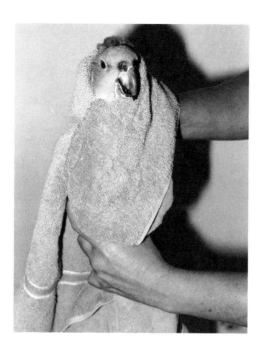

To capture the bird inside the cage, first remove toys and perches. Depending on the size and temperament of the bird, either one or both hands are placed behind the open towel. The "writing hand" takes charge of the head, while the other hand holds and wraps the body. For example, if righthanded, use this hand to catch the bird's head. Second, the towel is brought into the cage and quickly draped over the bird. Next, the bird is grasped by the head, with the thumb and index finger protected by the towel. The fingers should be pressing directly on the bird's jawbone. The palm of the hand is resting on the back of the neck. The opposite hand quickly wraps the towel around the body of the bird. After this the bird is removed from the cage. The two-hand technique works well for medium-size and larger birds. A modification involving only one hand is used with small birds.

Once the bird is out of the cage, adjust the towel as needed and uncover the face. Allow the bird to chew on the towel. This keeps the bird occupied, and it can blame the towel, not the holder, for the indignity.

Outside the Cage

The technique outside the cage is very similar to catching a bird inside a cage. Remember to coax the bird into a corner. The kitchen or another room with a tiled or linoleum floor works best. Carpeting can catch toes, and it's not as easy to clean up "messes." As previously discussed, quickly drape the towel over the bird and immediately reach for the head. Frequently, the head will be missed on the first try and the entire process will need to be repeated.

Towels are the best way to catch and hold a bird. The larger the bird, the larger the towel needed.

Unfortunately, some birds will roll over on their back when approached with a towel. If this should happen, the risks of getting bitten are greater. First, reach for a thicker towel or fold the towel you have in half. Both hands must be used to "pin" the head against the floor. Immediately, slide one hand around and in back of the head. Be sure to continue to press the head against the floor with the other hand. As soon as the head is under control, lift the bird up and rearrange the towel. There will be more wing flapping, so it might help to press the bird's body against the holder's chest during the towel arranging. This is going to be the most difficult situation encountered during restraint.

The "Three-Point Hold"

For more control of the head, as might be needed for beak trimming or administration of oral medications, try this technique. The only difference is that three fingers are restraining the head, instead of two. Begin by using the same capture method as described previously. But once the bird is safely restrained in the towel, the finger positions on the head will be changed. Instead of holding the head with the thumb and index finger only, also use the middle finger, for additional restraint. Simply slide the index finger up and around to the very top of the head. Move the middle finger up to the same place that the index finger was and keep the thumb in the same spot.

Once the bird has been caught, reposition the towel to cover both wings and fold the towel back to uncover the face. For added restraint, the bird can also be cradled against your body.

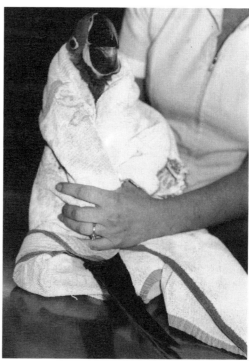

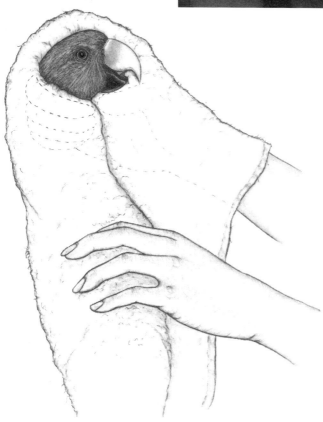

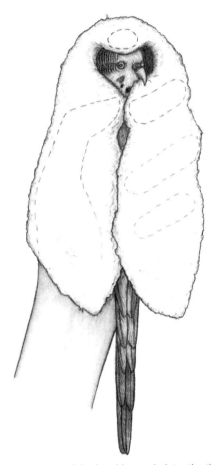

When more control of the head is needed, try the three-point hold.

"HE OR SHE WHO HESITATES GETS BIT" AND OTHER TIDBITS TO REMEMBER

- Most importantly, there is a fine line between too little and too much restraint. There is a need to be firm, but also gentle. Pressure can easily be applied to the jawbones with the fingers holding the head. On the other hand, very light pressure is sufficient around the body. The towel will help to cushion the hold around the bird.
- "He or she who hesitates gets bit!" Don't be timid. Be quick and decisive from the time the first move is made.
- Remember, it's only the beak that bites. Therefore, when catching a bird always take control of the head first, followed by the body. When releasing, let go of the body first, the head last.

For small birds, bare hand restraint can be used.

- Practice restraining your bird *before* there is a need to do so. It's easier to learn in a calm and relaxed setting than under the pressure of having to do it. A second person may be helpful, not only for moral support, but also for adjusting the towel around flapping wings. Practice makes perfect!

8

Grooming

Feathers, Nails and Beak

WE HUMANS have always been fascinated with the ability of birds to fly. Free of any mechanical aids, they soar the skies, peering down at us from their lofty places. So envious were we of their ability that Icarus, in Greek mythology, built a flying suit of wax and feathers. However, when he approached too close to the sun, the wax melted and he fell to the ground.

The radiance, beauty and function of feathers is truly one of the wonders of the world. When birds live in their natural setting, their feathers become their key to survival and are maintained in near perfect condition. Caged birds, on the other hand, often need help in maintaining their feathers in clean and healthy condition.

This chapter will assist bird owners with the care and maintance of feathers, nails and beaks.

FEATHERS

Most bird owners would never dream their beautiful feathered friends are closely related to reptiles. In fact, the feathers of birds actually evolved from the scales of reptiles. Scales protect a reptile's skin just as feathers do for a bird's. Feathers play many different roles, including beauty, sexual attraction, warmth, waterproofing, protection, and not least of all the ability to fly. Feathers allow a bird to cover enormous areas in search of food, as well as to escape quickly from predators.

The condition and appearance of the feathers can be an excellent "win-

An African Grey parrot preening its tail feathers.   *(Animal Environments)*

dow'' to a bird's overall health. A well-nourished, healthy bird will have a magnificent coat of shiny, glossy feathers to show off. Birds with dull, off-colored, broken or tattered feathers are prime suspects for disease.

Preening is work a bird does on its feathers to maintain their beauty and function. Birds have two to three thousand feathers, and each of these must be cleaned of dust and dirt, untangled, fluffed, lubricated and properly replaced in its special position every day. This is work. A healthy bird will spend much of its waking hours caring for its "coat." Owners can help encourage this very important activity by following the suggestions below.

Bathing

Bathing is an excellent way to encourage preening. In the wild, birds are often seen splashing in puddles or playing on wet grass and leaves. There are many ways to bathe birds. Every bird will have its own preference when it comes to bathing. If your bird does not appear to like bathing, chances are the preferred method has not been discovered. Here are some bathing suggestions:

- Bowl filled with water
- Plant mister, an ideal method for larger birds (try experimenting with different spray settings)
- Water faucet, making sure the water doesn't get too hot
- Wet foliage (lettuce leaves, etc.), great for "budgies" and other small birds

Bathing can play an important part in good grooming.
(Animal Environments)

- Sprinklers outside on a warm day
- ''Steamy'' bathroom
- ''Shower with a buddy'' (larger birds usually love it!)

Bathe your bird during the warmest part of the day. Daily bathing is ideal, but a realistic schedule is two to three times weekly.

Commercially available bird bathing solutions are available. However, "plain old" fresh water usually works best. Soap or other cleaning agents should not be used. Even in small amounts, these products could destroy the protective oil coating on the feathers.

Molt

Molting is the term given to the shedding or loss of old feathers simultaneous with the growth of new ones. Molting is a very stressful period in a bird's life, and there are several reasons for this. For birds flying free, it's the time when they are most susceptible to predators. This lack of security carries over to pet birds as well.

Growing new feathers requires considerable energy. If the bird is already on a good diet, no change is necessary. However, a marginal diet may need to be "boosted" during this time. See Chapter 4 for general dietary recommendations.

Feathers provide insulation from the cold. When many feathers are lost, birds require additional warmth around them. As new feathers grow in, increased preening is necessary to bring the feathers to their final stage of maturity. The keratin sheath protecting the young feather is removed, which allows the new adult feather to emerge.

RECOMMENDATIONS DURING MOLTING

- Minimize stress: Allow for rest and relaxation, increase the feeling of security.
- During a heavy molt, increase room temperature; 75° to 80°F is ideal.
- Good nutrition is essential.
- Encourage preening.

Wing Trimming

Properly done, a wing trim should prevent flight. Wing trimming will prevent a bird from flying away, avoid injuries commonly associated with flying and make training easier. On the other hand, flying is an important form of exercise and will help allow a bird to escape a house dog or cat bent on "birdie mayhem." After weighing all the pros and cons, pet birds are better off with their wings trimmed.

There have been several methods described for trimming wings. Some birds will retain the uncanny ability to fly, regardless of the trimming method used. The preferred technique is to trim *both* wings. By trimming the flight feathers of both wings instead of just one, a bird can still have a safe, controlled glide to the floor. When only one wing is trimmed, balance is poor, directional ability is lost and dangerous "crash landings" can occur.

Extend the wing and work from the "top side." Begin cutting from the wing tip and work inward. *Cut the first five to eight primary flight feathers on both wings.* Trim the feathers along the line created by the bottom of the dorsal major wing coverts.

The appearance of properly trimmed wings.   *(Bonnie Jay)*

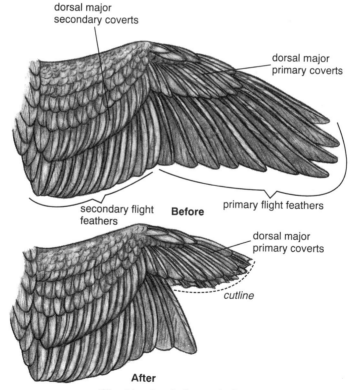

Wing trimming, before and after.

Wing trimming, in order to be effective, *must be done on a regular basis.* Many a "trimmed" bird has flown away because the owner forgot that new feathers continually grow in or because the feathers were not trimmed correctly. There are many pet birds flying wild today for this very reason, much to the dismay of their previous owners.

There is *no* prescribed timetable for trimming wings. Every bird is different. It is recommended that the wings be checked at least every three to four months.

WING-TRIMMING TIPS

- Don't cut blood feathers. These "baby" feathers maintain a fairly large blood supply. They grow out in a sheath made of a hornlike substance called keratin, which is similar to fingernails. Running along the length of the feather is a small blood vessel that can give it a pinkish appearance. If a blood feather is accidentally cut, it will bleed (for first aid for a bleeding feather, see Chapter 11).
- Wing trimming requires good restraint and two people. It is more difficult than it first appears. Therefore, at least consider having a professional trim the wings the first few times. Watch carefully to learn the technique.

These are "blood feathers." Before cutting any feathers, examine them to make sure no blood feathers are present. They should never be cut. However, after these feathers mature, they can then be safely trimmed. *(Bonnie Jay)*

NAILS

With birds, as with other animals, toenails grow continuously. Normal activity is often sufficient to maintain proper length. However, in a cage environment, toenails may grow too long and require periodic trimming. Overgrown nails can make perching difficult, as well as catch on carpeting or cause foot problems.

The nails may also be just very sharp, but not overgrown. This is readily felt once a bird is perched on an arm. Cutting the very tips off, ''blunting,'' is all that is necessary.

Nail Trimming

To check for overgrown nails, a good rule of thumb is that the toes should not be elevated off the ground when the feet are placed on a flat surface. A normal claw will curve down and form a right angle to the end of the toe. The quick is the living portion of the nail containing the blood and nerve supply. It extends two thirds to three fourths of the way down the length of the nail. In light-colored nails, the quick can be seen as a pink coloration inside the claw. In dark-colored nails, the quick is not visible.

If the nails need to be shortened, be prepared for bleeding. *Before* attempting to trim nails read First Aid for Bleeding Nails or Beak in Chapter 11. Make sure to have styptic powder handy before starting.

Human nail clippers work very well on small birds. For very large birds, dog nail clippers are preferred. Two people, one for restraint, are required. Since bleeding usually occurs, begin by cutting off only a tiny amount. Continue to trim off tiny amounts until the proper length is achieved or the first sign of

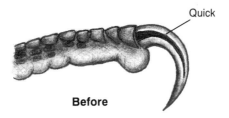

Before

After

Nail trimming, before and after.

Overgrown toenails.

bleeding is observed. If bleeding occurs, use styptic powder as directed. Watch to make sure the bleeding has stopped, then continue with the other nails. Cut off less on the next nails to avoid additional bleeding.

NAIL TRIMMING TIPS

- If the nails bleed and are still too long, wait about two weeks and trim them again. Each time nails are cut the quick recedes a little.

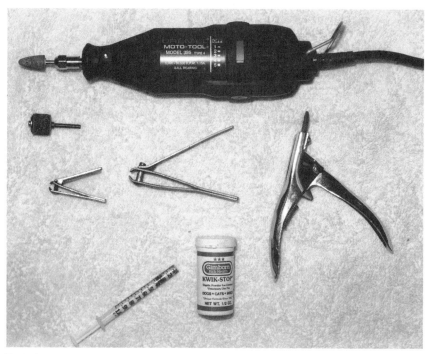

Tools for nail trimming include: hand-held electric grinder with attachments, human fingernail and toenail clippers, a standard dog nail trimmer and styptic powder (a syringe with the tip cut off can be used to pack the powder onto the nail).

110

- Nail trimming is more difficult than it appears. Consider watching a professional trim nails the first few times.
- After trimming, the bird may hold one of its feet up off the perch. The toes may be sore. Don't worry—this should last only for a day or so.

BEAK

The beak is a marvelous, versatile tool used to grip, grab, grind, groom, pry, crack, crush, attack, defend, feed young and make noise, as well as give affection. It is important for a bird's survival that the beak be able to function effectively.

The beak is composed of hollow bone, with sinuses on the inside and the outer covering a thin layer of keratin. There is a nerve and blood supply present. The beak grows from the top (where it connects to the head) and out from the center line, not from the tip, as is usually thought. Average growth for a "budgie's" beak is said to be one-quarter inch per month or three inches per year. The lower beak grows more slowly.

As the beak grows, the outermost layer of keratin begins to flake and peel. This is a normal process of shedding the oldest layers and does not indicate a health problem. For appearances, a light "sanding" with an emery board will help to remove these flaking layers. This does require *good* handling skills and should not be performed by novices.

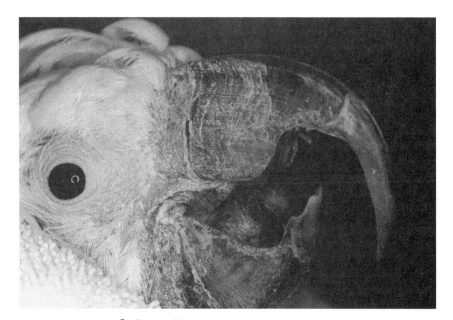

Cockatoo with overgrown upper and lower beak.

Chewing is a favorite activity enjoyed by most birds. It not only helps to keep the beak worn down, but is also important for keeping birds mentally "fit." Branches, knuckle bones (cow's, not yours!), mineral blocks, cuttle bones and lava rocks are all good for conditioning the beak.

Normally, the hingelike action of the upper and lower beak will maintain proper length. If for some reason the "hinge" is not perfectly aligned, the beak will become overgrown and misshapen. Affected birds must have their beaks trimmed periodically to maintain proper function.

Note: Trimming beaks is difficult and practice is required to do a good job without injuring the bird or getting bitten. If trimming is not done correctly, it could interfere with the bird's ability to eat. Beak trimming is an art. It is strongly recommended to have a professional do the trimming, especially on larger birds.

Medicine

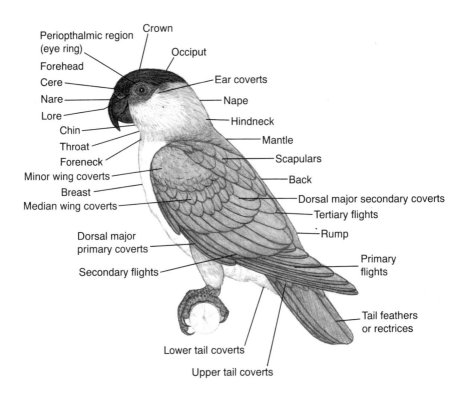

Periopthalmic region
(eye ring)

Crown

Occiput

Forehead

Cere

Nare

Lore

Chin

Throat

Foreneck

Minor wing coverts

Breast

Median wing coverts

Ear coverts

Nape

Hindneck

Mantle

Scapulars

Back

Dorsal major secondary coverts

Tertiary flights

Rump

Dorsal major
primary coverts

Secondary flights

Primary
flights

Tail feathers
or rectrices

Lower tail coverts

Upper tail coverts

9

Anatomy and Physiology
The Basics

"I T'S ONLY through understanding the normal, can you better understand the abnormal." This statement was heard repeatedly throughout our years in veterinary school. It is with this thought in mind this chapter has been written.

This chapter is a *very* brief introduction to the body of information that explains the structure and function of the various "parts" of our fine feathered friends. Specifically, each of the major organ systems will be discussed along with how birds differ from mammals.

First of all, remember that a bird's body, in its most basic form, is *very* similar to that of a mammal. Obviously, birds are unique when compared to other animals. The ability to fly and other remarkable characteristics have helped make birds the *most* successfully-adapted creatures on earth!

To begin with, the body in its smallest unit is composed of millions and millions of cells, all invisible to the naked eye. Cells are the "workhorses" of the body, performing all the various responsibilities needed to sustain life. Tissues and organs are groups of cells with specific functions. An organ system is a set of interconnected organs working together for a common purpose. A group of cells form the heart. The heart is an organ. It is also a part of the cardiovascular system, which includes other organs and tissues such as the blood and blood vessels. The systems—respiratory, digestive, cardiovascular and reproductive, to name a few—are *all* interconnected, each with their own responsibilities, but working together to sustain life.

Anatomical Differences in Birds as Compared to Mammals

SKIN	MUSCULOSKELETAL	REPRODUCTIVE	RESPIRATORY	CARDIOVASCULAR	URINARY SYSTEM	DIGESTIVE TRACT	LYMPHATIC
Very thin and nearly transparent	Lightweight and air-filled bones	Egg laying	No vocal cords	"Basic" design similar	No urinary bladder	No teeth	No lymph nodes
Beak	Sternum large and keeled	No mammary glands	Syrinx for talking and noise production	Large heart	Urine is semisolid	Crop	
No sweat glands	Pectoral muscles massive in size	No penis	Small, compact and nonexpandable lung	Very fast heartrate		Two-part stomach	
Feathers	Numerous fused bones in legs and wings	Functional ovary and oviduct left side only	No diaphragm				
	"Wishbone" is fused, clavicles	Female determines sex	Air sacs				
		Testicles internal					

NERVOUS SYSTEM

Birds and mammals have similar nervous systems. To coordinate the multitude of cellular functions and chemical reactions occurring throughout the body, good communication is essential. The brain is the body's central computer. It integrates and coordinates all these activities. The nerves are the messengers that relay information from every part of the body to and from the brain. These messages are transmitted, interpreted and answered in minute fractions of a second!

ENDOCRINE SYSTEM

The endocrine system, like the nervous system, communicates with and controls many of the organs in the body. Hormones, secreted from glands, travel through the bloodstream and have specific effects on the activity of a certain organ or organs. Hormones exert very powerful influences on the body. When they are secreted in abnormal amounts, the results can be some of the most dramatic seen in the body.

The pituitary gland is thought of as the master gland because it stimulates secretions of hormones from other glands. The thyroid glands exert powerful control over body growth, metabolic rate and molting. The parathyroids and ultimobrachial glands control calcium metabolism. The adrenal glands play important roles in electrolyte balance and carbohydrate and fat metabolism. The pineal gland responds to changes in amount of light (changing seasons), and exerts influence over the reproductive cycle.

The pancreas, testes, ovaries, liver, small intestine, kidneys, uterus and a few other organs also secrete hormones, in addition to their other functions.

THE "SENSES"

Vision

The basic structure of the eye is similar to that of mammals. Some of the more important differences will be discussed.

The eyes of birds are relatively large and well developed. Their ability to see detail (i.e., sharpness of vision) is better than that of mammals. Colors *are* detectable.

The eyes operate independently of one another. The eyeball's range of motion, the ability to move in different directions, is very limited. This is compensated for, however, by the tremendous mobility of the head and neck. The eyelashes have been replaced with tiny bristlelike feathers called semiplumes.

The iris regulates the amount of light that enters the eye. It gives the eye its characteristic color. The iris is brillantly colored in some species of birds. In many parrots, the iris is darker in the young bird, but lighter and more pigmented

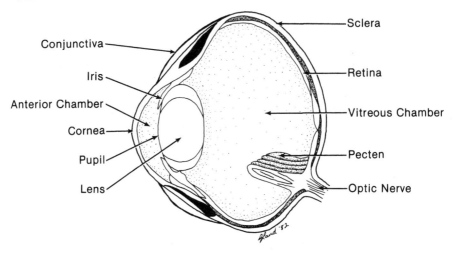

Cross-section of eyeball.

in the mature bird. In cockatoos, iris color is *often* an indicator of gender—in males, the iris is black or dark brown and in females it's reddish or burnt orange.

Birds have three eyelids, similar to some mammals, such as dogs. The upper and lower eyelids move up and down. The third eyelid, nictitating membrane, moves horizontally, sweeping across the eye from the inner corner. Birds do not blink like humans. When a bird blinks, their third eyelid flicks across the eyeball. This occurs up to thirty to thirty-five times per minute.

Hearing

Ears are the organ of hearing and balance in all animals. In birds, they are hidden from view. To find the ears, look behind and below the eye. The feathers directly over the ears have a slightly different texture and appearance. Part them and the ears will be apparent. Notice there are no pinnae (ear flaps).

The discrimination of sound waves and ability to localize the direction of sound are well developed and similar to that of humans. However, birds appear less sensitive to higher and lower vocal tones as compared to humans. Their ability to differentiate various sounds is ten times faster than humans. In other words, a canary's song would have to be slowed down ten times before the human ear could identify all the notes that are learned by a canary chick. Most birds, including parrots, do not hear ultrasonic vibrations.

Smell

The sense of smell is present, but poorly developed. Odors quickly fade above the ground where birds are flying.

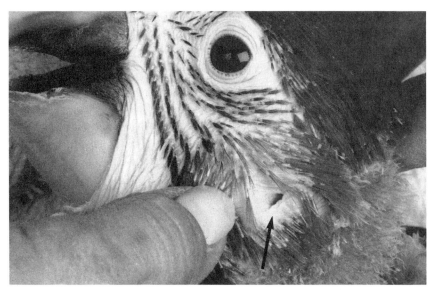

The location of the ear. Notice there is no "flap," or pinna. A baby macaw is the subject of this picture. *(Bonnie Jay)*

Taste

Birds can taste, but compared to mammals, this sense is poorly developed. The number of taste buds in birds is much less than in humans and other animals. Taste buds in birds are found on the roof of the mouth, *not* the tongue.

In a study involving birds, but *not* specifically parrots, they were able to distinguish tastes. Bitter and salt flavors were disliked. Sour flavors were accepted, but varied with the species. Sweet flavors were inconsistently accepted.

INTEGUMENT (SKIN)

A bird's skin is different from a mammal's. It's very thin and delicate, and appears nearly transparent. The red hue seen when looking at the featherless areas is actually the underlying muscle being seen through the skin. The beak, cere (nasal area), claws, and scales on both the feet and legs are all modifications of the skin.

During nesting, the lower chest area loses its feathers, develops an enriched blood supply and thickens to form a brood patch. This area provides extra warmth to the eggs during the incubation period. The cheek patch is a featherless area on the face of some parrots, such as macaws. It often will "blush" or redden with excitement or stress. A few minutes after the stimulus is gone, the color returns to normal.

The uropygial gland (*u-ro-pi-je-al*, preening gland) is located on the lower back, at the base of the tail. It is found in all parrots, except Amazons. It produces an oil that's spread over the feathers by the beak during preening (grooming).

119

The oil waterproofs and increases the durability of feathers. It also appears to help prevent skin infections. Amazons, although lacking this gland, ordinarily maintain healthy and strong feathers in any case.

Unlike mammals, there are *no* sweat glands. To cool themselves, overheated birds breathe rapidly (pant) and lift their wings away from their body. Birds that are cold will fluff their feathers and crouch to conserve heat

Feathers

Feathers are part of the skin and similar to hair in mammals. The "budgie" has between two and three thousand feathers on its body. Feathers primarily insulate and help maintain the normally high body temperature in birds. They are also used in courtship and aggressive displays, as nest material and, of course, for flight.

Feathers grow from feather follicles arranged in tracts or rows called pterylae (TER-i-la). In contrast, mammalian hairs grow randomly. The bare or unfeathered areas between the tracts are called apteria (AP-te-RI-ah).

Primary feather types are contour, plume and semiplume.

Contour feathers cover the contour, or outline, of the body, including the tail and wings. They are divided into flight feathers and body feathers. The primary flight feathers are the longest ones at the end of each wing. Next to these are the secondary flight feathers. There are about ten primaries and ten secondaries. The body feathers, or coverts, cover most of the body and base of the flight feathers.

Down feathers cover the newly hatched chick and are the "fluffy" feathers of adult birds. They form the "undercoat" and provide insulation. Unique to cockatoos, cockatiels, and African Greys is powder down. These feathers grow in "patches" on both sides of the flank, just above the attachment of the legs. The white powdery dust resulting from these feathers appear to help with water repellency. The dust can often be found on the cage and on everything else around it. Excessive powder down could aggravate an owner's allergies or lung disease.

Semiplume feathers are bristlelike and found along the edges of the feather tracts. This includes areas around the beak, nose and eyelids. They help with insulation and *may* have a sensory function similar to whiskers in mammals.

Feather Growth: For a new feather to begin growing, the old feather must first fall out. The earliest indication of a developing feather is a thickened, pointed projection of skin. Soon afterwards the emerging feather, called a pin or blood feather, appears, wrapped in a protective keratin sheath. Each of these young growing feathers contain their own artery and vein. If this new feather is damaged or broken, bleeding will occur. When the feather is completely grown in, its blood supply "dries up." The sheath then falls off or is removed by the bird. The feather, now fully mature, is essentially a dead structure.

If a feather is pulled out—plucked—the follicle will be damaged slightly. However, a new feather will still usually begin to grow. If a mature feather is

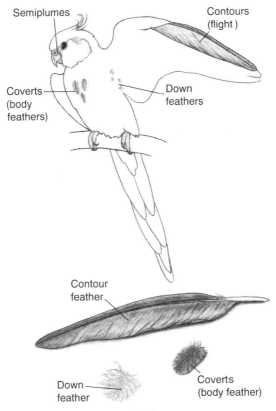

Semiplumes

Contours
(flight)

Coverts
(body
feathers)

Down
feathers

Contour
feather

Down
feather

Coverts
(body feather)

Common feather types.

Numerous immature or pin feathers.

cut, as with wing trimming to prevent flight, the feather shaft remains and a new feather will *not* develop until the next molt.

Molting: Molting is simply the process of losing old feathers and replacing them with new ones. Factors influencing the frequency and extent of the molt are time of year, temperature, photoperiod (natural and artificial light cycles), nutrition, reproductive cycle and species. After hatching, chicks pass through a series of molts, eventually producing adult plumage. Thereafter, wild birds usually molt once a year, after the breeding season. Pet birds rarely show this classic pattern of molting. They either continuously lose a few feathers at a time, or pass through a series of "light" molts two or three times a year. The reasons for this are the relatively constant temperatures and lighting patterns in our homes.

During a molt, birds do *not* lose all their feathers at one time. If this were so, they would be bald, cold and flightless. Feathers are lost in an orderly pattern and the process takes about six weeks.

Molting is a stressful time. Nutritional requirements are greater and resistence to disease is weaker. Follow the recommendations in Chapter 8.

Feather Color: Feather color results from pigments within the feather and light reflecting off their surface. These colors can be altered by dirt, oil from hands, bleaching agents, age, disease, hormones, diet, physical damage and temporarily by water.

MUSCULOSKELETAL SYSTEM

Muscles and bones protect, support and move the body. They also play critical roles in swallowing, blood circulation, respiration, elimination, egg laying and much more. The marrow cavity, found within some of the bones, produces the red and white blood cells and platelets (involved in blood clotting).

The ability to fly has resulted in many changes in the structure and function of the bones and muscles. Here are a few of the more important and interesting adaptations:

- Certain bones called pneumatic bones contain air sacs. They are actually part of the respiratory system. The ribs, vertebrae, pelvis, sternum, humerus and sometimes the femur are pneumatized.
- Bones are very light and thin walled. Fractures (broken bones) can easily occur. Think of it like "snapping a toothpick."
- During the breeding season, the females' bones become more dense as the cavities are filled with new bone, and the weight of the skeleton can increase by 20 percent. The extra calcium needed for egg shell production is stored in this way.
- Bones of the skull have fused together, giving added strength and power to the beak. Spinal bones in the neck have formed in a unique manner, creating a long, extemely flexible neck. As a result, the head can actually rotate about 180 degrees. The sternum, or breastbone, is massive and

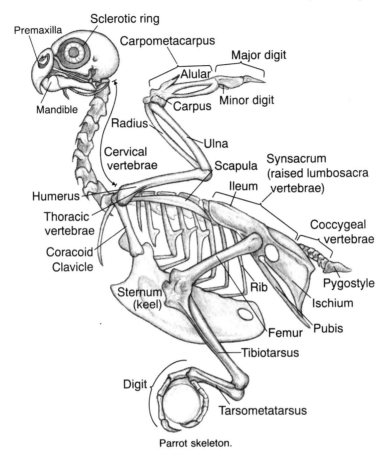

Parrot skeleton.

along with the powerful pectoral muscles enables birds to develop the powerful forces needed for flight.

- In passerines (canaries, finches, and mynahs) three toes point forward and one backward. In parrots, two toes point forward and two point backward. These adaptations help birds catch and hold prey or vegetable food sources, much like a hand.
- About 20 percent of a bird's body weight is due to its pectoral (breast) muscles.
- The basic structure of the muscles is similar to that of mammals. One interesting difference, however, is the existence of both red and white muscles. Red muscle fibers use fat rather than carbohydrate as their source for energy. Since fat releases more energy than carbohydrates, red muscles are better adapted for sustained exercise. In strong fliers, such as parrots, the pectoral muscles contain mostly red fibers, accounting for its deep red color. In chickens, which are poor fliers, white is the predominant fiber and the color is very pale (i.e., "the breast is white meat").

123

CARDIOVASCULAR SYSTEM

Transportation of oxygen and nutrients to the cells is the cardiovascular system's primary responsibility. In addition, carbon dioxide and other waste products are carried away from the cells by the cardiovascular system. Water, electrolytes, hormones, enzymes and antibodies are all transported throughout the body via the bloodstream.

The "design" of the heart, arteries and veins is similar to that of mammals. The heart has four chambers, two atria and two ventricles. The heart is relatively large, and the heart rate is *much* faster than that of mammals. A human heart beats 60–80 times per minute. *At rest*, a canary's heart beats 500 to 1,000 times per minute, and 150 to 300 beats per minute for a large parrot! Cardiac output is the amount of blood pumped through the heart each minute. It has been estimated to be *seven* times greater in a flying "budgie" than in a human exercising at maximum capability! Their circulatory systems working in unison

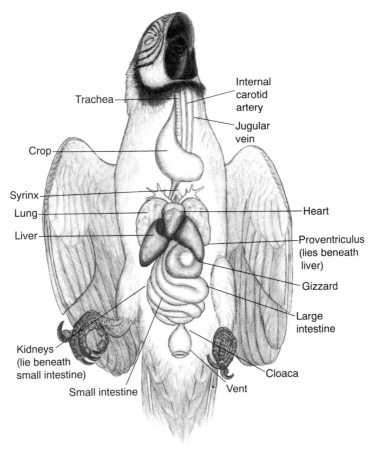

The location of some major internal organs.

with the other organ systems has enabled birds to utilize tremendous amounts of energy very efficiently.

Blood is composed of three different types of cells, suspended in a liquid called plasma. Red blood cells carry oxygen to the body's cells. White blood cells combat the invasion of foreign organisms and produce, and transport antibodies. Platelets are responsible for normal blood clotting.

RESPIRATORY SYSTEM

Respiration is simply the exchange of the gases, oxygen and carbon dioxide, in the lungs. Oxygen provides fuel for cells to produce energy. Carbon dioxide is the waste product of this exchange. Birds have a very high requirement for oxygen, especially during flight.

Air enters the nostrils, which are the paired openings in the cere. These structures are located just above and behind the beak. Air passes through cavities

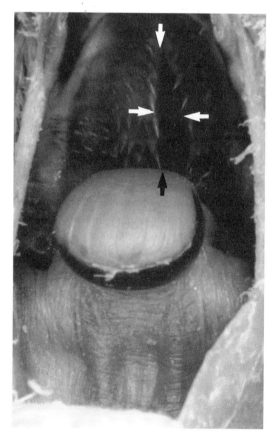

The choanal slit along the roof of the mouth.

inside the upper beak and skull, called the sinuses. It then flows into the pharynx (throat).

Above the pharynx, and easily seen along the "roof of the mouth," is a slitlike opening called the choana (ko-A-nah). This is part of the *nasal cavity*. Acting like a mini-filter, humidfier and heater, the nasal cavity cleans, moisturizes and warms the incoming air.

Once in the mouth, air passes through the larynx and into the trachea ("windpipe"). Vocal cords are *not* found in birds. The syrinx is the bird's "voice box" and is located at the base of the trachea in the neck area. It is the vibrations of the syrinx membrane that produce sound. Veterinarians unfortunately are sometimes asked to surgically curtail a parrot's ability to make sounds, especially with an unusually noisy bird. The location and structure of the syrinx is such that a safe and effective procedure has *not* been developed.

Passages called bronchi split off from the trachea and continue to channel air into the lungs. In birds, unlike mammals, the lungs do *not* expand and contract with each breath. Assisting the lungs are unique structures called air sacs. These are hollow spaces located in the body cavity and in some of the bones.

A bird's lungs exchange gases, oxygen and carbon dioxide more efficiently than those of any other animal. The actual mechanics of breathing, compared to mammals, is strikingly different. Birds have no diaphragm separating the chest cavity from the abdomen. The chest and abdominal cavities unite into a single large space called the coelom (SE-lom).

Respiration works similar to a bellows system, with the body wall expanding and contracting on each breath. When a bird breathes and its body wall expands, air is filling the air sacs, not the lungs. The bellows action is pulling and pushing air in and out of the lungs.

In mammals, one complete breath is required to circulate air through the entire respiratory tract. In birds, two complete breaths, two inspirations and two expirations, are required! Humans breathe at a rate of twelve to sixteen breaths per minute. Compare this with a canary that takes sixty to one hundred breaths per minute at rest and a large parrot at twenty-five to forty breaths per minute.

Birds are magnificent athletes. However, because their respiratory system is more complex, they are more susceptible to respiratory disease. Even a simple respiratory infection can quickly become serious, even life-threatening.

LYMPHATIC SYSTEM

The lymphatic system is actually part of the circulatory system and consists of lymphatic vessels and lymphatic tissues. Lymphatic fluid transports water, electrolytes, fats, hormones and proteins from the tissues and returns them to the general circulation.

Parrots do *not* have lymph nodes. Lymphatic tissues include the thymus, cloaca bursa (often called the Bursa of Fabricius), and spleen. Lymphocytes,

126

produced by these tissues, manufacture the antibodies necessary for immunity (resistence to disease). The spleen removes "old" red blood cells from the circulation. It does *not* appear to be a reservoir for blood, as it is in mammals.

DIGESTIVE SYSTEM

Digestion is the process whereby food is converted into simpler compounds so it can be absorbed into the bloodstream and used for fuel by the cells.

The energy requirements of birds are incredibly high, and conversion of food into energy must be very rapid. A small bird will eat upwards of 20 percent of its own body weight daily. It would be similar to a 150-pound person devouring 30 pounds of food in a single day! The by-product of all this food being turned into energy is heat, for this reason: The body temperature of birds is very high compared with mammals (104° to 112°F degrees for birds versus 98.6°F degrees for humans).

A bird's digestive tract functions similar to a mammal's. However, there are some important differences. Birds lack teeth, but use the beak and tongue to prepare food for swallowing by crushing, hulling and tearing. Hard, ridgelike structures on the base of the upper beak and inside the mouth aid in crushing hard food. Parrots can also use a foot to grasp food and raise it up to the beak.

Parrots have relatively dry mouths, since only a small amount of saliva is produced. The esophagus, connecting the mouth to the stomach, contains glands that moisten and lubricate food. The crop is a saclike, esophageal enlargement, located at the base of the neck. The crop continues the process of food softening and also functions to slowly supply a continuous amount of food to the stomach.

Birds have one stomach divided into two distinct portions. The proventriculus, "true" stomach, adds digestive juices to the food as it passes through. The gizzard, a muscular stomach, then pulverizes the food as it moves along. In the small intestine, the digestive process continues, and the "food" is finally absorbed into the bloodstream. It is transported throughout the body to provide "fuel" for the cells. The solid wastes, unusable portions of the food, pass on to the large intestine, then through the cloaca (klo-A-kah). The cloaca is the common chamber into which fecal, urinary and reproductive elements pass through before explusion from the body. It opens to the outside through what is called the vent.

The pancreas, located alongside the small intestine, supplies the enzymes necessary to digest protein, carbohydrates and fats. The liver has many various functions, and it works very closely with many other organs. Some of its more important jobs include filtration of blood, producing and storing energy in the form of carbohydrates and numerous other metabolic functions.

In birds droppings are frequent, as they can only store small amounts of feces in their cloaca. It only takes a few hours for food to pass through the entire digestive tract.

URINARY SYSTEM

The urinary system of birds consists of paired kidneys and ureters. There is *no* bladder or urethra. Urine is produced in the kidneys, transported via the ureters into the cloaca, and subsequently eliminated.

The kidneys are the filtering system for blood, removing poisonous waste materials. They play a critical role in regulating the balance of water and electrolytes (sodium, chloride and potassium).

Urine is only partially liquid. The primary portion is the white semipasty material, uric acid or ''urates'' mixed with the feces. Uric acid is the end product of protein metabolism. It is manufactured in the liver, transported by blood and eliminated through the kidneys. Since no bladder is present, storage is limited and birds must urinate frequently.

Birds and reptiles have evolved a unique pattern of blood flow, different from mammals. Blood returning from the legs, reproductive system and lower intestines passes through the kidneys *before* entering the general circulation. This is important to understand because an infection in one of these organs could also cause a kidney infection. Also, injected drugs should *not* be given in the legs or lower abdomen. The kidneys could inactivate the drug *before* it has a chance to circulate through the body.

FEMALE REPRODUCTIVE SYSTEM

In birds and mammals, the female reproductive tract consists of the ovary, oviduct and vagina. In mammals, both the left and right ovaries and oviducts are fully functional. In birds, the left ovary and oviduct develop normally. However, the right ovary and oviduct are underdeveloped, and not functional. Interestingly, female birds determine the sex of newborns, whereas in mammals males have this distinction.

Depending on the stage of the breeding cycle, the reproductive system varies considerably in size and shape. Stimulation of reproductive activity is influenced by environmental factors, with increasing periods of daylight being most important. Hormones similar to those found in mammals control ovulation.

The oviduct is actually divided into *five* distinct regions. It is here that both fertilization and growth of the egg occur. The uterus produces the calcified shell around the egg. The vagina pushes the egg through the cloaca and on to the outside. This entire process, from ovulation to egg laying, requires about twenty-five hours.

Eggs can be laid spontaneously, without fertilization and without another bird in the cage. Cockatiels, especially, can be prolific and lay multiple clear, or infertile, eggs throughout the year.

MALE REPRODUCTIVE SYSTEM

The male bird's reproductive tract consists of paired testes, epididymis and the ductus deferens. There is no prostate gland. The testes are located within the abdominal cavity next to the kidneys. The increased temperature in the abdomen does not affect sperm production in birds, as it would in mammals. Testosterone is the primary hormone in male birds.

A true penislike structure does not exist in parrots. Mating still occurs through joining of the cloacas. Ejaculated semen is deposited on the everted cloaca of the female. The volume of semen is only one or two drops. It can retain its fertilizing powers for many days and sometimes even weeks.

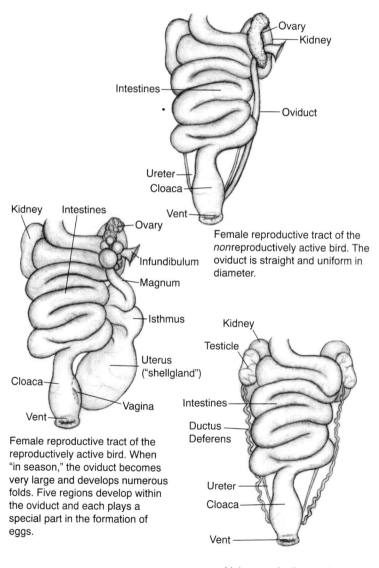

Female reproductive tract of the *non*reproductively active bird. The oviduct is straight and uniform in diameter.

Female reproductive tract of the reproductively active bird. When "in season," the oviduct becomes very large and develops numerous folds. Five regions develop within the oviduct and each plays a special part in the formation of eggs.

Male reproductive tract.

10

Home Physicals

. . . in Sickness and in Health . . .

BIRDS ARE generally very healthy and resistant to disease. However, like all living beings, pet birds are going to become ill. It may not happen tomorrow, next month or even next year, but unfortunately it will happen. Even pet birds that are never exposed to another bird, or never venture outdoors, will become sick. With good loving care, common sense and a little luck, hopefully the effects of disease can be minimized.

This chapter is designed to assist in the recognition of diseases in their *early* stages. The survival instinct in birds is very strong. In spite of being sick, birds in the wild will continue to act normally for as long as possible. This "act" continues even in pet birds. In most instances, birds that "just got sick yesterday" have in fact been ill for some time.

Read, and reread, this chapter. It is perhaps the most important chapter in this book for pet bird owners to understand. *The sooner diseases are recognized and treatment started, the better the odds for a speedy recovery.*

Author's Note: Throughout the text only the word *sign* is used and never *symptom* to describe a particular appearance in a sick bird. Symptoms are a subjective feeling described by the patient. Signs are the objective evidence observed by a person about their pet. Since birds cannot communicate with us, they always show signs, never symptoms. There have been "sooo" many times in my career that I yearned for my patient to simply "tell me where it hurts."

SICK BIRDS: THE SIGNS OF ILLNESS

Many of these signs will not be obvious to the casual bird owner. As an owner becomes more familiar with the *normal* appearance and behavior of his/her bird, these signs will be easier to detect.

Change in Activity (Personality or Behavior): Less active, less talking and/or singing, more sleeping, decreased responsiveness to various stimuli

Change in Appearance: Ruffled feathers, weakness, not perching—remaining on cage floor, bleeding, injuries, convulsions, distended abdomen

BREATHING PROBLEMS

Noisy breathing: wheezing, constant panting or "clicking" sounds
Heavy breathing: shortness of breath, open-mouth breathing, tail bobbing
   (pronounced up-and-down motion of the tail)
Nasal discharge or area surrounding eye swollen
Loss of voice

DIGESTIVE PROBLEMS

Vomiting/regurgitation
Diarrhea (specifically, loose stool), may contain blood, mucus, or undigested seeds
Straining to eliminate

A seriously ill Amazon parrot. Notice its posture (leaning to the side), wing droop and fluffed-up feathers. Also, the eyes are closed and a nasal discharge is evident.

MUSCULOSKELETAL PROBLEMS

Lameness
"Droopy" wing
Change in posture

EYE PROBLEMS

Eyelids swollen or "pasted" closed
Increased blinking. Any eye discharge, including excessive tearing
Cloudiness of eyeball
Squinting
Rubbing eye or side of face

SKIN PROBLEMS

Any lumps or bumps
Excessive flaking of skin or beak
Overgrowth of beak or nails

FEATHER PROBLEMS

Prolonged molt
Picking at or chewing feathers
Damaged feathers: broken, twisted, crushed or deformed

Change in Food or Water Intake: *Most* sick birds will eat and drink less; weight loss and dehydration are common. An exception is diabetes and a few other diseases, where there will be an *increase* in food and water consumed.

Change in Droppings: Any variation in the number, consistency or color (see the discussion of droppings later in the chapter).

THE "HANDS OFF" EXAMINATION

Learning the daily routine and normal behaviors of your bird is essential. The longer your bird is in your home, the easier this will become. Any change or variation from these usual routines could suggest a problem.

Every day you or another family member will, at the very least, walk by your bird's cage. Someone will probably feed the bird, clean its cage and, hopefully, include some playtime. During these times, observe your bird and its surroundings. Take a moment, to *look* and *listen*. A few seconds is all it takes.

A "oneness" will soon develop between you and your bird. A "sixth sense" will begin to develop. When that "voice inside" is talking, or even whispering something is wrong, listen to it! Your instincts are probably correct.

This very brief daily routine should include asking yourself a few questions. Look at the bird:

- Is there *anything* out of the ordinary?
- Has any daily routine or ritual changed? For example, first thing in the morning, is your bird greeting you about the same as always?
- Eating habits normal?
- Vocalizing pattern, if any, about the same? If there is any variation, a problem *could* be developing. Birds are creatures of habit and generally follow established routines.

Look at the cage. In just a moment's glance:

- Food eaten?
- Water drunk?
- Are there any missing or chewed objects?
- Is there anything present that normally does not belong in the cage?

Look at the cage floor:

- Are the droppings normal? Check the location of the droppings. An active bird will leave droppings all around the cage. If the dropping are all piled up in one or two places it could indicate an inactive and depressed bird.
- Are there any feathers or blood on the floor?

Look at the food dishes:

- Are the seed cups full of uneaten seed? Remember, if seeds are fed, the dish could appear full when it's actually near empty. Seed hulls could be all that are present. A finger could be used to stir the seeds around to check.
- Is the water clean? If it becomes dirty with droppings on a regular basis, move the water dish to a different location in the cage.

Nervous System

The signs to watch for with a nervous system problem are varied. They will depend on the underlying cause, the part of the nervous system affected and other organ systems that may be involved.

SIGNS TO WATCH FOR

- Changes in behavior, responsiveness or coordination (loss of balance or clumsiness)
- Abnormal head positions
- Postural changes
- Unusual eye movements
- Blindness
- Paralysis (loss of movement or sensation)
- Seizures
- Lameness

Healthy birds rarely fall off their perch. If this occurs, consider that there could be an underlying problem. However, many young birds naturally tend to be a little clumsy.

A lameness or paralysis in one or both legs could suggest a tumor or egg in the abdomen. In "budgies," tumors in the abdomen can put pressure on the sciatic nerve and result in lameness. A concussion (violent shock or jarring of the brain) can occur when birds collide with a window or mirror.

Endocrine System

There are many glands and organs, each producing specific hormones. Therefore, the signs to watch for are variable.

SIGNS TO WATCH FOR

- Increased appetite or thirst
- Abnormal growth
- Bone and reproductive problems

There are more signs than are listed, but they are too numerous and nonspecific to mention here. For instance, hypothyroidism can be present in

135

many different ways, including obesity and feather problems. Diabetes, another endocrine disease, also has many presenting signs, but classically dramatic increases in appetite and thirst are seen.

"The Senses"

Vision Both eyes should *always* appear similar in color, size and shape. Compare one with the other; if there is a difference, it suggests a problem. A complete eye exam requires special instruments and testing procedures.

Note: Eye problems are potentially serious; consult your veterinarian immediately.

SIGNS TO WATCH FOR

- The eyelids should be open wide, appear smooth and clean. They should *not* be crusted, or "pasted" closed. The feathers surrounding the eyes should be clean, lie in neat rows and *not* be "caked" together.
- The conjunctiva (delicate membrane lining the eyelids) should be pink and glistening. It should not appear red or swollen.
- The cornea (transparent outer covering of eyeball) should appear clear and radiant. If injured it becomes cloudy and loses various degrees of its transparency.
- The pupils should both be the same size and shape. The size of the openings should adjust with the amount of light. Stimulation or excitement causes dilation of the pupils.
- The lens is located immediately behind the iris and on the back side of the pupil. It is transparent and normally cannot be seen. A white "spot" in the center of the pupil suggests a cataract (see Chapter 12).

Hearing Ear diseases are uncommon.

SIGNS TO WATCH FOR

- The *internal ear canal* controls balance. Watch for head held constantly "bent" or in an awkward position, or problems with balance.
- The *external ear canal* should be clean and dry, and no swelling should be present. Watch for discharge, and rubbing or scratching the area around the affected ear. This could be suggested by the feathers over the ear being wet, ruffled or "stuck" together.

Smell Signs to watch for are general and nonspecific. Plugged nostrils ("stuffy nose") would probably affect the sense of smell and could affect appetite.

Taste Signs to watch for are general and nonspecific. An upper respiratory infection could affect the sense of taste. Appetite could be decreased.

Integument

The skin is very thin and nearly transparent. Don't be fooled by its normal reddish-purple appearance. This is normal because the muscles can be seen through the skin. There are few blood vessels in the skin, and therefore bleeding is usually very minimal.

SIGNS TO WATCH FOR

- Examine the skin for any wounds, cuts or bruises. An area of wet or matted feathers could suggest a skin problem.
- Any swellings, "lumps or bumps" on the skin are abnormal.
- A thickening of the skin or a soft, smoothly rounded mass felt beneath the skin could suggest fat. It usually "builds up" in the upper chest and abdominal areas. "Budgies," cockatiels and Amazons are particularly prone to developing obesity.
- A whitish honeycomblike crusting at the corners of the mouth, around the beak and sometimes the legs could suggest mites (see Chapter 12).
- Watch for overgrown toenails or beak (see Chapter 8).

Feathers The appearance of the feathers are a good indicator of a bird's overall health. Sick birds usually develop a ruffled and unkempt appearance.

SIGNS TO WATCH FOR

- The feathers should be arranged in neat rows. They should all appear in good condition and have a nice shiny glow.
- Watch for signs of feather picking (see Chapter 12). Areas on the chest, back, wings and legs are the sites affected. The feathers on the head and upper neck remain undisturbed and should appear normal.
- If blood is found on the feathers, it usually suggests a damaged immature feather or a skin injury.

Musculoskeletal

Palpation (feeling with the fingers) of the pectoral muscles provides an excellent indication of weight. The muscle should be full, rounded slightly and about even with the leading edge of the sternum (keel bone.) If underweight, the pectoral muscle begins to take on the shape of an "arrowhead" and the keel feels "sharp" and more prominent. If overweight, the muscle becomes rounded and extends slightly above the keel.

SIGNS TO WATCH FOR

- The joints should flex easily, and there should be no evidence of pain or swelling.
- The wings should be at equal height and lie adjacent to the body. An injured wing will "droop" and be held slightly away from the body.
- Both legs should bear weight equally when the bird is standing.

137

This parrot is leaning toward its right side, showing reluctance to bear full weight on its left leg. This can be a subtle indication of an injury to the left leg.

Coelom

The coelom is the body cavity. The major organs, including the heart, lungs, liver, gizzard and kidneys are contained within this space. Although it is hidden from view, there are still signs to watch for that would suggest a problem within the body cavity.

Become familiar with your birds' normal abdominal shape. Simply move your index finger around the area just above the vent. It should feel flat or even slightly indented.

SIGNS TO WATCH FOR

- Labored breathing, suggested by forceful and pronounced expansions of the body wall or "tail-bobbing" (pronounced up-and-down movements of the tail)
- An enlarged or distended abdomen, a "potbellied" appearance

These are serious problems; consult your veterinarian.

Cardiovascular

SIGNS TO WATCH FOR

- Tiring easily, coughing and abdominal swelling. These could suggest a heart problem.
- Bleeding. This is a medical emergency; *contact your veterinarian immediately.*

Estimating heart rate is very difficult. The heart beats very fast, and this, combined with relatively tiny blood vessels, makes it nearly impossible to locate a pulse on most birds. The heart can be heard using a stethoscope placed on the far side of the chest wall. However, since the heart rate is incredibly fast, murmurs are very difficult to hear.

Respiratory

SIGNS TO WATCH FOR

- Stand a few feet from the cage and observe the pattern of breathing. It should be easy, smooth and rhythmic. Watch for rapid breathing, gasping for breath, holding wings out and away from the body, open-mouth breathing and panting at rest.
- The nostrils should be clear of debris and the area around them clean. There should be no swelling, redness, or discharge.
- Listen for unusual sounds. Sneezing can be pronounced like an "achoo" or as subtle as a soft "click." Wheezing sounds similar to a "wet" whistling noise. A cough is softer but similar to a human's. A change in pitch or tone of the voice could suggest a syrinx or lower tracheal problem.
- Swelling below one or both eyes could suggest sinusitis (infection of sinuses).

Diseases of the lungs and air sacs are nearly impossible to diagnose without X rays and other diagnostic tests.

Author's Note: Be very careful when handling birds with respiratory disease. If capture and restraint are necessary, keep the time to an absolute

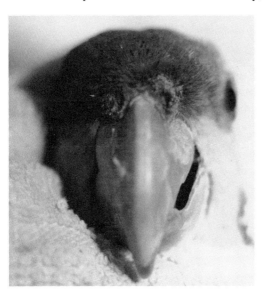

Notice the right nare is "plugged" and there is discharge around it.

minimum. If giving medicines, have the proper dosage drawn up and ready to go *before* handling the bird.

Lymphatic System

Signs of lymphatic system disease are vague and nonspecific. Diagnosis is difficult and requires diagnostic testing.

Digestive System

SIGNS TO WATCH FOR

- The normal shape and length of the beak varies with each species. Compare your bird's beak with other birds of the same species.
- Swallowing of food should be effortless. Birds having difficullty will stretch their necks and hold their heads back. If a swallowing problem is suspected, the mouth needs to be examined.
- The mucous membranes lining the mouth and throat should appear pink. There can also be various amounts of black pigmentation normally seen. Look for problems such as white, creamy patches covering the roof of the mouth. Bleeding is always abnormal. Any odor from the mouth suggests a problem.
- Vomiting or regurgitation is usually not normal. Regurgitation can also be a sign of a courtship behavior.
- Become familiar with the appearance of your birds' droppings (see discussion later in this chapter).
- In young, hand-fed baby birds, watch for a crop that empties very slowly or not at all (see Chapter 5).

Cloaca and Vent

SIGNS TO WATCH FOR:

- The area around the vent should be clean and dry. There should be no matted feathers or accumulation of droppings.
- The vent sphincter should be tightly closed.
- There should not be any tissue or growth protruding from the vent.

Urinary System

Urine and urates should be normal color and consistency (see discussion later in this chapter).

Female Reproductive System

SIGNS TO WATCH FOR

- Acute swelling of the abdomen. Excessive straining, squatting or walking like a penguin. This could suggest an egg-laying problem. A history of recent egg laying or breeding along with these signs would be very suspicious.

- Excessive straining could result in a cloaca prolapse.

Note: These problems are a medical emergency. Contact your veterinarian immediately.

Male Reproductive System

There are *no* specific signs that suggest a problem with the male reproductive system.

THE "HANDS ON" EXAMINATION

The last part of the examination involves actually capturing the bird and performing a complete physical examination. This last step of a complete physical exam is *best left to a veterinarian*. It takes years of study and practice to understand the technique, which includes developing a systematic approach, differentiating normal from abnormal, interpreting the findings and making recommendations toward the best course of action. Also, proper restraint, for everyone's safety, requires a great deal of training and experience.

DROPPINGS: A REFLECTION OF YOUR BIRD'S HEALTH

Bird droppings are a mess, and they're unsightly. However, they also reveal a great deal of information about the overall state of a bird's health. A change in the appearance, color or quantity of the droppings is one of the *earliest* signs recognized in sick birds. Unfortunately, owners frequently overlook this important clue. In birds, unlike dogs with a digestive problem, there are no foul odors, no "messes" to clean up, no "mistakes" in the house. A similar problem in birds could easily go unnoticed for long periods of time.

Pet bird owners should get into the habit of taking a moment to look over their bird's droppings on a daily basis.

Normal Droppings

It is important to become familiar with the appearance of your bird's normal droppings. Within any given period of time, the droppings will vary slightly. Learn to recognize these normal variations. Factors such as diet and stress can quickly change their appearance.

Unlike mammals, birds urinate and defecate at the same time. In fact, the digestive, urinary and reproductive tracts all empty into the same receptacle, the cloaca.

The droppings consist of three distinct portions:

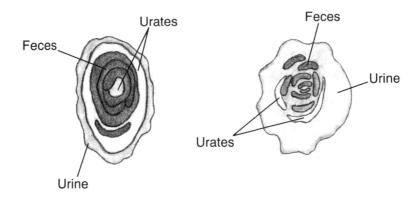

Normal dropping   **Increased urine output**
                                       ("wet droppings")

The "wet" droppings have too much urine. The feces are formed; therefore this is *not* diarrhea. "Wet" droppings can be seen with stress, many diseases and diets high in fruits.

1. Feces ("stool") are the unusable solid waste material from food. The feces should be tubular in shape and formed into a coil. Their color and consistency is affected by diet. A diet consisting mostly of seeds produces a dark green to near black-colored feces. Formulated diets ("pellets") yield a more brownish stool.
2. Urine ("water") is the liquid portion. It is normally clear. Diets high in fruits and vegetables will produce more urine.
3. Urates, also called uric acid, is the creamy-white or chalklike substance on top of and around the feces.

Abnormal Droppings: Interpretation

Once the appearance of the normal droppings are known, recognizing abnormal ones will be much easier.

Feces: Abnormal Changes in Appearance

DIARRHEA (soft or liquid feces): Diarrhea is uncommon. An increase in urine, which produces wet droppings, is frequently mistaken for diarrhea. Remember, if the feces are solid and formed, it is *not* diarrhea. Increased urine can cause the feces to become wet and slightly loose. *Diarrhea is not a disease. It is only an indication that there is a problem affecting the digestive tract.*

CAUSES OF DIARRHEA

- Diet (sudden change in diet, addition of new food, spoiled food), intestinal infection, parasites, ingestion of foreign object or poison
- Diseases of other organs
- Egg ready to be laid or egg binding

- Abdominal hernia
- Overtreatment with antibiotics
- Stress
- Parasites

BLOODY (red, reddish-black, or "tarry"): Bleeding in digestive tract, severe intestinal infections, bleeding disorders, some poisons such as lead, cloaca papillomas, tumors, ingestion of foreign object, parasites, egg laying.

UNDIGESTED FOOD (whole seeds or pieces of pellets in feces): Poor digestion, parasites, intestinal infection (e.g., proventricular dilation), pancreatic disease, oil ingestion.

INCREASED VOLUME ("bulky" feces): Egg laying, poor digestion.

DECREASED VOLUME (small, scant and dark feces): Appetite loss or shortage of food, intestinal obstruction.

Urine: Changes in Volume

INCREASED URINE OUTPUT (wet droppings, polyuria): Normal with increased stress, diets high in fruits and vegetables; abnormal with infections, diseases (i.e. diabetes, kidney), poisons, drug reactions.

DECREASED URINE OUTPUT: Dehydration.

Urates: Changes in Color: Remember, urates should *always* be white or whitish-beige in color. Color changes indicate a serious problem.

YELLOW OR YELLOW/GREEN DISCOLORATION: Liver disease.

RED OR REDDISH/BROWN DISCOLORATION ("bloody"): Poisoning (e.g., lead), liver disease.

11

Emergencies

Spills, Thrills 'n' Oops . . .

THIS CHAPTER is a useful guide to the recognition of, basic first aid for, and prevention of the most common emergencies seen in pet birds. The *best* way to utilize this information is to become familiar with its contents. In this way, when a problem strikes you'll have a better idea on how to deal with it. Also, simply being aware of and knowledgeable about the potential dangers will help to prevent them.

As the reader becomes familiar with the information contained in the medical chapters, an important reality should begin to emerge. It is that there are a wide range of illnesses affecting pet birds, but *only* a handful of signs are actually ever observed. In other words, many different types of injuries and illnesses will "look" similar. A correct diagnosis is difficult because pet birds can't communicate with us, and they hide signs of disease very well. Even an experienced avian veterinarian will often have difficulty determining the actual cause of the signs seen. The importance of establishing a correct diagnosis cannot be overemphasized. This helps ensure the most effective treatment can be provided.

Author's Note: The medical information, including first aid suggestions, are *not* meant as a substitute for veterinary care. The recommendations are generally safe and simple methods of treatment. However, they are *not* going to work in every case. The disease process is very complex, and it's strongly encouraged that a veterinarian *always* be consulted *prior* to initiating treatment of any kind. Remember, your fine feathered friend is fragile, and even the act of restraint and administering medicines can be dangerous. Above all, when it comes to health problems, my hope is that you'll be able to detect the *early* warning signs of disease *before* they become life threatening.

HANDLING THE SICK OR INJURED BIRD

Sick or injured birds must *always* be handled as little as possible. These birds need peace and quiet. However, the benefits of medical treatment often outweigh the risks associated with the stress of handling. When handling is necessary, plan ahead—have all medications and other treatments ready to go. Handle the bird cautiously and gently, and always use a reassuring voice. Dimming the lights can also be helpful. (See Chapter 7.)

Author's Note: Just a word of caution. Birds, even loving, tame pets, if sick or injured, may be more apt to bite. Fear, pain, and sickness could cause unexpected changes in behavior. Therefore, be careful! Be prepared, don't rush and think clearly before reaching out to catch a sick or injured bird.

TRANSPORTING THE SICK OR INJURED BIRD

Call your veterinarian *before* leaving the house. When the phone is answered, say "This is an emergency." Explain the nature of the problem so the hospital staff can be prepared. Ask if there will be a veterinarian available

Bring the bird in its *own* cage, if possible.

- Food and water should be within easy reach. Remove water just prior to leaving the house to avoid its spilling.
- Consider removing perches and toys from the cage. This will help eliminate the possibility of the bird being injured during transport.
- Cover the cage with a blanket or towel. This helps provide warmth and reduces stress.
- *Do not clean the cage.* Your bird's living environment might yield some important clues about the nature of the problem.

If moving the cage isn't possible, use a cardboard box or other, similar container.

- Use a towel to pad the floor.
- If it is cold outside, place a hot water bottle under the towel to provide warmth.
- Be sure there's plenty of fresh air. Puncture holes in the box if needed.
- Fold up the cage paper and bring it along.

If any medications have been given, bring them as well.

Author's Note: Throughout this chapter, the term *general supportive care* is frequently mentioned. This refers to the range of possible treatments and care most sick birds require. In order to avoid repetition, the reader is referred to the pages listed below for a complete explanation of general supportive care.

Home Care for the Sick Bird (page 251) discusses the types of supportive care possible in the home.

Therapeutics: The Art and Science of Healing (page 239) discusses the types of general supportive care used in a veterinary hospital.

EMERGENCIES

A medical emergency is a serious and/or potentially life-threatening injury or disease. *Immediate care is required.* In some instances, such as bleeding, first aid at home may actually be the best *first* course of action. In addition to any home care given, contact your veterinarian immediately.

EMERGENCY SITUATIONS

In many instances, it's difficult to know whether a problem is truly an emergency. Follow your instincts and good common sense. If in doubt, it's an emergency!

Remember—*emergencies need immediate attention.*

Shock

Any emergency can lead to shock. This widely used term describes the circulatory system's failure to supply adequate blood flow to meet the body's needs. When this occurs, nutrients and oxygen are unable to reach the cells, and the normal buildup of toxic waste products cannot be removed.

Any severe insult to the body can result in shock. Common causes include bleeding, dehydration, prolonged vomiting or diarrhea, severe infection, trauma and poisoning. If untreated, shock will lead to death.

In mammals, the signs of shock are relatively easy to determine. They include severe weakness and/or unconsciousness, weak or rapid pulse, pale or "muddy-colored" gums, low body temperature (i.e., cold hands and feet).

Signs of Shock in Birds: The signs are difficult to determine. If a bird is depressed, weak, "fluffed up" and has rapid shallow breathing, shock should be suspected.

Birds in shock are emergencies and treatment must be started immediately. Call your veterinarian!

First Aid for Shock: Unfortunately, there is *no* effective first aid treatment for shock. The best thing to do is keep your bird warm, cover the cage, minimize handling and promptly transport it to your veterinarian.

Call ahead so the hospital staff can be prepared.

Avian Veterinary Care: The therapy for shock is very sophisticated and will probably include:

- Fluids to increase volume. Given intravenously (within a vein) or intraosseously (within a bone).
- Oxygen for breathing difficulties. It is usually given by face mask or in a special oxygen cage. Another technique involves placement of a breathing tube directly into the air sacs from a small skin incision in the abdominal area.
- Warmth—80° to 85°F.
- Drugs—antibiotics, corticosteroids and other medicines as indicated.
- Close monitoring and frequent evaluation of the patient. This is critical.
- General supportive care.

Treatment must also be guided by the underlying problem. Sometimes the cause of shock is obvious. When it isn't, diagnostic tests are essential. However, often these have to wait until the patient is more stable and better able to handle the added stress of collecting the samples.

INTERPRETATION OF EMERGENCY SIGNS

Breathing Difficulties

Respiratory problems are one of the most common ailments in pet birds. Any problem that interferes with normal breathing must be regarded as potentially life threatening (see Chapter 12).

SIGNS TO WATCH FOR

- Noisy breathing: wheezing, constant panting or "clicking" sounds
- Heavy breathing: shortness of breath, open-mouth breathing, tail bobbing (pronounced up-and-down motion of tail) or outstretched neck
- Nasal discharge or area surrounding eye swollen (suggests sinus infection)
- Loss or change of voice

First Aid for Breathing Difficulties: If serious breathing problems are present, call your veterinarian immediately.

1. Keep the bird warm and rested. Minimize stress.
2. Wipe any discharges from nostrils if bird can be *easily* handled.
3. Steam vaporization is helpful.
4. Provide general supportive care.
5. Contact your veterinarian for further advice.

Avian Veterinary Care: A thorough history and physical exam is essential. Diagnostic tests recommended may include X rays, blood tests, and culture

Birds usually breathe through their nostrils. Prolonged open-mouthed breathing such as this usually indicates a respiratory problem. *(R. Woerpel, D.V.M.)*

and sensitivity. Treatment is based on the underlying cause and may include antibiotics, antifungals, and medications to open the airways and make breathing easier. More serious cases may require oxygen and nebulization. General supportive care should be provided as needed.

Coma (Loss of Consciousness)

A coma is a state of unconsciousness where the patient cannot be aroused regardless of the stimulation. A coma is *not* indicative of a particular problem. It is not a diagnosis. There are many causes, including head trauma, brain disease, heat stroke, liver disease, kidney disease, poisoning and metabolic problems such as diabetes.

First Aid for Coma: There is no first aid that would be beneficial. *Call your veterinarian immediately and follow directions exactly.*

Avian Veterinary Care: A coma is a difficult and challenging problem to diagnose and treat. A thorough history and physical exam is essential. Intensive care, including fluids with glucose added, medications for shock and infection, oxygen and general supportive care will be administered as needed. Diagnostic tests and hospitalization will also be recommended.

Convulsions (Seizures, "Fits")

A convulsion is an abrupt and uncontrolled burst of skeletal muscle activity. The muscle contractions may be intense. It is not a diagnosis, but rather a result

149

of some serious underlying problem. The causes are many and include lead poisoning (see discussion later in this chapter), severe infection, some nutritional deficiencies, hypoglycemia (low blood sugar), hypocalcemia (low blood calcium), heat stroke, head trauma and epilepsy (brain malfunction causing recurring seizures).

Even though it may seem like an eternity, seizures usually last only seconds or sometimes up to a minute. Immediately afterward, the bird usually appears dazed and very tired, and may remain on the cage floor for several hours. Convulsions generally recur unless the underlying cause is eliminated or controlled. The frequency of seizures can vary from only minutes apart to days or even months.

SIGNS TO WATCH FOR

- Apprehension and restlessness (possible precursors of a seizure)
- Muscle trembling, "jerking" or entire body in violent muscle spasms (twitching leg, flapping wing, "wandering" head or entire body in uncontrolled shaking and flopping)
- Loss of balance (may fall off perch or appear very unsteady)
- Loss of consciousness

First Aid for Seizures: *Seizures cannot be prevented or controlled with first aid alone.*

1. Prevent injury to the bird. Quickly remove objects such as toys, cups and perches which could get in the way.
2. Move quietly, calmly and gently.
   - If the bird is in its own cage, cover the cage with a towel.
   - Dim the lights and avoid loud noises
3. *Call your veterinarian immediately.*
4. Provide general supportive care.

Avian Veterinary Care: A thorough history and physical examination are important. Diagnostic testing is recommended and will vary depending on probable causes. For example, X rays and blood tests are indicated if lead poisoning is suspected. Treatment might include medication to control seizures, corticosteroids for shock, antibiotics, glucose, calcium and general supportive care as needed. Specific treatment can be initiated if the actual cause is known.

Prolonged Appetite Loss

Birds eat frequently throughout the day. Normal patterns for food preferences and mealtimes should be well established for every bird. Problems should be suspected if there is a dramatic change in established routines. If a large bird (Amazon, cockatoo, macaw) stops eating for twenty-four hours or a small bird ("budgie," cockatiel, lovebird) for twelve hours, a problem should be suspected. Remember, a bird's very fast metabolic rate can lead to rapid weight loss and weakness when eating stops.

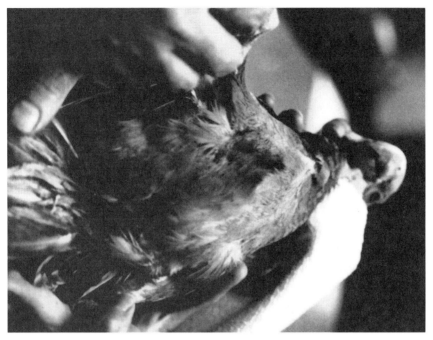

This parrot is very thin. Note the severe muscle loss resulting in a prominent keel bone.

A decrease in appetite is also serious, but is more difficult for an owner to notice. This is especially true if the appetite decreases gradually. Learn to monitor food and water dishes, number and appearance of droppings and general activity levels.

First Aid For Loss of Appetite

1. Provide general supportive care.
2. Call your veterinarian.

Avian Veterinary Care: A thorough history and physical exam are essential. It's important to remember that appetite loss is a result of a problem and *not* the problem itself. Diagnostic tests will be recommended and are especially important if there are no obvious clues as to the nature of the primary illness. General supportive care, including force feeding and medication to stimulate the appetite, may be necessary. Specific treatment can be started once the cause has been established.

Vomiting and Regurgitation

A sign of disease? Or simply of affection?

Regurgitation is the backward flow of *undigested* food, usually from the crop. Vomiting is the forcible expulsion of *digested* food from the stomach

151

through the mouth. Since birds have a crop, it's rare for them to actually vomit. Therefore, regurgitation is what normally occurs, *not* vomiting.

Regurgitation can indicate a crop infection or a blockage in the upper digestive tract. It can also occur in perfectly healthy birds, especially "budgies," and be a normal sign of affection and courtship. This natural behavior reflects a mother bird feeding her young. It can be directed onto a toy, mirror, or a beloved owner. Removing the object of affection will often stop the regurgitation. However, if the owner is the recipient of this affection, little can be done to change it!

In many instances the actual act of regurgitation will not be seen. However, after regurgitating birds will often shake their heads back and forth, and the feathers on top of the head will become sticky and "stuck" together. Also, there is an obvious distinction between the appearance of droppings and regurgitated food.

Regurgitation in the sick bird can be caused by a number of different ailments, most of them involving the upper digestive tract (see Chapter 12). These include dietary changes, crop infection, foreign object ingestion, poison, other digestive tract problems (e.g., proventricular dilatation) and thyroid gland enlargement.

First Aid for Regurgitation in the Sick Bird: As mentioned above, there are many causes for regurgitation. Therefore it's very difficult to generalize about recommendations for first aid. Since this is often a problem seen in very young birds, it could rapidly become life-threatening

1. Provide general supportive care.
2. To help soothe and protect the inflamed lining of the digestive tract, try Kaopectate or Pepto-Bismol. Use a plastic medicine dropper. The dosage is as follows:

Finches/canaries	4 drops every 4 hours
"Budgies"	6 drops every 4 hours
Cockatiels	10 drops every 4 hours
Amazon parrots	20 drops (1cc) every 4 hours
Cockatoos and macaws	30 drops (1.5cc) every 4 hours

3. If there is no improvement within twenty-four hours, or if your bird continues to do poorly, contact your veterinarian.

Avian Veterinary Care: A thorough history and complete physical exam are important. Since there are numerous causes, diagnostic tests are helpful to establish the correct diagnosis. Radiographs can screen for conditions such as foreign bodies, impaction, lead poisoning and proventricular dilation. Also, sampling of the crop contents for the presence of bacteria and yeast will often be recommended. Treatment is, of course, directed at the primary problem in combination with general supportive care. For crop disorders in young birds, see Chapter 5.

TRAUMAS AND INJURIES

Animal Attacks

When birds are kept along with dogs and cats, there is the potential for unexpected problems to occur. In most instances pets get along well, but sometimes accidents do happen. If they do, it can lead to serious, if not fatal, injury, most often for the bird.

In too many instances, owners believed either that their pets *always* got along well or they had a foolproof system for keeping their pets separated. See Chapter 2 for a discussion on how to safely keep different pets together.

Animal bites, whether or not the skin appears broken, are a true emergency. Puncture wounds can be very difficult and sometimes nearly impossible to find beneath the feathers. Most people realize the seriousness of a bite wound. However, in birds, it is even more serious, and often life threatening. Even if a bird looks normal immediately following an attack, it could die shortly afterwards. Internal injuries can easily be sustained from the animal's bite crushing the bird's body. Birds are also very susceptible to the bacteria from an animal's claws or mouth.

First Aid for Animal Attacks: No first aid can be recommended. There is no home treatment effective against a serious infection and internal injuries. Time is crucial. *Call your veterinarian first and immediately drive to the hospital.*

Avian Veterinary Care: A thorough history and physical exam are essential. Treatment for shock, if needed, and antibiotics should begin immediately. The first forty-eight hours are especially critical, and the bird must be closely monitored. Hospitalization may be recommended. X rays may be suggested if fractures or internal injuries are suspected. General supportive care is provided as needed. Once the patient is stable, any wounds present will be cleaned and treated.

Bleeding

Blood, whether seen on a bird, splattered around the cage or in any other area, is *always* a cause for concern. Stop the bleeding first, then try and determine the cause.

Blood Volume and Blood Loss (Hemorrhage): Blood volume is the total amount of blood in the body. It accounts for 6.5 to 10 percent of total body weight—in other words, 6.5 to 10 milliliters for each 100 grams of body weight. A healthy bird *can* very easily lose 10 percent of its blood volume without any danger. Losses of 20 to 30 percent are relatively easily tolerated. A strong and

Blood Loss as a Percentage of Body Weight

SPECIES	WEIGHT*	TOTAL BLOOD VOLUME	10% BLOOD LOSS	30% BLOOD LOSS
"Budgie"	30 g. (1 oz.)	3/5 tsp. (60 drops)	6 drops	20 drops
Amazon	450 g. (1 lb.)	9 tsps. (900 drops)	1 tsp. (90 drops)	2.7 tsp. (270 drops)
Macaw	1,000 g. (2.2 lbs.)	20 tsps. (2,000 drops)	2 tsps. (200 drops)	6 tsp. (600 drops)

*Weights are approximate and meant only as a helpful reference.

otherwise healthy bird could even sustain a loss of 50 percent or slightly more and survive. On the other hand, mammals cannot survive these higher levels of blood loss.

Where could bleeding originate from?

- Externally: beak, nail, feather or skin
- Internally, or from a source *within* the body, including from the nares, mouth or vent

External Bleeding

External bleeding is usually the result of an injury. These include: broken blood feather, flying into a wall, self-trauma (e.g., from picking or chewing on a feather, skin or nail), human induced (i.e. trimming the beak, wings, or nails) and numerous other "freak" accidents.

First Aid for Bleeding Nails or Beak

1. If the bleeding appears minimal, do nothing and see if it stops on its own.
2. If bleeding continues, catch the bird (see Chapter 7).
3. Apply direct pressure. Use a towel, paper towel or finger.
4. Use bleeding "stopper," for example, styptic powder (available at most pet stores). Firmly pack it onto the bleeding area. If a beak is bleeding, keep styptic powder out of the mouth. Other "stoppers" that can be used in an emergency include baking powder, cornstarch, or even flour. As a last resort, sear the site with a red-hot needle.
5. Once the bleeding has stopped, observe the bird for at least one hour. The bleeding could start again.
6. Provide general supportive care.
7. If blood loss seems considerable or the bird appears weak and listless, *call your veterinarian immediately*. If possible, one person should be available to drive to the veterinarian so someone else can control any bleeding.

First Aid for a Bleeding Feather: When an immature feather breaks, the rest of the feather needs to be removed. It should not be left in, or cut, since it could start bleeding again or become infected. Two people are usually required to do this, one for restraint.

1. Act immediately and restrain the bird (see Chapter 7).
2. Using firm pressure and sturdy tweezers or needle-nose pliers, pull the feather out. Grasp the feather as close to the skin as possible. Be gentle and apply smooth, even pressure. If it's a broken wing feather, be sure to firmly hold and support the wing as the feather is pulled out.
3. After the feather is removed, bleeding from the empty follicle may occur. If this happens, apply direct pressure for one or two minutes using a towel or cotton ball.
4. Once the bleeding is controlled, observe the bird for at least one hour. The bleeding could start again.
5. Provide general supportive care.
6. If blood loss seems excessive or the bird appears weak and listless, *call your veterinarian immediately.* If possible, have another person drive so there is someone to control any bleeding.

First Aid for Minor Skin Wounds (Bleeding or Not): Blood loss is usually minimal unless a blood vessel has been cut.

1. Act immediately and restrain the bird (see pages 93–106, 146).
2. Apply direct pressure to the bleeding area with a small towel.
3. Clean the wound. Flush the area with an antiseptic solution such as 3% hydrogen peroxide, Betadine, or chlorhexidine (Nolvasan). A moist-

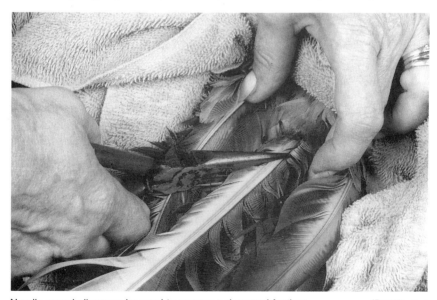

Needle-nosed pliers can be used to remove a damaged feather.   *(Bonnie Jay)*

ened cotton-tipped applicator (Q-tip) can be used to help clean and remove debris. Be gentle and keep the surrounding area clean and dry.

4. Apply a topical antibiotic spray or powder. *Do not* apply to the skin any medications that appear greasy or oily.
5. Provide general supportive care.
6. If there are questions or your bird is weak and listless, *contact your veterinarian immediately.* Further care such as surgery to repair the wound or bandaging to protect it may be necessary.

Avian Veterinary Care for External Bleeding: Stop the bleeding first. Some of the more common methods include applying styptic powder (constricts blood vessels), cautery (seals bleeding vessels with heat or electrical current), bandaging and even surgery when necessary. A broken or cracked beak or nail may require simple trimming or, if severe, surgery. The shaft of a broken feather will need to be removed. A cut or laceration may require surgery. A thorough history and physical exam is essential. Diagnostic tests might include a blood sample to determine the amount of blood lost. Additional testing or treatment would be dependent on the suspected problem and overall condition of the bird. Medication is available to help stimulate the bone marrow to produce more red blood cells. If blood loss is excessive, hospitalization and general supportive care might be suggested.

Internal Bleeding

Internal bleeding is usually more serious. Blood may be seen in the droppings, or coming from the mouth, nose or vent. It can also be one of the many causes of a distended or bloated abdomen. There are many causes for internal bleeding, and these include trauma to an organ, bleeding disorder (blood fails to clot normally), some cancers and poisons, and ingestion of a foreign object. Bleeding from the mouth could suggest a cut on the tongue, or it could be coming up from the lungs.

First Aid for Internal Bleeding: There is no first aid for internal bleeding. However, if the bleeding is from the nose or mouth it may stop within a short time if it's simply a minor injury. Blood in the droppings or coming from the vent may be noticed only intermittently. This does indicates a serious problem.

It's best not to handle your bird or create any other unnecessary stress. Call your veterinarian immediately.

Avian Veterinary Care for Internal Bleeding: The source of the bleeding, amount of blood loss and general health of the patient must first be determined. A thorough history and physical exam is very important. Diagnostic testing such as blood tests and X rays is usually required. Treatment, in addition to controlling the bleeding, may include fluids to replace the blood loss, medication to stimulate increased production of blood cells and improve blood clotting ability, general supportive care and treating the underlying problem.

Burns

Burns are an injury to tissue caused by exposure to high temperatures (i.e., flame, hot objects, hot liquids or steam), electricity or chemicals (i.e. acids, bases such as chlorine bleach). Birds allowed flight in the home, especially the kitchen, may land in a pot of boiling water or grease or on a hot stove. Chewing on electrical cords (i.e. Christmas tree lights) can result in burns around the beak and mouth. Household chemicals are numerous and can cause not only burns, but also poisonings.

SIGNS TO WATCH FOR

- Reddened, painful skin
- Greasy or burnt feathers
- General signs of a "shocky" bird (see discussion earlier in this chapter)

First Aid for Burns: These recommendations are for mild, superficial burns in a bird that still appears relatively bright and alert. If your bird is "shocky," contact your avian veterinarian immediately.

1. Spray the affected area with cool water. If it can be done with minimal stress, immerse the burned area in cool water to help relieve pain.
2. Allow the area to dry, then apply a light coating of an antibiotic cream, powder or spray. *Do not* apply any medications that appear greasy or oily, including butter.
3. For *acid burns*, apply a light coating of baking soda paste (baking soda mixed half and half with water).
4. For *alkali (base) burns*, apply a light coating of vinegar.
5. For *hot grease burns*, apply a light coating of flour or cornstarch *before* rinsing with cool water.
6. Provide general supportive care.
7. If the burn is extensive or the bird is doing poorly, contact your avian veterinarian.

Avian Veterinary Care for Burns: A thorough history and complete physical exam are important. If there are any signs of shock, treatment must be started immediately. Antibiotics are necessary to control infection. The wound may be bandaged with special dressings. Once the bird is stable, collaring may be necessary to prevent picking at the wound. General supportive care as needed must also be furnished.

**"Night Frights"/"Cockatiel Thrashing Syndrome"/
"Earthquake Trauma"**

These are different names for the same problem, but regardless of the name preferred, the signs are the same. Birds, primarily cockatiels, for unknown reasons, will thrash around in their cages. It may be in the middle of the night or following an "earth-shattering" experience. Most commonly, these frightened birds are bruised to various degrees on the wing tips, feet, chest and abdomen. If the thrashing occurs during the night, a small night light may help prevent these episodes.

First Aid for Earthquake Syndrome

1. Provide general supportive care.
2. Call your veterinarian.

Avian Veterinary Care: A complete history and physical exam are very important. Shock, if present, would be treated first. Any injuries requiring treatment would be managed next. If internal injuries are suspected, such as broken bones, X rays would be recommended. General supportive care as needed would be furnished. Bandaging the affected area may be helpful.

Eye Problems

Any eye problem, although usually not life threatening, should be considered serious. A minor irritation can rapidly progress to irreversible damage and even blindness (see Chapter 12 for eye disorder).

SIGNS TO WATCH FOR

- Eyelids swollen and/or "pasted" closed
- Increased blinking
- Eye discharges, including excessive tearing
- Cloudiness of eyeball
- Rubbing eye or side of face

First Aid for Eye Problems

1. Carefully examine the eye. Towel restraint (see Chapter 7) will probably be necessary. If the eyelids are "pasted" closed, they can be gently separated. Warm water may help. A bright light and magnifying glass are helpful. Look for a foreign object in the eye. If found, it might be able to be removed with a moistened cotton-tipped applicator (Q-tip).
2. The surface of the eyeball and eyelids can be rinsed and cleaned with plain tap water. Apply with a plastic eye dropper or drip it off a wad of cotton or tissue paper. Artificial tears (available at drug stores) can also be used.
3. Over-the-counter eye drops containing boric acid or antibiotics *without* a *steroid* (cortisone) can safely be applied to the eye three to five times daily. *Never* use any medication in the eye unless it specifically states "for ophthalmic use" or has some similar statement, or has been prescribed by your veterinarian. Medication in ointment form should be avoided.

A cockatiel with a severe infection around the eye.

4. Provide general supportive care.
5. *Call your veterinarian.* Remember, irreversible damage, including blindness and even loss of an eye, can occur in the early stages of an infection.

Avian Veterinary Care: A thorough history and physical exam are essential. An important distinction must be made between a problem involving the tissue immediately around the eye versus an actual eye problem. An ophthalmoscope is used to examine the interior parts of the eye. A green dye, fluorescein, will probably be applied to the eyeball to determine if the cornea is damaged. Medications and other treatments used will depend on the nature of the problem. Surgery to repair an eye laceration or, if severely injured, enucleation (removal of eye) is occasionally necessary. General supportive care is furnished as needed.

Fractures (Broken Bones)

A bird's bones are brittle and, like toothpicks, can be easily broken. Pet birds *most* commonly fracture bones in their legs, and occasionally in their wings. The tibiotarsus (shin bone), tarsometatarsus (foot bones), digit (toe) and, less commonly, the femur (thigh bone) are affected. However, fractures of the skull, spine (backbone) and other bones can occasionally occur.

Fractures are usually caused by accidental injuries. These include collisions or falls, attacks by another animal and all sorts of "freak" accidents. Poor nutrition and some other diseases can weaken bones and make them more susceptible to fracturing.

159

There are specific names given to particular types of fractures. Some of the more common terms are mentioned. Incomplete fractures, such as so-called greensticks (one side of a bone is broken and the other side is bent), most often affect young birds whose bones are growing and are still relatively soft. Complete breaks are divided into simple and compound. Simple (closed) fractures do *not* produce an open wound in the skin. Compound (open) fractures penetrate the skin and the bone is visible. The exposed bones become contaminated and bone infections can occur. Also, since birds have some pneumatic (hollow) bones, these infections can travel into the lungs and air sacs. A comminuted fracture is a bone splintered or crushed into several pieces.

SIGNS TO WATCH FOR

- Nonweight bearing (holding leg up), leg held in awkward position ("crooked") or difficulty in perching, indicating a leg fracture
- One wing (the affected one) hanging lower than the other (droopy), indicating a wing fracture
- Sudden onset of bruising or swelling at the affected site
- Loss of function or movement of affected limb
- Dangling or floppy limb

OTHER PROBLEMS THAT CAN MIMIC A FRACTURE

- Arthritis (inflammation and pain in a joint)
- Dislocation (joint rupture and displacement of bone)
- Soft tissue injury (muscle, ligament, or tendon)
- Abdominal tumor causing lameness in one or both legs (common in "budgies")
- Foot problems

First Aid for Broken Bones

Attempts at home repair cannot be recommended. Many factors have to be considered, and there are also many complications that can result. Frequently, bandages alone will not heal the fracture. Also, if bandages are improperly applied, they can do more harm than good!

1. Observe the bird for any other problems that may have resulted from the injury (i.e., bleeding, breathing difficulties or shock).
2. Do not attempt to handle the bird unnecessarily. Any movement can cause more bruising and damage to the affected area.
3. Confine the bird. If out of its cage, gently place it back in the cage. A small transport carrier can also be used. Line the floor with an oversized towel. Remove perches.
4. Provide general supportive care.
5. *Call your veterinarian.*

Avian Veterinary Care: A thorough history and complete physical exam are very important. Fractures are usually not life threatening, but if a bird is in shock, this must be treated first. Once the patient is stable, X rays will be necessary to determine which bone is fractured and how seriously and the best course of treatment. For fractures to heal properly, the pieces must be realigned and rigidly held together to prevent internal movement. External stabilization (bandages and splints) is often adequate. In some instances, internal stabilization (surgery) using metal pins and wires will be necessary. Broken bones heal in about four weeks. General supportive care (see page 146) should be provided as needed.

Frostbite (Hypothermia, Cold Exposure)

Frostbite could result from prolonged exposure to low temperatures. The feet and toes are most commonly affected. Birds kept outside in snow and ice conditions or those perching on frozen metal surfaces are at the greatest risk. The frozen tissues appear dry and pale and are very cold to the touch.

First Aid for Frostbite

1. Bring the bird in from the cold and keep it warm.
2. If possible, warm the damaged area by placing it in a circulating water bath. Over about a thirty-minute period, continue to slowly warm the water until it reaches the normal body temperature (about 104°F).

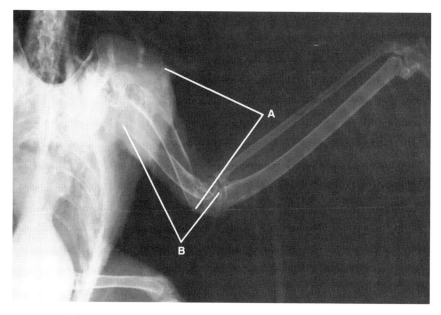

An X ray of a blue-and-gold macaw, Zoltar, with a spiral fracture of the humerus of the wing. (A) indicates the upper fragment of the fracture and (B) shows the lower fragment. There is marked overlapping of the two pieces of bone. Bandaging alone was not enough for this type of fracture. Surgery was required.

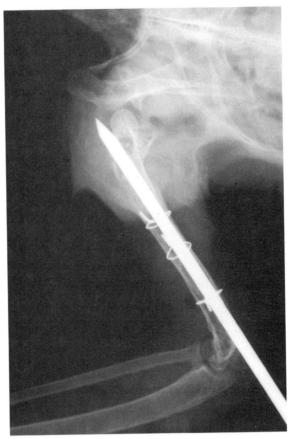

This X ray was taken immediately after surgery while the bird was still under anesthetic so that any changes could be made. A metal pin and three metal wires were used to repair this fracture. The X ray shows good positioning and stabilization of the fracture. However, the pin needed to be backed out a little to prevent joint problems and also cut shorter.

3. Provide general supportive care.
4. *Contact your veterinarian.*

Avian Veterinary Care for Frostbite: Life-threatening problems, such as shock, would be treated first. The bird would be warmed as noted in the preceding list. In addition, it would be placed in an incubator and given warm intravenous fluids. A thorough history and physical exam are essential. General supportive care is furnished as needed. Once the bird is stable, if tissue damage is severe, amputation of the "dead" limb might be required.

Heat Stroke (Overheating)

Heat stroke is caused by prolonged exposure to high temperatures. The body loses its ability to regulate its own temperature. As a result, the body

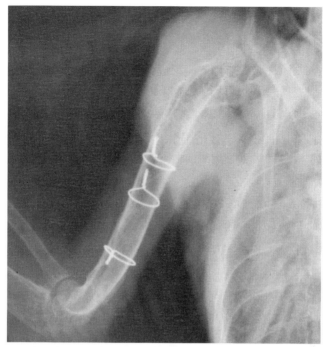

This X ray was taken three weeks after surgery, after the pin was removed. The wires are left in the bird for life. Otherwise, surgery would be required to remove them, and they shouldn't cause any harm.

Zoltar five weeks after surgery.

overheats. Some of the causes include direct sun without shade or water, humid and unventilated rooms and being closed up in a parked car on a hot summer's day. Overweight or older birds have an increased susceptibility to the harmful effects of higher temperatures.

SIGNS TO WATCH FOR

- Heavy panting and outstretched wings
- Extreme weakness, head "wandering"
- Collapse, coma and shock

First Aid for Heat Stroke

Body temperature must be lowered immediately to avoid permanent brain damage or death.

1. Remove the bird from the hot enviroment.
2. Reduce the body temperature.
   - Place the bird in an air-conditioned room, near an open window and/ or in front of a fan.
   - Use a spray bottle with cool water and drench the feathers (prevent chilling).
   - Have the bird stand in a bowl of cool water.
3. Offer cool water to drink or use a dropper to squirt small amounts into the mouth.
4. Provide general supportive care.
5. *Contact your veterinarian.*

Avian Veterinary Care: Provide emergency care, including treatment for shock and dehydration. A thorough history and physical exam are very important. History should confirm the diagnosis. Oxygen and cool-air humidification may also be beneficial. General supportive care is furnished as needed. Close monitoring for twenty-four hours is important.

Leg Band Problems

The reasons for applying leg bands were discussed in Chapter 1. The decision on whether or not to remove leg bands is not a simple one. Closed bands should *never* be removed. They are a "birth certificate" for a bird. On the other hand, removing open bands may well help to prevent injuries. Bands can catch on cage wires, toys and other objects. Also, if the leg is injured and swells, the band can actually cause additional damage. In either case, a tight band will intefere with normal blood flow.

However, this recommendation is subject to your state laws and your veterinarian's opinion.

If the band is going to be removed, *never* attempt to remove a band yourself. It's definitely a two-person job. However, removing these bands is difficult, and serious leg injuries can result. It is for this reason that *only* an avian veterinarian or other experienced person be allowed to remove them.

164

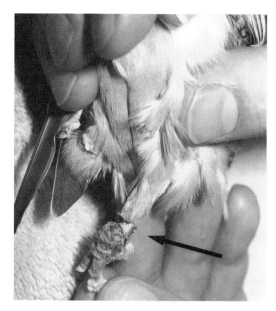

When leg bands are left on, they should be loose-fitting. This bird suffered an injury to its leg, and with a snug-fitting band, the damage became worse.

First Aid for Leg Band Problems

1. If the band is caught around a cage wire, toy or other object, first try and remove the object to free the bird. Cut it or pull it apart if necessary.
2. *Do not* attempt to remove the band.
3. *Call your veterinarian.*

Avian Veterinary Care: If the leg is severely swollen or bleeding, the band would be removed first. This can be a difficult and delicate procedure, especially if the band is tight around the skin. Anesthesia is often required. Bandaging the leg may be necessary. A thorough history and physical exam are important. Diagnostic tests are generally not needed unless other problems are suspected. General supportive care is furnished as needed.

Oil Contamination of Feathers

It's well known that oil-soaked wild birds often die from chilling, exhaustion, starvation and drowning. However, even pet birds are susceptible to feather damage from oils. Free-flight birds allowed out of their cage are most susceptible. Grease and oils from cooking or machinery can accidentally get onto the feathers. Once this occurs, the insulating properties and temperature regulation of the feathers are lost. There can also occur breathing difficulties, eye problems and, if the oil is ingested, poisoning.

First Aid for "Oiled" Feathers

The method discussed below is very involved. It is very stressful for the bird and requires excellent restraint skills. Instead, consider taking the bird to a veterinarian and allowing him or her to clean the feathers and stabilize the bird.

A cockatiel that fell into a pot of cool cooking oil. Oil-soaked feathers can be life-threatening.

1. Dust oiled feathers with cornstarch or flour. This helps to soak up much of the oil. Keep the powder away from the eyes and nose. A suggested method is to place some cornstarch or flour in a small pillowcase or bag. Place the bird inside the bag with its head exposed. Hold the bag around the bird's neck and shake *gently* to dust the feathers. Allow the powder to stay on for about thirty minutes. Brush off excess.

2. Wrap the bird in a towel. This reduces heat loss and prevents ingestion of the oil.

3. Remove oil from nostrils, mouth and around eyes with a moistened cotton swab (Q-tip).

4. Fill a sink with warm water and add a very small amount of mild dishwashing soap (preferably Dawn or Lux Liquid Amber; in Canada try Joy II). Protect the eyes. Immerse the bird in the water. Handling the feathers gently and following their natural contour, wet all affected feathers. Dip the bird slowly in and out of the soapy water for one to two minutes. Rinse the feathers well with fresh warm water. Repeat as needed.

5. Blot dry with towels. Do not rub. A hair dryer on the low setting is also very useful.

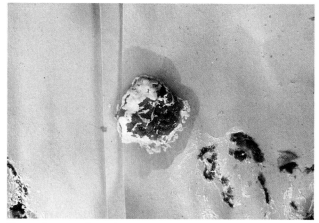

Normal parrot droppings   (Bonnie Jay)

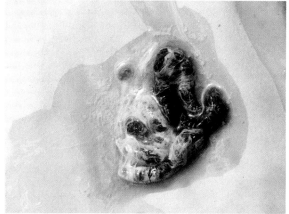

"Wet" droppings may or
may not be normal. These
droppings can be seen
with stress, many diseases
and diets high in fruits.
(Bonnie Jay)

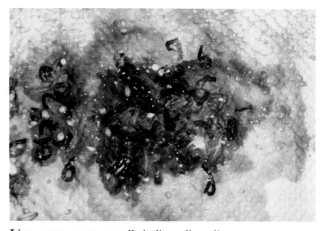

Lime-green urates usually indicate liver disease.

Yellow urates also usually indicate liver disease.

Blood in the feces.

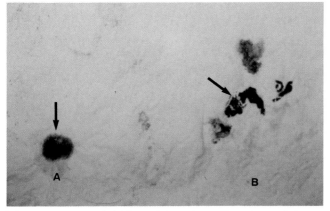

(A) Regurgitation. (B) Normal droppings. There is an obvious distinction between the two.

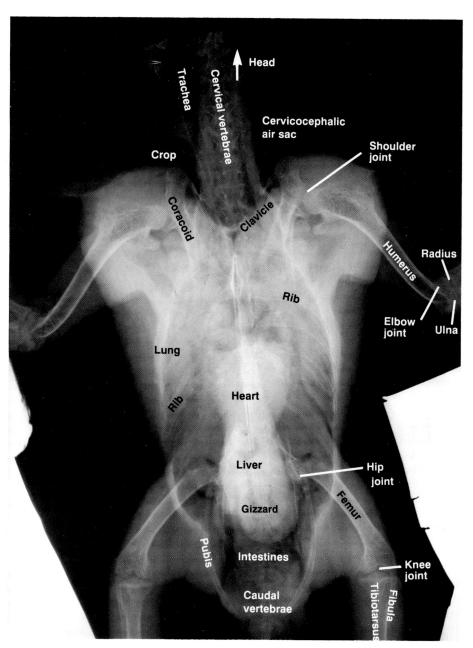

Normal macaw X ray. Positioning is with bird on its back.

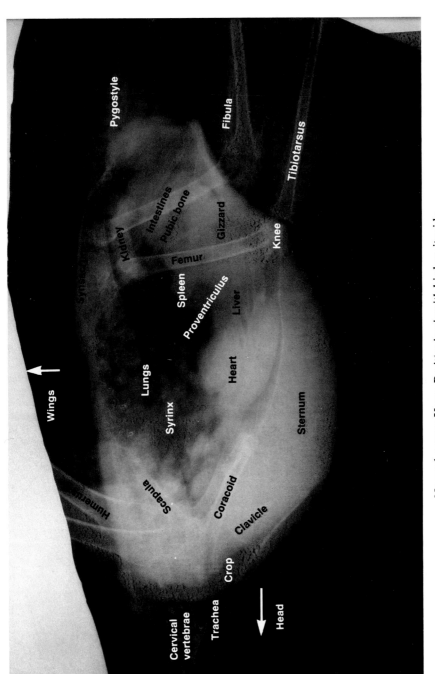

Normal macaw X ray. Positioning is with bird on its side.

6. Wrap the bird loosely in a towel and place it in a warm cage, aquarium or box. Increase the environmental temperature to 85° or 90°F. Avoid drafts.
7. General supportive care follows these steps.
8. If oiling is severe, do not try and remove it all at one time. The above steps may need to be repeated over several hours or perhaps even days.
9. Observe the bird closely over the next several hours. Shock and dehydration are serious concerns.
10. Call your veterinarian.

Avian Veterinary Care: Shock, dehydration and chilling are the most serious threats and would be treated first. A thorough history and physical exam are important. Oil on the feathers would be removed similar to the methods noted herein. Anesthesia may be useful and will help eliminate stress. General supportive care (see page 146) is furnished as needed. Hospitalization and close monitoring over the next twenty-four to forty-eight hours may be recommended.

Egg Binding

Birds generally lay eggs without difficulty. However, on occasion, an egg may get "stuck" inside and may not be laid on schedule. The exact cause is often unknown, but contributing factors may include lack of exercise, obesity, laying multiple eggs over a short period of time, calcium deficiency, soft-shelled eggs, oversized eggs, disease and stress. A "stuck" egg can cause kidney, urinary and intestinal problems. It can also rapidly develop into a life-threatening situation.

History is very helpful. A hen with a previous history of egg-laying problems, along with some of the following signs, should be especially suspect for egg binding.

SIGNS TO WATCH FOR

- Weakness, depression, fluffed-up appearance
- On bottom of cage, not on perch, and exhausted
- Abdominal swelling
- Straining, squatting in a "penguinlike" position
- Paralysis, stiffness or weakness of one or both legs, or waddling like a duck
- Panting, shortness of breath
- Egg visible or bleeding from vent

First Aid for Egg Binding

First aid can be attempted for egg binding. However, precious time will be lost if no egg is produced. Therefore, it would be better to contact your veterinarian.

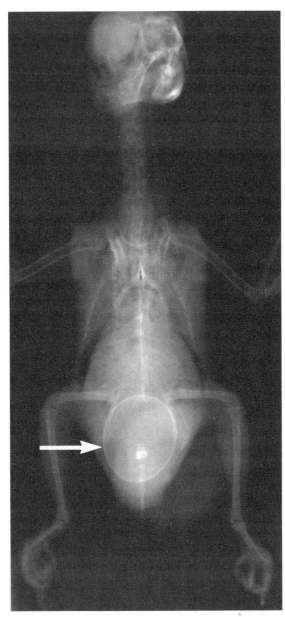

An X ray of an egg-bound cockatiel. This egg is fully calcified and should have been passed before this bird came to the veterinarian "not doing well."

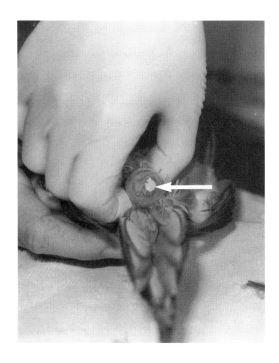

Under anesthesia, the egg is carefully being eased out. Complications could arise if the egg should crack during this delicate procedure.

The egg has been successfully removed. Sometimes the egg cannot be removed with this method and surgery must be considered.

1. Place the hen in a small cage, box, or aquarium.
2. Increase the temperature to 85° to 90°F.
3. Increase the humidity:
   - Place the cage in a bathroom or erect a small tent over the cage using plastic sheeting.
   - Create steam in the bathroom with hot water or use a steam vaporizer.
   - Wet toweling on the floor of the cage will also help.
   - Do *not "overcook" bird*. Consider fifteen-to thirty-minute treatment periods.
4. Supply an energy and calcium supplement in the bird's drinking water:
   - Calcium supplements to dissolve in water include powdered milk, ground cuttlebone, calcium tablets, Neo-calglucon syrup (over the counter from the pharmacy).
   - Quick energy supplements to dissolve in water include honey, Karo syrup, sugar, Gatorade.
5. Provide general supportive care.
6. If no response within a few hours or even less, *call your veterinarian*.

Avian Veterinary Care: A thorough history and physical exam are essential. A radiograph may be necessary to confirm the diagnosis and determine the size and shape of the egg. Injections of calcium and oxytocin may be given to stimulate contractions. Sometimes gentle manipulation of the egg and inserting lubrication may be attempted. This may be done under anesthesia. In other instances, needle and syringe can be used to empty the contents of an egg. This will make removal easier. Sometimes surgery (C-section) is required. General supportive care is furnished as needed. Although not a commonly performed procedure, a hysterectomy (spay) could be suggested in birds frequently laying eggs.

POISONING

> *All substances are poisons. The right dose differentiates a poison and a remedy.*
>
> —Paracelsus (1493–1541)

Birds by nature are curious creatures. "Mouthing," chewing, tasting and even swallowing dangerous liquids or objects are all possible. If birds are allowed free flight in the house, the risks are even greater. Any product labeled poisonous for humans will be poisonous to birds.

ROUTES OF POISONING

Ingestion (by mouth)
Inhalation (by breathing)
Topical (contact with skin)

Suspect poisoning if your bird is sick *and* you observe:

- Contact with a known poisonous substance, including: chewing or playing with the packaging, exposure to fumes or odors
- Opened or spilled containers of any poisonous substance
- Toxic plants recently chewed on
- A foreign substance noted on feathers

SIGNS TO WATCH FOR

- Sudden onset of regurgitation, diarrhea, coughing, breathing problems and/or depression
- Bloody droppings
- Redness or burns around the mouth
- Convulsions
- Paralysis
- Shock

Author's Note: Remember there are *many* diseases and other problems that also present with the above signs. Many are discussed in this book. Therefore, unless it's obvious, poisoning should only be considered a possibility and not the definite diagnosis. If, however, your bird, or other pet, is poisoned, a veterinarian or owner can contact The National Animal Poison Control Center at the University of Illinois in Champaign/Urbana. Its phones are answered twenty-four hours a day, and each call is handled by a veterinarian with special training in animal poisonings. There is a charge for calls, but it could save your pet's life! The two numbers are 800 548-2423 (billed as a flat fee) or 900 680-0000 (billed on a per-minute basis)

First Aid for Poisonings

1. Remove the poison to prevent further ingestion.
2. For eye contact, flush the eye with lukewarm water. For skin contact, flush the area with water. For fume intoxication, ventilate the room immediately—open windows, use a fan or, better yet, remove the bird from the area altogether.
3. Call your veterinarian.
   - Bring a sample of the poison and its packaging
   - Bring a sample of the bird's most recent droppings.
4. Provide general supportive care.

First Aid for Poisonings When No Veterinary Care Is Available

If no veterinary care is immediately available, the bird is conscious and you are sure that the poison was ingested, not just played with, follow the directions below:

1. Call the National Animal Poison Control Center, phone number listed herein. Information on virtually every toxic product is readily available.
2. Refer to the tables on pages 173–176 to determine the type or category of poisoning.

If acid, alkali or petroleum products are swallowed, try one of the following:

- Milk or raw egg white mixed with Kaopectate or Pepto-Bismol
- Activated charcoal (available at pharmacies), mixed with a few drops of mineral oil and enough water to make a pasty consistency

Suggested amounts to give orally:*

Canary or "budgie"	3–6 drops
Cockatiel or similar size	20–40 drops (1–2 cc)
Large parrots	60–120 drops (3–6 cc)

If another type of poison is swallowed, if the poison has been ingested *within* previous 30 minutes or 1 hour maximum, try to induce regurgitation/vomiting. Use equal parts 3% hydrogen peroxide and water. Place a few drops on the middle of the tongue and repeat, if needed, every five to ten minutes two to three times.

Avian Veterinary Care: A thorough history and physical exam are critical. Regardless of the type of poisoning, the general approach to treatment remains the same. An antidote (remedy for counteracting a poison), if available, would be given immediately. The next step would be to reduce absorption of an ingested poison by removal, or dilution. Activated charcoal, mineral oil or another product might be used to irrigate the digestive tract to dilute and reduce the absorbtion. It also will act as a laxative to speed the passage through the digestive tract. If a poison has recently been ingested, surgery or endoscopy might be performed to remove it from the crop and, possibly, even the proventriculus or gizzard. For inhaled toxins, an oxygen-enriched environment is beneficial. For topical poisons, see the discussion of burns earlier in this chapter. General supportive care is furnished as needed.

A discussion of some specific poisons follows.

Lead

Lead poisoning is one of the most common toxicities occurring in pet birds. There are a number of potential sources of lead in most homes. This type of poisoning could frequently be prevented by simply recognizing the common sources of lead in the environment.

SOURCES OF LEAD FOR PET BIRDS

Bird toys weighted with lead, old costume jewelry, lead caulking in stained-glass windows, fishing weights, curtain weights and some types of screens and wires cause the majority of lead poisoning in pet birds. Newsprint, lead pencils and paint manufactured within the last twenty years will not cause poisoning.

---

*Can be given with a plastic dropper.

TABLE 11.1

Common Poisonous Substances That Are Acids, Alkalis or Petroleum Products

Dishwasher detergent	Oven cleaner
Drain cleaner	Paint remover
Floor polish	Paint thinner
Furniture polish	Shoe polish
Gasoline	Toilet bowl cleaner
Kerosene	Wax (floor or furniture)
Lye	Wood preservative

Source: Sheldon Gerstenfeld, *The Bird Care Book* (Reading, Mass.: Addison-Wesley, 1981).

TABLE 11.2

Common Household Poisons

Acetone	Herbicides
Ammonia	Hexachlorophene (in some soaps)
Antifreeze	Indelible markers
Ant syrup or paste	Insecticides
Arsenic	Iodine
Bathroom bowl cleaner	Kerosene
Bleach	Lighter fluid
Boric acid	Linoleum (contains lead salts)
Camphophenique	Matches
Carbon tetrachloride	Model glue
Charcoal lighter	Mothballs
Clinitest tablets	Muriatic acid
Copper and brass cleaners	Mushrooms
Corn and wart remover	Nail polish
Crayons	Nail polish remover
Deodorants	Oven cleaner
Detergents	Paint
Disinfectants	Paint remover
Drain cleaners	Paint thinner
Epoxy glue	Perfume
Fabric softeners	Permanent wave solutions
Garbage toxins	Pesticides
Garden sprays	Photographic solutions
Gasoline	Pine oil
Gun cleaner	Plants
Gunpowder	Prescription and nonprescription drugs
Hair dyes	Red squill

TABLE 11.2 (*Cont.*)

Rodenticides	Strychnine
Rubbing alcohol	Sulphuric acid
Shaving lotion	Suntan lotion
Silver polish	Super Glue
Snail bait	Turpentine
Spot remover	Weed killers
Spray starch	Window cleaners

Source: Adapted from Gary Gallerstein, *Bird Owner's Home Health and Care Handbook* (New York: Howell Book House, 1984); Sheldon Gerstenfeld, *The Bird Care Book* (Reading, Mass.: Addison-Wesley, 1981); and Margaret L. Petrak, ed., *Diseases of Cage and Aviary Birds*, 2nd ed. (Philadelphia, Lea and Febiger, 1982).

TABLE 11.3

Plants Considered Harmful to Birds

PLANT NAME	SCIENTIFIC NAME	PARTS KNOWN TO BE POISONOUS
Amaryllis	*Amaryllidaceae*	Bulbs
American yew	*Taxus canadensis*	Needles, seeds
Azalea	*Rhododendron occidentale*	Leaves
Balsam pear	*Memordica charantia*	Seeds, outer rind of fruit
Baneberry	*Actaia* spp.	Berries, roots
Bird of paradise	*Caesalpina gilliesii*	Seeds
Black locust	*Robinia pseudoacacia*	Bark, sprouts, foliage
Blue-green algae	*Schizophycaea* spp.	Some forms toxic
Boxwood	*Buxus sempervirens*	Leaves, stems
Buckthorn	*Rhamnus* spp.	Fruit, bark
Buttercup	*Ranunculus* spp.	Sap, bulbs
Calla lily	*Zantedeschia aethiopica*	Leaves
Caladium	*Caladium* spp.	Leaves
Castor bean (castor oil plant)	*Ricinus communis*	Beans, leaves
Chalice vine	*Solandra* spp.	All parts
Cherry tree	*Prunus* spp.	Bark, twigs, leaves, pits
Christmas candle	*Pedilanthus tithymaloides*	Sap
Clematis	*Clematis* spp.	All parts
Coral plant	*Jatropha multifida*	Seeds
Cowslip	*Caltha polustris*	All parts
Daffodil	*Narcissus* spp.	Bulbs
Daphne	*Daphne* spp.	Berries
Datura	*Datura* spp.	Berries
Deadly amanita	*Amanita muscaria*	All parts
Death camas	*Zygadenis elegans*	All parts
Delphinium	*Delphinium* spp.	All parts

174

TABLE 11.3 *(Cont.)*

PLANT NAME	SCIENTIFIC NAME	PARTS KNOWN TO BE POISONOUS
Dieffenbachia	*Dieffenbachia picta*	Leaves
Egglant	*Solanaceae* spp.	All parts but fruit
Elephant's ear (taro)	*Colocasis* spp.	Leaves, stem
English ivy	*Ilex aquafolium*	Berries, leaves
English yew	*Taxus baccata*	Needles, seeds
False henbane	*Veratrum woodii*	All parts
Fly agaric mushroom (deadly amanita)	*Amanita muscaria*	All parts
Foxglove	*Digitalis purpurea*	Leaves, seeds
Golden chain (laburnum)	*Laburnum anagyroides*	All parts, especially seeds
Hemlock, poison	*Conium* spp.	All parts, especially roots and seeds
Hemlock, water	*Conium* spp.	All parts, especially roots and seeds
Henbane	*Hyocyanamus niger*	Seeds
Holly	*Ilex* spp.	Berries
Horse chestnut	*Aesculus* spp.	Nuts, twigs
Hyacinth	*Hyacinthinus orientalis*	Bulbs
Hydrangea	*Hydrangea* spp.	Flower bud
Indian turnip (jack-in-the-pulpit)	*Arisaema triphyllum*	All parts
Iris (blue flag)	*Iris* spp.	Bulbs
Jack-in-the-pulpit	*Arisaema triphyllum*	All parts
Japanese yew	*Taxus cuspidata*	Needles, seeds
Java bean (lima bean)	*Phaseolus lunatus*	Uncooked beans
Jerusalem cherry	*Solanum pseudocapsicum*	Berries
Jimsonweed (thornapple)	*Datura* spp.	Leaves, seeds
Juniper	*Juniperus virginiana*	Needles, stems, berries
Lantana	*Lantana* spp.	Immature berries
Larkspur	*Delphinium* spp.	All parts
Laurel	*Kalmia, Ledum, Rhododendron* spp.	All parts
Lily-of-the-valley	*Convallaria majalis*	All parts, including the water in which they have been kept
Lobelia	*Lobelia* spp.	All parts
Locoweed	*Astragalus mollissimus*	All parts
Lords and ladies (cuckoopint)	*Arum* sp.	All parts
Marijuana	*Cannabis sativa*	Leaves

TABLE 11.3 (*Cont.*)

PLANT NAME	SCIENTIFIC NAME	PARTS KNOWN TO BE POISONOUS
Mayapple	*Podophyllum* spp.	All parts, except fruit
Mescal bean	*Sophora* spp.	Seeds
Mistletoe	*Santalales* spp.	Berries
Mock orange	*Poncirus* spp.	Fruit
Monkshood	*Aconitum* spp.	Leaves, roots
Morning glory	*Ipomoea* spp.	All parts
Narcissus	*Narcissus* spp.	Bulbs
Nightshades (all types)	*Solanum* spp.	Berries, leaves
Oleander	*Nerium oleander*	Leaves, branches, nectar of blossoms
Philodendron	*Philodendron* spp.	Leaves, stem
Poison ivy	*Toxicodendron radicans*	Sap
Poison oak	*Toxicodendron quercifolium*	Sap
Poinsettia	*Euphorbia pulcherrima*	Leaves, flowers
Pokeweed (inkberry)	*Phytolacca americans*	Leaves, roots, immature berries
Potato	*Solanum tuberosum*	Eyes and new shoots
Privet	*Ligustrum volgare*	All parts, including berries
Rhododendron	*Rhododendron* spp.	All parts
Rhubarb	*Rheum rhaponticum*	Leaves
Rosary pea (Indian licorice)	*Abrus precatorius*	Seeds (seed illegally imported to make necklaces and rosaries)
Skunk cabbage	*Symplocarpus foetidus*	All parts
Snowdrop	*Ornithogalum umbellatum*	All parts, especially buds
Snow-on-the-mountain (ghostweed)	*Euphorbia marginata*	All parts
Sweet pea	*Lathyrus latifolius*	Seeds and fruit
Tobacco	*Nicotinia* spp.	Leaves
Virginia creeper	*Pathenocissus quinquefolia*	Sap
Western yew	*Taxus breviflora*	Needles, seeds
Wisteria	*Wisteria* spp.	All parts
Yam bean	*Pachyrhizus erosus*	Roots, immature pods

Source: Adapted from *American Medical Association Handbook of Poisonous and Injurious Plants* (Chicago: American Medical Association, 1985); R. Dean Axelson, *Caring for Your Pet Bird* (Poole-Dorset, England: Blandford Press, 1984); Gary Gallerstein, *Bird Owner's Home Health and Care Handbook* (New York: Howell Book House, 1984); Greg J. Harrison and Linda R. Harrison, eds., *Clinical Avian Medicine and Surgery* (Philadelphia: W. B. Saunders, 1986); and John M. Kingsbury, *Poisonous Plants of the United States and Canada* (Englewood Cliffs, N.J.: Prentice-Hall, 1964).

As strange as this may seem, inspect branches to be used as perches before placing them in the cage. There have been cases of birds finding and ingesting buckshot embedded in the wood.

SIGNS TO WATCH FOR

- Depression, weakness
- Blindness
- Seizures, "walking in circles," "head wandering"
- Regurgitation
- Droppings: excessively wet, may even be bloody ("tomato juice–colored" urine)
- General signs of a sick bird

Other Problems That Mimic Lead Poisoning: Any disease or infection involving the nervous, digestive, or urinary systems could easily be confused with lead poisoning.

First Aid for Lead Poisoning: Unfortunately, there is no first aid available. In most instances, the pet owner is not even aware the bird has ingested lead. Treatment is very specific, and veterinary care must be initiated as soon as possible.

Avian Veterinary Care: If lead poisoning is suspected, tests should be performed to confirm the diagnosis. X rays and blood lead levels are the preferred methods. Calcium versenate (abbreviated CaEDTA) is the antidote and is given daily until all lead is gone from the body. If large amounts of lead are found, surgery to remove it could be the best approach. Tube-feeding Metamucil, peanut butter or other "bulking agents" can be used to minimize absorption and help speed passage through the intestinal tract. General supportive care, including antiseizure medication, will be administered as needed.

"TEFLON TOXICITY" OR POLYMER FUME FEVER

Polytetrafluoroethylene (PTFE) is a synthetic polymer used as a nonstick surface in cookware. The brand names Teflon, Silverstone and T-Fal are the best known, but PTFE-coated products are also manufactured under other trade names.

As Dr. Peter Sakas states:

Under normal cooking conditions, PTFE-coated cookware is stable and safe. When PTFE is heated above 530 degrees Fahrenheit, however, it undergoes breakdown and emits caustic (acid) fumes. Most foods cook at lower temperatures: Water boils at 212 degrees, eggs fry at 350 degrees, and deep frying occurs at 410 degrees. But when empty PTFE-coated cookware is left on a burner set on the high setting, it can reach temperatures of 750 degrees or greater. Thus, if a pan is being preheated on a burner and forgotten, or if water boils out of a pot, breakdown of the PTFE can occur. In other words, PTFE-coated cookware has to be "abused" to emit

177

toxic fumes, but this is not as rare as it might seem; many people fall asleep after they put pots or pans on the stove to heat.

Birds kept in areas close to the kitchen will usually die very shortly after breathing the fumes. Even birds kept in another room are at great risk. Severe breathing difficulties, such as gasping for breath, may be seen just prior to death. Humans, dogs, cats and other mammals are somewhat less sensitive to the very serious effects of these fumes.

First Aid for Teflon Toxicity

1. Remove the affected bird immediately from the home and supply lots of fresh air. Unfortunately, other than this, no first aid exists.
2. *Call your veterinarian immediately*

Avian Veterinary Care: An oxygen-enriched environment and shock therapy should begin immediately. A thorough history and physical exam are important. General supportive care (see page 146) is furnished as needed.

Insecticide Poisoning

The most common insecticide poisoning in pet birds occurs when the house is sprayed ("fogged" or "bombed") for various pests. As already mentioned, birds have very sensitive respiratory systems. *Always* take birds and their cages out of the house *before* spraying. When the spraying is finished, open all doors and windows to help remove the odors. Use fans if needed. Do not bring your birds back in the home for at least twenty-four hours. Consult your veterinarian for the safest and most effective foggers.

First Aid for Insecticide Poisoning

1. Remove the bird immediately and supply lots of fresh air.
2. Provide general supportive care.
3. Call your veterinarian immediately.
4. Bring the insecticide along.

Avian Veterinary Care: An oxygen-enriched environment and shock therapy would begin immediately, if needed. If an antidote is available, it will be given. A thorough history and physical exam are important. General supportive care is furnished as needed.

Author's Note: Our homes "house" many dangerous products. There's a very real risk for pets getting into them. For birds, the kitchen poses the *greatest* peril. See pages 21–25 for a discussion on designing a bird-safe home.

12

Diseases

Aches, Pains and Problems

$\mathbf{D}$ISEASES, BY DEFINITION, have a specific cause and recognizable signs and, to varying degrees, prevent the body from functioning normally. This sounds rather simple. In reality, however, so many *different* diseases have *similar* causes and presenting signs. These similarities often make identifying the *actual* disease very challenging. There is no such thing as a standard or ''cookbook'' approach to disease recognition and treatment. The ''art of practice'' has been so named because it involves combining the science of medicine with the finely honed skills necessary to ''bring to light'' the correct diagnosis and approach to treatment.

This chapter is meant only as a *brief* introduction to many of the common diseases affecting pet birds. The purpose is *not* to teach the pet bird enthusiast how to recognize and treat disease, but rather to introduce bird owners to the diversity of illnesses affecting pet birds. It is hoped this increased awareness will allow for earlier recognition of problems. This is very important. The longer a disease is allowed to run its course, the more damage occurs, and the more difficult it will be to effectively treat.

HOW DISEASES GET STARTED

The body is exposed to or virtually ''bombarded'' every day by potential disease-producing organisms. Why is it that birds and other animals are, for the most part, healthy? The body's ability to successfully fight off so many different diseases is influenced by a number of different factors. In addition, the onset of disease, its signs and severity will also be affected by the same elements.

179

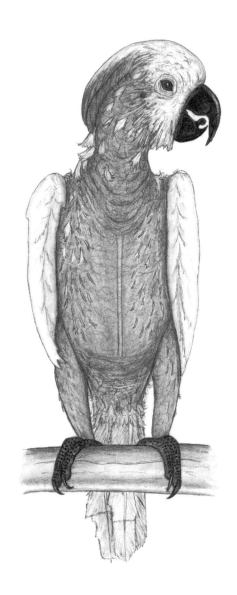

In the body these include general health status, which is influenced by age, sex, species, diet, stress and heredity, elements that will all have an effect on the immune system. It is this system that must be kept strong and healthy to protect the body against disease.

With regard to the organism, its ability to penetrate the body's defenses is influenced by its unique characteristics, which can actually vary within the same group of organisms, the number of organisms present and the length of time the organism has to invade the body.

Transmission or spread of an infection can occur by many different routes, including through food and water, via the air, through contact with other animals and contamination of objects within the living environment, and even occasionally on the hands and clothing of a loving, conscientious owner.

CLASSIFICATION OF DISEASES

Diseases are classified into major categories based on their underlying cause. These include:

Infectious

Infections are caused by microorganisms too small to be seen by the naked eye. Those of medical importance include bacteria, viruses and fungi (including yeast).

Bacteria and fungi survive on dead tissue. Viruses, on the other hand, must live *inside* the cells of living things. Viruses live "protected" within the cell, and this makes them *very* difficult, if not nearly impossible, to treat, since any drug used to kill viruses will usually also kill the cell in which it is living. Fortunately, vaccines to prevent some viral diseases are available.

Metabolic

Metabolic problems are the result of abnormal chemical and physical processes occurring within the body. These would include all the steps involved with the production and utilization of energy. Examples of diseases in this category include diabetes, allergies and thyroid gland problems.

Nutritional

Nutritional problems would result from an excess or deficiency of essential nutrients. Vitamin A deficiency is a commonly seen example. Also, in some cases the body cannot properly utilize the nutrients provided in the diet. Although there are frequently metabolic reasons for this, nutrition-related disease occurs. Hypocalcemia seen in African Grey parrots would be an example.

Parasitic

Parasites are tiny living organisms that live on or in another living creature. Parasites obtain food and/or shelter at the expense of their host. Mites and worms are examples of parasites.

Toxic

A toxin is any poisonous substance that irritates, damages or weakens the body's normal activities.

Cancerous

Describing the abnormal and uncontrolled growth of cells that invade and destroy surrounding tissue. Cancer can also spread (metastasize) via the bloodstream and lymphatics, and even spread throughout the body cavities. As a result, serious organ damage occurs. Other problems such as bleeding, obstructions and infections can result.

Developmental and Degenerative

Developmental disease is associated with problems during the growth phase from egg through adulthood (e.g., birth defects). Degeneration is a process by which tissue deteriorates and loses functional activity—"the aging process" (e.g., arthritis).

DIAGNOSING DISEASE

One of the many challenges in diagnosing disease is the way in which the body responds to disease. The body is able to respond to disease in only a limited number of ways. In other words, a variety of different diseases will "look alike" and cause similar damage to the tissues. For this reason, in addition to a thorough history and physical examination, diagnostic tests are usually necessary to help identify the underlying cause. Other factors that also make diagnosis in birds difficult include their inability to "tell us where it hurts" and their very effective ability to "hide" signs of disease.

Within each of the various bird species, certain diseases are more common than others. Knowing these tendencies makes diagnosis easier. In this book, however, with few exceptions, the identification of species most prone to certain diseases has not been included. The reason for this is to encourage the pet bird owner to consider disease possibilities with an open mind. Remember, *any* species and *any* bird can develop any of the illnesses mentioned.

Author's Note: Remember, just because a bird is exhibiting signs that appear "identical" to a particular disease described in this book does *not* mean it has that disease. It could, very likely, be any number of other diseases that manifest similar signs.

Diagnostic tests will generally be recommended when attempting to determine the cause of the problem. However, even with thorough testing, there are times when an accurate diagnosis simply cannot be made. In these cases, a lot of useful information will still be learned about the general health status of a bird and the range of possible diseases will be narrowed down. There are also times when, for financial reasons, few and sometimes no diagnostic tests can be performed. In these instances, there is always the option of treatment based solely on the findings from the history and physical exam.

Above all else, remember that the early recognition of a problem, followed by good medical care, is the key to success in treating any disease.

EYE DISORDERS

SIGNS TO WATCH FOR

- Eyelids swollen and/or pasted closed
- Increased blinking
- Eye discharges, including excessive tearing
- Cloudiness of the eyeball
- Squinting
- Rubbing the eye or side of the face

Any eye problem could be an emergency (see Chapter 11).

Conjunctivitis (Pinkeye): Conjunctivitis is an inflammation of the membrane covering the inside of the eyelids and outer surface of the eyeball. When only one eye is affected, an injury from a small seed, feather or piece of dirt might be suspected. If both eyes are involved, an infection, allergy or air contamination from dust or smoke should be suspected. On the other hand, conjuctivitis could be suggestive of a more serious problem affecting the entire body.

SIGNS TO WATCH FOR: Normal pink color of membrane of tissue surrounding the eye becomes a deeper red; there is usually a discharge from the eye.

AVIAN VETERINARY CARE: Eye problems require immediate treatment. The eye is closely examined for the presence of foreign objects and corneal abrasions (see below). If a simple conjunctivitis is present, eye medication containing both antibiotics and corticosteroids may be prescribed for use in the eyes and administered several times daily.

Corneal Abrasion ("Scratch" or Ulcer on the Surface of the Eyeball): Injuries to the cornea can be very serious and painful. Some of the causes include trauma, infection, irritating substances and self-inflicted injuries from excessive rubbing of the eye.

SIGNS TO WATCH FOR: Squinting is common, and the cornea may appear "cloudy" or lose its transparency

DIAGNOSIS: Ulcers are usually *not* visible to the naked eye; they are detected with the combination of a special stain, light source and magnification.

AVIAN VETERINARY CARE: Immediate veterinary care is required, and antibiotic eye medications will be instilled in the eye several times daily. Medications containing corticosteroids should *never* be used. They delay the healing process and can cause more serious problems. Surgery to repair a deep ulcer is occasionally necessary.

Cataract: Cataracts most commonly develop in older birds. They are usually hereditary, but can also result from diabetes or trauma to the eye.

SIGNS TO WATCH FOR: A "whitening" of the lens suggests a cataract. The lens is normally invisible because it is transparent. If a cataract is present, the normally seen "black hole" of the pupil appears white.

AVIAN VETERINARY CARE: An examination is needed and a blood test may be recommended to rule out diabetes. If diabetes is not the cause, treatment is usually *not* necessary, unless *both* eyes are affected and vision is severely impaired. Surgery to remove the lens is the only option available. When the lens is removed, vision is restored, but since no lens is present to focus light, objects appear blurry.

RESPIRATORY SYSTEM DISORDERS

SIGNS TO WATCH FOR

- Noisy breathing: wheezing, frequent panting or "clicking" sounds
- Difficulty breathing: shortness of breath, open-mouth breathing, tail bobbing (pronounced up-and-down motion of tail), or frequent stretching of neck
- Nasal discharge or matting of feathers around cere
- Swollen area surrounding eye (may suggest eye problem or sinus infection)
- Loss or change of voice

As previously discussed, a bird's respiratory system is markedly different from that of a mammal. Therefore, a basic knowledge of a bird's respiratory anatomy and physiology is vital to understanding its unique problems.

Respiratory infections in pet birds are common. A human's "common cold" should *not* be confused with similar problems seen in birds. Since birds have a highly specialized breathing system, problems are, unfortunately, more involved and more difficult to treat. Even a simple "runny" nose or sneeze should be taken seriously. Problems can quickly become life threatening, and treatment is always best started when signs first appear.

Rhinitis/Sinusitis: These are an inflammation of the membranes in the nose or sinuses. An infection in the nose frequently extends into the sinuses. Sinus infections can be *very* difficult to treat and can easily become a long-term problem.

SIGNS TO WATCH FOR: "Plugged" nares, "runny nose," sneezing; sinus infections may show "puffy" cheeks or swelling around one or both eyes.

DIAGNOSIS: Sinus infections are more difficult to diagnose. X rays can be helpful, also a culture and sensitivity or gram stain of the nose or sinus area may be suggested.

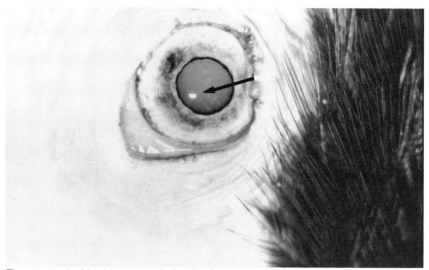

The cataract in this older macaw is the cloudy appearance of the pupil (or black part of the eye).

AVIAN VETERINARY CARE: Simple infections are treated with antibiotics. Depending on the severity, other options include decongestants, anti-fungals, sinus flushes and nebulization. Sinus infections can frequently become a long-term problem, and aggressive treatment is recommended.

Vitamin A deficiency (Hypovitaminosis A): Vitamin A is needed for the maintenance of healthy skin, good vision, bone development and even reproduction. Since a type of skin (epithelium) lines the inside of the respiratory and digestive tracts, a deficiency often causes problems in these areas. The reason for this is the weakening of the skin's normal defenses against microorganisms. Poor nutrition, such as with an all-seed diet, is the most common cause. *Seeds contain little or no vitamin A.*

SIGNS TO WATCH FOR: General signs of a respiratory problem, poor vision, frequent yeast infections, poor fertility and hatching problems. One of the more commonly recognized problems, especially in Amazon parrots, are sores in the mouth. These appear along the roof of the mouth and under the tongue. Look for white, "cheesy" patches or lumps.

DIAGNOSIS: History suggesting poor diet, signs as mentioned above, microscopic exam of affected tissue and a "throat" culture.

AVIAN VETERINARY CARE: Vitamin A supplementation is given, usually by injection. Infections are also frequently present and must be treated. Surgery is sometimes needed to lance abscesses, especially if eating or breathing becomes difficult.

PREVENTION: Improving the diet is essential. Cod liver oil is a good oral source, and it can be added to food. However, it spoils rapidly, and treated foods should be discarded after about twelve hours. Animal sources of vitamin A include liver, fish oils and egg yolk. Plant sources include those vegetables that are deep green or orange in color (such as sweet potatoes/yams, spinach, broccoli,

White "cheesy" patches along the edges of the choanal slit are suggestive of a vitamin A deficiency. A sample of these plaques may be submitted to the lab for microbiological analysis. Gauze strips are being used to hold the beak open safely.

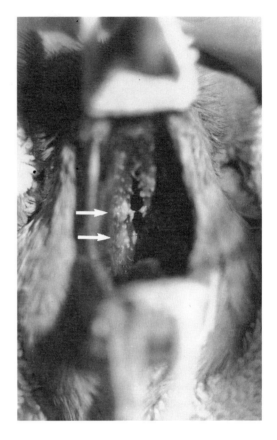

carrots, squash, red peppers, endive and parsley). Fruit sources include papaya, cantaloupe and apricots. Remember, vitamin A in excess can also cause problems. Consult your veterinarian for recommendations on supplements.

Laryngitis, Tracheitis, Syringitis, Bronchitis, Pneumonia and Air Sacculitis: These terms are used to describe an inflammation of a specific area of the lower respiratory tract. In actuality, *most* illnesses involve two or more of these areas at the same time. Bacterial and fungal infections are the most common cause.

SIGNS TO WATCH FOR: General signs of respiratory problems.

DIAGNOSIS: Diagnosis presents many challenges. Among them is "listening" to the lungs and heart with a stethoscope. In mammals, this simple instrument yields a tremendous amount of very useful information. However, in birds the instrument is not as useful. The reasons include massive pectoral muscles, very rapid heart rate, nonexpanding/contracting lungs and the small size of the organs.

Culture and sensitivity, Gram stain, blood counts and X rays may be needed for an accurate diagnosis.

AVIAN VETERINARY CARE: Depending on the cause and severity this could

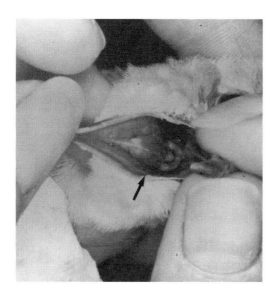

Look carefully to see the small seed lodged in the trachea of this bird. This picture was taken after the bird died.

include antibiotics, antifungals, decongestants, nebulization and oxygen therapy.

Air Sac Infections: These deserve special mention. Diagnosis and treatment are especially difficult. Air sacs are at the "end of the line," so to speak, of the respiratory system and form a convenient reservoir for contaminated air. Blood supply is scant, and therefore the accumulated debris escapes most of the body's normal waste-removal mechanisms. Treatment is difficult because oral and injectable drugs require a good blood flow to carry them to the site of the problem. In the early stages birds usually do not appear sick. As a result, by the time the illness is recognized the condition is well established in the body. Infections caused by the fungus aspergillus is one of the more common causes.

DIAGNOSIS: Requires X rays, cultures and often endoscopy.

AVIAN VETERINARY CARE: Nebulization is the most effective method of "delivering" drugs to the air sacs. Oxygen therapy may be necessary. Surgery, on occasion, may be recommended to cut out and remove diseased air sac tissue.

Some Other Common Respiratory Problems

Allergies: Although allergies in birds have not been proven, there is considerable evidence to suggest they do indeed occur. Birds are probably similar to mammals in that virtually anything could trigger an allergic reaction. However, the most likely causes would include certain types of seeds, cage coverings, odors, perfumes and branches used as perches. Also, simply keeping a bird outside or near an open window would expose it to many different potential allergens.

SIGNS TO WATCH FOR: Sneezing, "runny" eyes and nose, and possibly digestive tract problems.

DIAGNOSIS: No tests are available. A good history is very important and could suggest possible causes.

AVIAN VETERINARY CARE: Medications such as steroids and antihistamines may be tried but are untested in the control of allergies in birds.

PREVENTION: Avoidance of suspected allergen.

Aspergillosis: Aspergillosis is a fungal disease that causes lower respiratory tract problems. The lungs and air sacs are the most common sites for infection. Birds with weakened immune systems associated with stress are particularly susceptible. Those kept in crowded, moist, poorly ventilated and unkempt areas are at greatest risk. The disease is transmitted by inhaling the fungal spores.

SIGNS TO WATCH FOR: General signs of respiratory disease, especially rapid breathing rate, voice changes and wheezing.

DIAGNOSIS: Fungal culture, aspergillosis blood test, X rays and endoscopy may also be helpful.

AVIAN VETERINARY CARE: Even with antifungal medications, this is a very difficult disease to treat. Months of therapy are often required. Medication given directly into the trachea or via nebulization can be very helpful.

Inhaled Foreign Objects: Small seeds can become lodged in a nostril, in the roof of the mouth, and even in the trachea. Small birds are most susceptible. Severe respiratory problems can result.

Mites: Found primarily in finches and canaries, mites can live in the trachea, lungs, body cavity and air sacs.

TRANSMISSION: Food or water, from one bird to another, including from parent to chick.

SIGNS TO WATCH FOR: Breathing difficulties with characteristic "clicking" sound, voice changes.

DIAGNOSIS: Microscopic exam of throat secretions, special lighting technique to visualize mites in the trachea.

AVIAN VETERINARY CARE: The drug ivermectin is very effective.

Psittacosis (Chlamydiosis, "Parrot Fever"): See pages 195–196.

Thyroid Gland Enlargement ("Goiter"): The paired thyroid glands are located alongside the trachea at the base of the neck. These glands will markedly enlarge if there is a dietary deficiency of iodine. As a result, pressure is placed on the trachea and breathing problems develop. "Budgies" seem to be affected most often.

SIGNS TO WATCH FOR: Breathing difficulties, increased swallowing movements, regurgitation.

DIAGNOSIS: X rays may show enlarged thyroid glands. Thyroid hormone levels in blood; but this may not be practical, especially in small birds. Therefore, when suspected, response to treatment is often the method used.

AVIAN VETERINARY CARE: Iodine supplementation.

Nonrespiratory Causes of Breathing Difficulties: Diseases of other organs, such as heart and liver problems, tumors in the abdomen, malnutrition and certain poisons can result in breathing difficulties.

Mimicking of Humans: When all else fails, remember a bird might be "faking" a cough. Many birds can learn to copy a cough or sneeze. Consider your bird's "talking" ability, exposure to coughing noises, health status and common sense to determine if this is possible.

DIGESTIVE DISORDERS

SIGNS TO WATCH FOR

- Vomiting/regurgitation
- Diarrhea (specifically loose stool); may contain blood, mucous or undigested seeds
- Straining to eliminate
- Droppings contain urine and *no* stool (consider constipation, obstruction and, of course, not eating)

As previously discussed, the digestive system of birds, is markedly different from that found in mammals. Therefore, a basic knowledge of birds' specialized digestive anatomy and physiology is vital to understanding their unique digestive problems.

Oral Cavity (Mouth) Problems

An examination of a bird's mouth is not as easy as it may seem. "Open up and say ahh" just doesn't work! To begin with, good restraint is essential (see Chapter 7). The best time to examine the mouth is immediately after "capture," when the bird is often vocalizing. Hold the head still, use a small flashlight or bright overhead light and possibly magnification. Instruments to forcibly open the mouth are not recommended, except in the experienced hands of an avian veterinarian. The normal membranes in the mouth are pink, shiny, slightly moist and with uniform coloration. Some species may also normally show various degrees of a black pigmentation.

SIGNS TO WATCH FOR: Presence of ulcerations, growths or white "cheesy" deposits in the mouth are abnormal. In addition, there may be appetite loss, voice changes or nasal congestion.

Vitamin A Deficiency: This can be a contributing factor in the development of oral infections.

Infections: Infections are very common. Bacterial and yeast are the most likely culprits.

SIGNS TO WATCH FOR: Redness, ulcerations or swellings in the mouth.

DIAGNOSIS: Bacteriological exams can be very helpful.

AVIAN VETERINARY CARE: Antibiotics or antifungals as indicated; growths or abscesses may require surgery.

Parasites: Parasites such as a protozoan named trichomonas (tri-KOM-o-nas) occasionally cause problems in the mouths of pet birds. It is more common in pigeons and raptors.

SIGNS TO WATCH FOR: White "cheesy" deposits or dry "scabby" lesions.

DIAGNOSIS: Microscopic exam of affected tissue.

AVIAN VETERINARY CARE: Antiprotozoan drugs.

Tumors: Tumors, such as benign papillomas, can be found along the roof of the mouth or in the back of the throat.

Crop Problems

The crop can normally be felt in the area around the base of the neck. It must be examined gently. If it is full, there is a risk of food being pushed up into the mouth and causing breathing difficulties. For this reason, only a veterinarian should examine this area.

Signs to Watch For: Regurgitation, unusual head and neck movements, unusually slow emptying of crop, swelling at the base of the neck, sour smell from the mouth, general signs of a sick bird.

Regurgitation is often not actually seen, but there are clues to suggest it has occurred. Look for food debris ''sprayed'' or ''caked'' over the face and head. Closely examine the cage paper. Regurgitation appears as a ''blob'' of semidigested food, which is very different from a dropping. Remember, regurgitation can be a normal sign of affection or courtship.

In young birds a large pendulous swelling at the base of the neck that fails to empty frequently suggests a problem (see Chapter 5).

Conditions that could be mistaken for an enlarged crop: fat deposits, especially in ''budgies,'' ruptured air sac and tumors in the neck area

Infections: Crop infections are more common in young birds. Bacteria and yeast (candida) are the most likely causes of crop infections.

Diagnosis: Microscopic analysis of crop contents.

Avian Veterinary Care: Antibiotics or antifungals as indicated; the crop may also need to be manually emptied and flushed to remove debris and microorganisms.

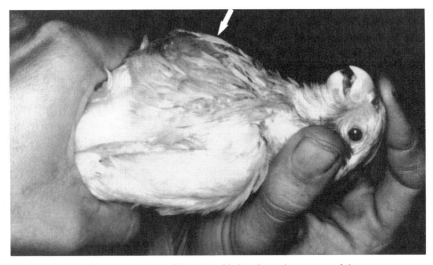

A cockatiel with an impaction of the crop. Notice the enlargement of the crop area.

Impactions: An impaction usually results from food getting "stuck" in the crop. The causes include infection, overeating of grit, dehydration, ingestion of a foreign object or any serious, debilitating disease.

SIGNS TO WATCH FOR: General signs of a sick bird.

DIAGNOSIS: A hard or "doughy" mass can usually be felt during examination; sometimes X rays may be helpful.

AVIAN VETERINARY CARE: The impaction will need to be removed from the crop. Manual removal is usually sufficient. This is accomplished by either "milking out" the impaction, or flushing and massaging to break it up. Occasionally surgery may be necessary to remove the impaction. Medications such as antibiotics or antifungals may be needed.

Other Possible Causes of Crop Problems: Enlarged thyroid glands prevent normal emptying of the crop. Lower digestive tract disorders can also lead to crop problems.

Proventriculus (Stomach)

The proventriculus is the "true" stomach in birds. It secretes the "juices" necessary to digest food. There is *no* simple way to diagnose problems of the proventriculus. The history, physical exam and the "signs to watch for" with all digestive tract problems are not specific enough. Diagnosis is therefore difficult, and diagnostic tests will be necessary. Most problems are the result of an infection or, occasionally, a tumor.

Proventricular Dilatation Syndrome (Macaw Wasting Disease): Proventricular dilatation syndrome (PVD) is a serious disease of the digestive tract. It was first discovered in macaws, but it has also been found in numerous other species of parrot. The death rate is near 100 percent. The cause at this time is not known, but a virus is suspected. The nerves to the digestive tract are affected, and this appears to cause most of the problems. As a result, food cannot be properly digested. PVD can be contagious from one bird to another.

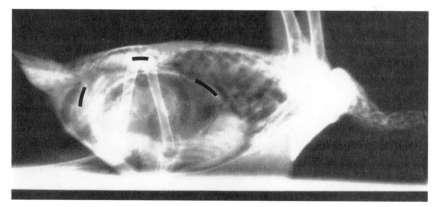

An X ray of a bird with proventricular dilatation syndrome (PVD). The three small lines show the border of the dramatically enlarged proventriculus.

SIGNS TO WATCH FOR: Regurgitation, undigested food in droppings, diarrhea, severe weight loss and possibly neurologic signs including loss of balance, paralysis and general weakness. Affected birds are *very* sick.

DIAGNOSIS: X rays reveal a distended, "balloonlike" proventriculus; biopsy may be necessary to confirm the diagnosis.

AVIAN VETERINARY CARE: No treatment is available. Mild cases may benefit with general supportive care, including a soft, easily digested diet.

Gizzard (Muscular Stomach)

The gizzard grinds up the food. As with proventricular disorders, there is no simple way of diagnosing problems in the gizzard. Most problems are the result of an infection, a foreign body or occasionally a tumor. Ingested foreign objects such as grit or lead will collect in the gizzard. Gizzard impactions sometimes occur.

DIAGNOSIS: X rays are necessary; endoscopy may be recommended.

AVIAN VETERINARY CARE: Grit impactions will frequently resolve on their own with good general supportive care, including antibiotics. Surgery of the gizzard is difficult and should be attempted only if there are no other options.

Intestines

The intestines normally harbor "good" bacteria to aid in the digestive process. During an infection, the gut linings become inflamed, allowing these bacteria to "escape" into the bloodstream. As a result, other organs can become involved. Also, diarrhea is common with intestinal problems. But with diarrhea there is loss of fluid, electrolytes, enzymes and nutrients. In extreme cases, shock can occur and a life-threatening problem develops. Therefore, immediate veterinary care is recommended.

Infections: Intestinal infections are common in pet birds. Primarily bacteria, but yeast and viruses can also cause intestinal disorders.

SIGNS TO WATCH FOR: Diarrhea and other general signs of digestive problems.

DIAGNOSIS: X rays, blood tests, fecal analysis, and bacteriologic exams.

AVIAN VETERINARY CARE: Variable, depends on the cause and condition of the bird; would include various medications, fluids for rehydration and nutritional support.

Parasites: There is a variety of "worms" that can cause intestinal disorders. Classically, most people think of parasites as appearing "wormlike." This is not always the case. In fact, many parasites are microscopic one-celled organisms. A fecal analysis is recommended on all newly acquired birds. However, once in the home environment, pet birds rarely have problems with intestinal parasites.

SIGNS TO WATCH FOR: Diarrhea, weight loss. Rarely are "worms" seen with the naked eye.

DIAGNOSIS: Microscopic exam of feces is necessary for identification.

AVIAN VETERINARY CARE: Many different medications are available depending on type of parasite.

Giardia is a relatively common intestinal parasite in pet birds. "Budgies" and cockatiels are most susceptible.

SIGNS TO WATCH FOR: Weight loss, diarrhea, dry flaky skin, itching and feather picking

DIAGNOSIS: Requires a *very* fresh stool specimen or a sample collected directly from the cloaca and immediately examined under a microscope; diagnosis is still difficult because these very tiny organisms are shed only intermittently in the feces.

AVIAN VETERINARY CARE: Specific medications are available.

Other Causes of Intestinal Problems: Malnutrition, cancer, metabolic diseases, poisons and disorders of other organs can result in diarrhea and other intestinal problems.

FIRST AID FOR "SIMPLE" DIARRHEA

1. If grit is being fed, remove it. Sick birds may overeat it and engorge themselves.
2. Offer soft, bland and nourishing foods such as cooked eggs, bread, pastas, rice, beans and cooked oatmeal. The food should always be served fresh.
3. Kaopectate or Pepto-Bismol can be given to possibly help soothe the inflamed digestive tract. Suggested amounts to give *orally*:

Finches/canaries	4 drops every 4 hours
"Budgies"	6 drops every 4 hours
Cockatiels	10 drops every 4 hours
Amazon parrots	20 drops (1cc) every 4 hours
Cockatoos/macaws	30 drops (1.5cc) every 4 hours

4. If no immediate response, contact your veterinarian.

Constipation: Constipation is actually *rare* in birds.

SIGNS TO WATCH FOR: *Consistently* no stool, or only tiny amounts, straining to eliminate. The causes for constipation would include dehydration, intestinal obstruction and external pressure on the intestines by an egg, a tumor, or obesity. *Remember, if a bird is not eating, little or no stool will be produced.* This is frequently mislabeled as constipation by concerned pet bird owners.

AVIAN VETERINARY CARE: Identify the underlying cause of the signs observed; treatment depends on the nature of the problem.

Foreign Bodies in the Digestive Tract: Swallowing of foreign objects *does* occur. However, most suspected cases presented to a veterinarian end up being false alarms. In other words, no object was ever ingested. Birds may frequently remove the back of an earring or play with a small object in their mouth, but they will usually *not* swallow it. If the "plaything" is all of a sudden missing, first *thoroughly* examine the entire area around the bird. If the object cannot be found, immediate veterinary care is warranted.

Cloaca

The cloaca is a saclike chamber that serves as the common reservoir for stool, urine and eggs. The vent is the outer muscular sphincter controlling the frequency of eliminations.

SPECIFIC SIGNS TO WATCH FOR

- Any protrusion of tissue from the vent
- Blood around vent, including actual picking or chewing of area

Cloaca Prolapse: This is the protrusion or "falling out" of tissue through the vent opening. The exposed tissue could be cloaca, lower intestines or uterus. Straining associated with persistent diarrhea, constipation or egg laying can be the underlying cause. Nerve damage to the vent, resulting in stretching, can also cause a prolapse.

SIGNS TO WATCH FOR: The exposed tissue, depending on how recently prolapsed, would appear pink, red, brown or even black. It could appear glistening or dry and "crusty." The bird will often pick at the tissue, and the tip of the beak will become bloodied

DIAGNOSIS: Physical exam.

TREATMENT: *Emergency veterinary care is required!* If the prolapse is minimal and has recently occurred, applying a little lubrication and gently pushing the tissue back "inside" will be effective. However, one or two sutures may be needed around the vent to help hold the tissue in place. If the prolapse continues to recur, surgery may be necessary. The procedure involves making

An anesthetized bird with a cloacal prolapse.

an incision into the abdomen and suturing the cloaca to the abdominal wall. This helps to hold the cloaca inside the body.

Cloaca Papilloma: Papillomas are benign growths of tissue. They can actually occur most anywhere on the body, but the cloaca, mouth and feet are the most common sites. They can be confined to the inside wall of the cloaca or they can protrude through the vent and be confused with a prolapse. A virus is the suspected cause, but this has not been proven.

SIGNS TO WATCH FOR: Straining to eliminate, droppings frequently bloody and may be seen "pasted" around the vent; severe bleeding can sometimes occur. If the tissue is exposed, it will appear "cauliflowerlike," and the bird will frequently pick at it and blood will be observed on the tip of the beak.

DIAGNOSIS: Physical examination. Biopsy is necessary to confirm diagnosis.

AVIAN VETERINARY CARE: Surgery is needed to remove the growth. Papillomas sometimes recur.

Two *very important* diseases that usually involve the digestive tract are psittacosis and tuberculosis.

Psittacosis: Psittacosis (sit-ah-KO-sis), also known as chlamydiosis (klahmid-e-O-sis), ornithosis and "parrot fever," is a relatively common and highly contagious disease of pet birds. Psittacosis can also be transmitted to humans. A bacteria called *Chlamydia psittaci* is the cause. *It is common in birds illegally smuggled into the United States.* Stress caused by crowding, chilling, shipping and numerous other changes in a bird's environment will lower resistance to disease, so newly acquired birds are at a higher risk of developing the disease than long-time pets.

TRANSMISSION: There are many ways the disease can be spread; these include contact with sick birds shedding the organism in respiratory discharges, droppings and feather dust, and contaminated food and water supplies. In addition, parents can infect their nestlings while feeding. Birds can also be carriers, showing *no* outward signs of the disease, but spreading the disease to other birds.

SIGNS TO WATCH FOR: *There are no signs that are distinctively characteristic for psittacosis.* However, the following signs in a bird *may* be suggestive: Any newly acquired bird that becomes sick should be suspect. Birds with psittacosis may have watery, yellow or lime green urates (see Chapter 11). In addition, look for general signs of a sick bird loss of appetite, weight loss, depression, listlessness, nasal discharges and sometimes just sudden death.

DIAGNOSIS: There are specific tests available for diagnosing psittacosis. It is recommended they be performed on *all* newly acquired birds and any other suspected cases. However, the results of the tests must be interpreted in conjunction with history, physical exam and other tests.

AVIAN VETERINARY CARE: Whenever psittacosis is suspected, treatment should begin immediately. The antibiotic tetracycline is the *only* approved drug for the treatment of this disease. It is available in different forms and has various routes of administration (oral, injectable, medicated pellets or as a food additive).

The type of tetracycline and its most effective route of administration will be determined by the veterinarian. Treatment must be continued for *at least* forty-five days. Very sick birds will also need general supportive care. Recovered birds can even become reinfected at a later time. Therefore, periodic testing of affected birds following treatment is advisable.

In addition to the treatment above, follow these other important steps: Isolate all sick birds, thoroughly clean and disinfect the cage and its surroundings (for disinfectants, see Chapter 3), keep circulation of feathers and dust to a minimum. Bird droppings and all contaminated equipment should be incinerated or saturated with disinfectant and placed in plastic bags before disposing. Human contact should be kept to a minimum.

PREVENTION

- All newly acquired birds should be examined by a veterinarian and tested for psittacosis.
- Buy birds only from reputable suppliers.
- Isolate all new birds from other birds for at least 30 days.
- Consider having your birds tested periodically for psittacosis; especially if they come in contact with other birds. Unfortunately, no vaccine is available.

PSITTACOSIS IN HUMANS: Birds carrying psittacosis, whether sick or not, can transmit it to humans. Fortunately, the spread of psittacosis to humans is uncommon, despite the high frequency of disease in pet birds, and most human cases are mild. However, immunosuppressed individuals (i.e., the elderly, AIDS patients, cancer patients) are at the highest risk.

Flulike symptoms are most common and include fever, headache, respiratory signs and weakness. In humans this disease can be misdiagnosed. If flulike symptoms persist, be sure to alert your physician to the fact there are pet birds in the home.

Tuberculosis (TB): Tuberculosis in birds is similar to the human form. However, in birds TB primarily involves the digestive system. This is in contrast to humans, where the respiratory tract is usually involved. The disease has a slow onset, and any signs will gradually appear over a long period of time. *Mycobacterium avium* is the cause of most TB in birds. Avian TB can infect humans; however, this rarely happens. Human TB could potentially infect birds as well.

TRANSMISSION: Sick birds spread the infection via their droppings. It is acquired through ingestion of contaminated food, water or soil. It can also be spread from a contaminated cage, perches or cups.

SIGNS TO WATCH FOR: The signs are extremely variable and depend on which organs are affected. *There are no signs that are distinctively characteristic for tuberculosis.* Signs that could be suggestive include chronic diarrhea, masses beneath the skin, joint problems or simply a bird that has been sick for a long period of time.

DIAGNOSIS: Reliable tuberculosis tests are available. The most commonly used one involves a microscopic exam with special stains of any suspected tissue. Routine screens for TB are usually done on feces. Complete blood counts and X rays can also be helpful.

AVIAN VETERINARY CARE: There are two distinct schools of thought at this time on whether or not birds with tuberculosis should even be treated. One opinion is that *all* TB-positive cases should be euthanized. The rationale is simply, that the disease can be transmitted to humans. Also, there are *no* drugs at this time that have been specifically tested for their effectiveness in avian TB.

The opposing view advocates treatment using medications effective for human TB, the rationale being that the disease is actually *rarely* transmittable to humans. There has also been success in treating these birds. Regardless of the approach taken, there are still human risks associated with exposure to avian TB, and persons with weakened immune systems (the elderly, AIDS patients, cancer patients) are most susceptible. Even birds under treatment can be contagious. All cases of TB should be thoroughly discussed with the veterinarian. Your physician should also be consulted.

Liver

Liver Disease: Common in pet birds. Problems can either begin in the liver itself, or, since the liver plays a role in filtering blood, diseases in other organs can easily spread to the liver. The term "hepatitis" simply means inflammation of the liver. It is *not* specific for any one particular type of liver disease. Most liver diseases, with the exception of psittacosis, are *not* going to be contagious to humans. They could, however, be spread to other birds.

DIAGNOSIS: Blood tests and X rays are very helpful. These tests can determine if liver disease is present, however, they *cannot* identify the actual cause. A liver biopsy would be necessary to determine this.

SIGNS TO WATCH FOR: Mustard yellow or green urates, appetite and weight loss, regurgitation/diarrhea, feather and beak changes, distended abdomen and breathing difficulties, general signs of a sick bird.*

CAUSES: Numerous microorganisms (i.e., bacteria, viruses and fungi) can cause liver disease. Psittacosis is one of the more common reasons for liver disease. Metabolic diseases such as obesity ("fatty liver"), hypothyroidism, diabetes, gout, allergies, poisons and drug reactions can all lead to liver problems. Heart failure, cancer and parasites can also cause liver disorders.

Pacheco's Disease: This is a viral hepatitis affecting *only* psittacines. Passerines, such as finches and canaries, are not susceptible. Also, individually kept birds are generally *not* at risk. This is a disease associated with facilities housing multiple birds in the same area, such as aviaries, pet shops and quarantine stations. Individual birds would be at risk only if they had *just* been acquired from one of these places. As is the case with many diseases, stress appears to play a major role. The stresses associated with shipping, quarantine and even

---

*Icterus/jaundice (classic yellow appearance of patient with liver disease) is very rare in birds.

introducing new birds into an established collection can trigger the disease. Some birds can be resistant to Pacheco's disease, but at the same time spread the disease to other birds.

SIGNS TO WATCH FOR: The most consistent sign is rapid death in one bird or as many as all the birds kept together. It frequently takes only hours and sometimes up to a day or two after the first hint of disease for the birds to die. They may act perfectly healthy and then suddenly "drop dead." The only signs prior to death may be diarrhea followed by appetite loss and depression.

DIAGNOSIS: The history of multiple birds kept together, especially with new birds recently introduced, and "signs to watch for" as noted above, should make Pacheco's highly suspect. The definitive diagnosis is usually made on post-mortem.

AVIAN VETERINARY CARE: Pacheco's is generally considered an untreatable disease, in part because it kills so quickly. However, some success in reducing death rates has been reported with an antiviral drug.

PREVENTION: There is a vaccine available for prevention of Pacheco's disease, but it is currently *not* recommended for individual pet birds. Vaccination should be considered in those birds, as noted above, that are at risk. Breeders and others who keep groups of birds are referred to other sources included in the bibliography for additional information on prevention and control of this disease.

Pancreas

The pancreas plays two important roles within the body. First, it supplies the enzymes necessary to digest the food being eaten. Second, it produces the hormones, insulin and glucagon, necessary to control carbohydrate metabolism.

There can be problems associated with the manufacturing of these enzymes. If they are absent or decreased, food cannot be properly digested.

SIGNS TO WATCH FOR: weight loss, feces that have become large and clay-colored, resembling puffed rice. Undigested whole seeds can be seen in the droppings.

AVIAN VETERINARY CARE: To help control this problem, digestive enzymes are available that can be added to the food. The diet should also be changed to one that is more easily digested.

Diabetes: Diabetes is also a pancreatic disorder (see below).

ENDOCRINE DISORDERS

Diabetes (Diabetes Mellitus, "Sugar Diabetes"): Glucose (sugar) is a simple carbohydrate and the body's preferred fuel source. Blood sugar levels are regulated by two hormones: insulin and glucagon. Insulin "carries" the sugar into the cells and thereby lowers blood sugar levels. Glucagon, on the other hand, stimulates sugar production in the liver and as a result raises blood sugar levels.

In mammals, diabetes is the result of a deficiency of insulin or other factors that prevent insulin from working as it should. In parrots, diabetes appears to be due to an excess of glucagon that keeps sugar levels abnormally high.

SIGNS TO WATCH FOR: Similar to mammals (always hungry and thirsty, seems to spend all day drinking, watery droppings, eats most of the day but still loses weight) and general signs of sick bird.

DIAGNOSIS: A complete history and physical exam are essential. The blood test will show an abnormally high blood sugar level; urine analysis will reveal a high sugar concentration.

AVIAN VETERINARY CARE: The *only* available treatment is daily injections of insulin. However, since diabetes is caused by an excess of glucagon, insulin therapy is not always effective in lowering blood sugar levels. It does help to control the severe weight loss that is often seen in diabetic birds. Hospitalization is necessary to determine the proper dosage of insulin. Once that is established, the injections can be given at home.

HOME CARE: There must be a strong commitment on the part of the pet owner. Dietary changes are usually necessary. Injections must be give *every day* and the bird will need to be monitored regularly for sugar levels. There is, unfortunately, no cure for diabetes. However, in many cases it can be controlled with medication and the bird can live a longer and healthier life.

Hypothyroidism (Thyroid Hormone Deficiency): The thyroid glands are located alongside the lower trachea near the base of the neck. The hormones they produce have important effects on nearly every organ in the body. In hypothyroidism, inadequate levels of thyroid hormone are produced.

SIGNS TO WATCH FOR: Obesity and, commonly, feather problems, which include delayed molt and poor feather growth, including changes in the size, color and structure of the new feathers. The delayed molt can cause the "old" feathers to appear worn out and discolored. There is an obvious lack of new pin feathers. Hypothyroidism can also cause an increased susceptibility to infections, "fatty tumors," decreased fertility, inactivity and a depressed mental attitude.

DIAGNOSIS: History, physical examination and routine blood tests will often alert the veterinarian to a possible hypothyroid condition. There are specific blood tests available to measure the level of thyroid hormone.

AVIAN VETERINARY CARE: Thyroid hormone replacement. The medicine can be added to the drinking water or, preferably, given directly into the mouth.

SKIN DISORDERS

The skin and its accessory structures—the feathers, beak, cere, nails and uropygial ("preening") gland—are affected by a variety of problems. These problems often cause owners their greatest concern. This is not necessarily because they are the most serious but, rather, because they are the most obvious! For this reason, skin disorders are usually recognized early in the disease process.

It is well worth remembering, regardless of how minor a skin problem may first appear, that treatment should be initiated as soon as possible. First, because the sooner any disorder receives proper medical attention, the easier it will be to treat. Second, birds tend to pick at wounds, and this can cause even the smallest

A bird showing primary skin disease. Note the lack of feathering on the head and neck area.

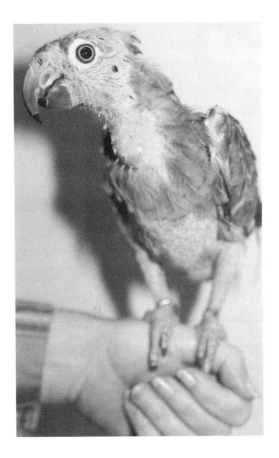

lesions to rapidly become worse. Third, once chewing or picking begins, a very undesirable habit can develop that can continue even though the initial cause is long gone.

The skin and its accessory structures have only a limited number of ways they can respond to an injury or disease. In other words, regardless of the underlying cause of the problem, the appearance of the skin will look very similar and many times identical. Therefore, it is *very* difficult to differentiate one skin disease from another without a thorough history, physical exam and often diagnostic testing.

There are many subtle clues concerning the actual underlying cause that can be uncovered with a thorough history and physical exam. This information is used to diagnose, or at least narrow down, the range of possible causes.

The following categories and questions to ask, along with observations from an examination, must be considered when attempting to correctly diagnose the underlying problem for any skin disease. This body of information, which includes the history, exam and diagnostic tests, in common medical language is referred to as the workup.

The Workup

History: History involves the "story" of the bird's past, including a chronological record of events surrounding the disease. It begins the process, one step at a time, of uncovering the source of the problem. Since our patients cannot communicate with us, the more aware and observent the owner, the more helpful the history.

OWNERSHIP: How long owned? Is the bird a pet or a breeder? Are other birds in the household? How many? What kind? Any sick birds?

LIFESTYLE: How much interaction ("playtime") with the bird? Has the amount of time changed recently (i.e., more or less time spent with bird)? How much sleep does the bird normally get? Is the cage covered? Regular bathing? Confined to cage or "free" in house? Regular grooming—beak, wings and nails? How often? Egg laying? If so, how often? When?

CAGING: Size of cage? Cage location in house? Cleanliness of cage? Toys available? What kind? Flooring material used?

DIET: Types of food offered? Types of food actually eaten? Food available all day long or part of each day? Appetite? Finicky eater?

ENVIRONMENTAL CHANGES: In other words, any recent stresses in the birds' life? Birds are creatures of habit, and *any* change can be very stressful. This can lead to chewing or picking. Has there been loss or addition of family members—human or animal? Recent move? Change in cage location? Remodeling or workman in house? Recent vacation?

PRESENT PROBLEM: What does the owner think is the cause of the problem? Duration? Initial appearance? Original location on body? Rate of progression of signs? Other health problems? Behavioral changes seen? Has owner actually seen picking or chewing? When was last molt?

HOME TREATMENT (if any): What has been used? Response?

Physical Examination: This is the next step on the ladder toward establishing the diagnosis. Unfortunately, in this area there is no substitute for experience. Frequently an owner will "see" one thing and an experienced avian veterinarian will recognize something very different. Magnification will help to better visualize some types of skin problems.

WHAT'S INVOLVED: Skin? Feathers? Or both? What about the beak? Nails?

LOCATION: What part of the body is involved? Single area? Multiple areas? Symmetrical? Entire body? Is the head involved? A bird *can't* pick its own head!

FEATHER APPEARANCE: Are the feathers broken, splintered or crushed? Are they dirty or lack a healthy sheen? For those birds with powdery down, are there normal amounts? Are there new feathers growing in? If so, appearance of these new feathers? Which feathers are involved—down, contours, or flight? A few feathers from different parts of the body should be removed and examined closely.

EXTERNAL PARASITES: Are there any seen? If so, are they on the skin or the feathers? Many skin parasites require microscopic exam to diagnose. *It is very important to remember that skin and feather parasites are extremely uncommon in pet birds!*

GENERAL HEALTH: A *complete* physical examination is essential. This involves the *entire* body, not just the affected area! Skin problems can result from disorders elsewhere in the body. Does the bird appear generally healthy? Are there any other problems? Is the weight acceptable?

Diagnostic Testing: Diagnostic testing is nearing the top step on the ladder. Frequently, the diagnosis is not clearly evident following the history and physical examination. In these instances, diagnostic testing would be recommended. There are a number of different tests available. In veterinary medicine, practical reasons, such as financial, often do not allow them all to be run. This is one of the reasons why a complete history and physical exam are so important. They allow the veterinarian to narrow down the range of possible causes, and as a result more selective testing can be done.

Below is a list of the *most common* diagnostic tests used for skin problems. Less commonly used tests will not be discussed. The interpretation of these test results is also briefly discussed.

- General health screen (blood tests, X rays): for detection of internal disease, which can cause skin and feather problems
- Blood tests for specific diseases: e.g., thyroid disease, psittacine beak and feather disease, tuberculosis
- Bacteriologic and fungal exams: Gram stain or culture and sensitivity of feather pulp or feather follicle, microscopic skin exam (commonly called "skin scraping")
- Fecal exam: for detection of *Giardia*, a common cause of feather picking in certain species
- Feather and skin biopsy: microscopic exam of tissue by an avian pathologist

Treatment: Sometimes, even with a complete history, physical exam and diagnostic testing, an exact diagnosis cannot be made. In these instances, treatment might be initiated based on a tentative diagnosis. This would probably be the top step on the ladder. Treat and determine whether the patient improves. This option is also used when, for financial reasons, few if any diagnostic tests can be performed. The hope is that the treatment will help cure the problem. It could also aid in identifying the underlying cause.

Beak Problems

The normal beak is hard, smooth and symmetrical. Its proper length, width and shape varies with each species. Beak problems, regardless of the cause, frequently result in a permanently misshapen beak. Since the beak grows continuously, when the upper and lower beak are *not* in perfect alignment, overgrowth will occur. However, with regular beak trimming, good diet and an ample supply of branches and other objects to chew on, birds should do well in this respect.

SIGNS TO WATCH FOR

- Misshapen (e.g., overgrown, "twisted")
- Flaky, soft, or roughened surface

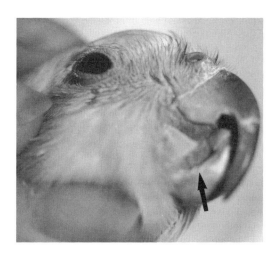

A lower beak fracture in this cockatiel has led to overgrowth of the upper beak.

- Chipped or cracked
- Change in color

Trauma: Injuries, such as puncture wounds and fractures, are the most common problems. Infections are a threat, even in the tiniest of wounds. Bleeding also commonly occurs at the injury site.

AVIAN VETERINARY CARE: If only the very tip is broken off or chipped, then simple filing and rounding off should be sufficient. The tip should grow back. Bleeding, if noted, will need to be controlled. However, any fractures, cracks or discolorations will probably require more extensive care. Any open wounds should be thoroughly cleaned first, then possibly covered with a medical acrylic (glue) to help prevent infection. Fractures or cracks can be repaired using acrylics with steel wire and pins for reinforcement.

Infections: Most often result from an injury, but can also be associated with diseases such as psittacine beak and feather disease (see page 218). Fungal infections are the most common.

AVIAN VETERINARY CARE: Open, clean and flush the affected area with antiseptic solution, apply topical antibiotic and/or antifungal medication; other treatments as needed.

Liver Disease: For unknown reasons, liver disease can lead to beak problems.

SIGNS TO WATCH FOR: Overgrowth of the beak (and nails), beak (and nails) softer than normal.

DIAGNOSIS: See page 197.

AVIAN VETERINARY CARE: Liver treatment depends on underlying cause; regular trimming and shaping of the beak will be needed.

Tumors: Tumors involving the beak are occasionally found.

SIGNS TO WATCH FOR: Look for any lump or bump either on the outside of the beak or along the roof of the mouth.

AVIAN VETERINARY CARE: Surgical removal of tumor, if possible.

Poor Nutrition: The beak (and nails) can become overgrown, with a flaky and rough surface.

Mites: See page 205.

Cere Disorders

The cere is the soft, rounded area behind the beak and surrounding the nares. Its appearance can change in response to a number of unrelated problems.

SIGNS TO WATCH FOR

• Swollen and reddened cere, sometimes caked with debris
• Thickened or hornlike surface
• Color change
• Change in size or shape

Infections: Upper respiratory infections can cause the cere to become swollen and inflamed. On the other hand, a long-standing respiratory infection could cause the cere to "shrink" in size. It could also lead to a change in the size or shape of the nares.

Brown Hypertrophy: This is seen most commonly in older female "budgies." The cause is unknown, but may be related to hormonal changes.

SIGNS TO WATCH FOR: The cere becomes thickened, almost hornlike and brown in color.

AVIAN VETERINARY CARE: It's not serious, and treatment is usually unnec-

Brown hypertrophy of the cere in a "budgie."

essary. However, occasionally the nares can become blocked. If this occurs, the build-up of the ''dead skin layers'' can be removed by gently peeling them away. Applying a little nongreasy moisturizing cream will help soften the tissue prior to removal.

Facial Skin

Conditions primarily affecting this area are varied.

Mites: Knemidokoptes [ne-mi-do-KOP-tez], or *scaly face mite*, is common in ''budgies.'' It's usually first noticed over the bare areas of the face, around the eyes, cere and beak. It can also be found on the legs and feet.

SIGNS TO WATCH FOR: whitish, honeycomblike crusting or growth.

DIAGNOSIS: Appearance of lesions are usually sufficient; occasionally microscopic exam of skin debris is necessary.

AVIAN VETERINARY CARE: Ivermectin is the safest and most effective remedy. The correct dosage is important. It is administered orally or directly onto the skin. Improvement is usually noticed within days. Many different over-the-counter medications are available, but most are not very effective.

Other skin and feather mites are very uncommon. Most owners think that mites or other ''bugs'' are the cause of any number of different skin problems. However, it is safe to assume the cause is *not* mites, unless proven otherwise.

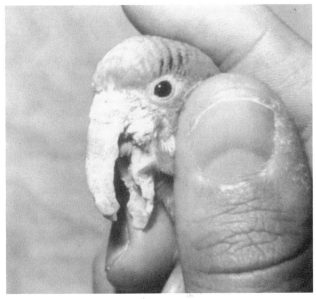

Severe beak deformity caused by the scaly face mite. Early treatment can prevent this disfiguration.

Infections

SIGNS TO WATCH FOR: Single or multiple scabs, crusts or firm swellings, sometimes feather loss.

DIAGNOSIS: Appearance of lesions may be sufficient; additional tests such as microscopic exam of skin debris, fungal culture or biopsy may occasionally be recommended.

AVIAN VETERINARY CARE: Medication as indicated, abscesses (accumulations of pus) require surgery.

Avian Pox: Avian pox is a viral infection usually transmitted by mosquitoes.

SIGNS TO WATCH FOR: Two different forms exist, the most common the *cutaneous form*, in which birds develop small raised swellings that can change in color from yellow to brown and become crusty; the lesions appear on the unfeathered skin around the eyes, beak, nose and even the lower legs and feet. The *wet form* develops small raised swellings in the mouth; swallowing and sometimes breathing can become difficult.

DIAGNOSIS: Biopsy of the lesions is necessary.

AVIAN VETERINARY CARE: There is no specific treatment. The lesions may actually resolve on their own in a few weeks.

PREVENTION: Vaccination is available. Mosquito control and cleanliness is important.

Trauma

SIGNS TO WATCH FOR: Cuts, scrapes, burns or bruises. Bruises develop a dark red to purple discoloration.

AVIAN VETERINARY CARE: Cannot be determined without examination by a veterinarian.

Insect Bites: Insect bites would be more common in birds kept outside or in unsanitary conditions. The actual biting is usually not observed by the owner. Skin reactions can be confused with various other problems.

SIGNS TO WATCH FOR: Localized swelling that rapidly develops, usually red and inflamed.

AVIAN VETERINARY CARE: May not be necessary; unless a bite is poisonous or other problems develop, swelling should resolve in about 24 hours.

Baldness: Baldness is most common in canaries, finches and lutino cockatiels. There are many possible causes, including heredity, infection, thyroid hormone deficiency and, in male canaries, a testosterone deficiency.

AVIAN VETERINARY CARE: Underlying cause would determine best treatment; some conditions are not treatable. Thyroid and testosterone hormone supplements are available. Good nutrition is important.

Legs and Feet

"Bumblefoot": "Bumblefoot" is the common name for an infection on the *bottom* of the feet. Some of the factors that can lead to the development of

this disease include poor nutrition, vitamin A deficiency, unsanitary conditions, sandpaper-covered perches and obesity.

SIGNS TO WATCH FOR: Initially, the skin on the bottom of the foot appears thinner than normal, red and inflamed. As the disease progresses, there is swelling and scab formation. Sometimes ulcers or obvious wounds are also noticed. As a result, the bird becomes lame and has difficulty walking.

AVIAN VETERINARY CARE: In advanced cases, surgery to open the wound, followed by removing the debris. Antibiotics, topical medications and bandages are usually needed. In addition, improving the diet and padding the perches are also helpful.

Papillomas: Papillomas are benign tumors. They can be found on the feet, legs, cloaca, wings, eyelids and preening gland.

SIGNS TO WATCH FOR: Small, raised growth with "fingerlike" projections or crusty and ulcerated lesions; susceptible to self-trauma and can bleed.

AVIAN VETERINARY CARE: Sometimes better left alone; however, if self-traumatized or other problems develop, surgical removal is recommended.

Hyperkeratosis: Hyperkeratosis (hi-per-KER-ah-TO-sis) is the excessive buildup or thickening of the outer horny layer (keratin) of skin. It is seen most commonly in canaries and finches. The cause is usually unknown, but sometimes mites are involved.

SIGNS TO WATCH FOR: Increased or heavy scaling on legs.

AVIAN VETERINARY CARE: Frequently no treatment is necessary; however, if the growths are excessive, they should be gently removed. See treatment of mites earlier in this chapter.

Gout: Gout in birds is associated with the kidney's inability to remove nitrogen waste products from the bloodstream. As a result, uric acid accumulates and begins to abnormally collect in different sites within the body.

There are two distinct forms of this disease. *Articular gout* usually affects the joints of the lower legs. It's most common in "budgies," where it appears as multiple cream-colored shiny swellings bulging up through the skin. It is painful, and the bird becomes lame and progressively crippled. Visceral gout affects the internal organs and is very difficult to diagnose.

AVIAN VETERINARY CARE: There is *no* effective treatment. Lowering the dietary protein level and feeding more fruits and vegetables may help. Drugs that lower uric acid levels in the blood have been used in birds with varied success. Pain medication and padding the perches may be beneficial.

Self-mutilation: For no obvious reasons, some birds simply begin chewing, picking and sometimes mutilating their legs and toes. A small wound or the stresses of captivity *may* have something to do with the onset of this problem.

DIAGNOSIS: A physical exam, biopsy, culture and sensitivity may be recommended to help identify the primary cause.

AVIAN VETERINARY CARE: This can be very frustrating and challenging to treat, as there is *no* consistently effective treatment; various options include treating wounds directly with antibiotics and anti-inflammatory medications, bandaging or an Elizabethan collar to help stop the chewing habit, hormones or behavior-modifying drugs to help alter unwanted behavior.

This is an example of self-mutilation on the leg.

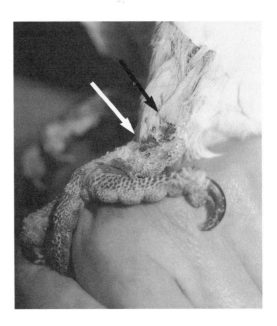

HOME CARE: Environmental factors (diet, caging and cleanliness) may need to be improved; approaching this as a behavioral problem may also be necessary (see the discussion of feather picking later in this chapter).

Mites: Refer to the discussion of mites earlier in this chapter.

Lumps and Bumps

The following are conditions that can occur most anywhere on the body.

Abscess: An abscess is a localized collection of pus, surrounded by a wall of tissue.

SIGNS TO WATCH FOR: Mammals produce a liquid pus; birds, on the other hand, produce a nonliquid, "cheeselike" material with no odor. The most commonly affected areas are just above the eye (look for a pea-size swelling), along the roof of the mouth (see page 189), below the tongue, in the preening gland or on the bottom of the foot (bumblefoot; see page 206).

AVIAN VETERINARY CARE: Bird abscesses cannot drain on their own; therefore, surgery is required to open, clean and remove the accumulated debris. Antibiotics are necessary.

Feather Cyst: A feather cyst is a soft swelling beneath the skin caused by an ingrown feather.

SIGNS TO WATCH FOR: A thick, lumpy swelling commonly seen beneath the skin and involving a feather follicle.

AVIAN VETERINARY CARE: Surgery is needed to open and remove the debris and instill antibiotics.

Hematoma: A hematoma is an accumulation of blood within a tissue that

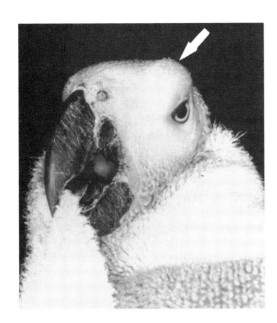

An African Grey with a swelling above the eye that turned out to be an abscess.

A canary with a feather cyst. Surgery is required to remove cysts.

forms a solid swelling. An injury is usually the underlying cause. In birds they are uncommon, but when found they are usually on the head or chest.

AVIAN VETERINARY CARE: Usually not needed; they generally disappear over a short period of time.

Hernia: A hernia is a protrusion of an organ or tissue through an abnormal opening in its surrounding wall. There are two types. Acquired hernias result from a tear in a muscle wall, usually from an injury, or straining to pass an egg; Their most common site is the abdominal wall, just above the vent. Congenital hernias are present at birth.

SIGNS TO WATCH FOR: The swelling should be soft to the touch; sometimes, even the "hole" in the tissue causing the hernia can be felt and protruding tissue can be pushed back through it.

AVIAN VETERINARY CARE: Surgery is needed to close the abnormal opening. Hernias can become larger over time, and early repair is recommended. If an organ should become "trapped" through the opening, its blood supply could be pinched off, creating an emergency situation.

Tumor: A tumor is an abnormal growth of tissue. It can develop anywhere in or on the body. A malignant tumor (cancerous) is the abnormal and uncontrolled growth of cells that invade and destroy the surrounding tissue. Benign tumors (noncancerous) once removed do not recur and the bird will have a favorable recovery, but if left untreated they can continue to grow and cause problems. One of the more common type of benign tumors is a lipoma ("fatty tumor"). It is found beneath the skin, usually on the chest or abdominal areas. It is also more common in overweight birds.

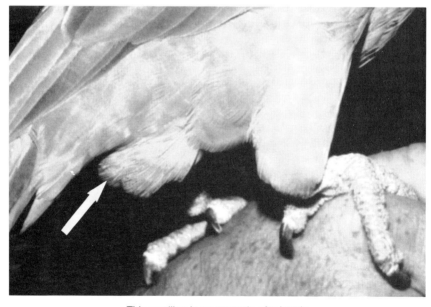

This swelling is an example of a hernia.

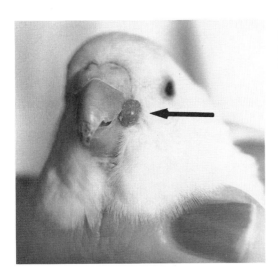

Tumors can occur anywhere on or in the body. This "budgie" has a small tumor on the skin at the corner of the beak.

DIAGNOSIS: Biopsy is required to determine whether a tumor is benign or malignant.

AVIAN VETERINARY CARE: Surgical removal is *always* recommended. Tumors should be removed when they are first noticed, because over time cancerous tumors are more likely to spread to other tissues. Also, as the tumor grows it becomes increasingly more difficult to remove.

Subcutaneous emphysema: Subcutaneous emphysema is an abnormal accumulation of air beneath the skin. The cause can be a tear in an air sac, a puncture wound through the skin or a broken bone. Whatever the cause, air escapes into the area beneath the skin.

SIGNS TO WATCH FOR: An easily compressible, balloonlike swelling.

AVIAN VETERINARY CARE: The underlying cause should be repaired, if possible; the trapped air is usually best left alone. However, sometimes large swellings might require lancing.

Feather Disorders

Self-mutilation, injuries and a variety of diseases can affect the appearance of the feathers. In response to any of these problems, the feathers could be pulled out or damaged, and may not grow back in. Damaged feathers could appear broken, twisted, crushed, splintered or deformed. These changes are usually not specific enough to positively identify the underlying cause. Using the workup approach as the guideline will help in establishing the correct diagnosis.

UNDERLYING CAUSES FOR FEATHER PROBLEMS: There are many varied causes for feather problems. It is not uncommon for a combination of factors to be responsible. For example, there could be a disease present damaging feathers and a behavioral problem present causing chewing or feather picking. This is one of the reasons why diagnosing and treating feather disorders is one of the most challenging pet bird problems seen by avian veterinarians.

A torn air sac caused subcutaneous emphysema in this canary. Notice the balloonlike swellings over the back and chest areas.

FEATHER PROBLEMS

Some of the contributing factors:

Inadequate Home Care

- Poor nutrition
- Inadequate caging (i.e., too small, lack of privacy, incompatibility with cagemates, dirty environment)
- Humidity too low

Psychological Problems

- Nervousness
- Sexual frustration
- Stress factors (see page 13)
- Emotional unhappiness (e.g., insecurity, boredom)

Medical Problems

- Any chronic or debilitating illness
- Internal medical disorders (e.g., infections, parasites and thyroid hormone deficiency)

- Skin disorders (e.g., infections such as psittacine beak and feather disease, folliculitis, injuries, tumors)

Species Susceptibility

- Within each species, certain types of feather problems are more common than others

"Stress Lines": "Stress lines" are seen most commonly on contour feathers of the wings and tail. They may be seen on one or several feathers. They appear as a grouping of tiny holes or bare spots across the length of the feather. Stress occurring during the growth phase of the affected feathers appears to be the cause. All feathers growing in during the stressful period should be affected.

Preening Problems: Self-grooming (i.e., preening) is essential for maintaining clean and healthy feathers. If this behavior becomes altered or stops altogether, the feathers will become unkempt and ragged. Factors that can prevent or interfere with the normal preening process include virtually anything causing excessive stress (see page 13), injuries (to the head, beak or neck), poor vision, long-term use of restraint collars and weakness from disease.

Molting Problems: Molting is the shedding or loss of old feathers with replacement of new ones. An abnormal molt should be suspected when the feathers lost are not replaced within the normal time (see pages 106 and 122), or the new feathers appear damaged in any way.

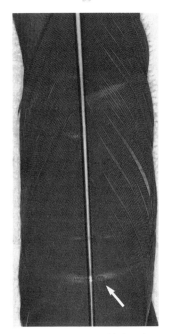
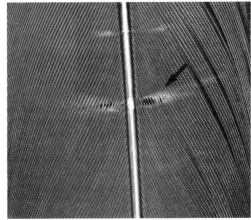

Notice the stress lines on the macaw tail feather.

A delay in the onset of a molt can cause the feathers to become excessively worn, dirty and frayed. Slow regrowth of the feathers during a molt will result in a longer-than-normal pin feather stage. The causes for either of these can include *any* disease, inadequate home care, malnourishment and stress. Thyroid hormone deficiency in an otherwise healthy bird can be another cause of molting problems.

Feather Picking: Feather picking is a condition characterized by a bird damaging its own feathers. Preening (see chapter 8) is a normal, healthy behavior. However, when this self-grooming process becomes exaggerated and obsessive, there is usually damage to the feathers. Sometimes the underlying skin becomes involved. The feathers are actually chewed on and sometimes pulled out.

Unfortunately, this is a disease of captivity, since wild birds with this condition would be unable to fly or keep warm, and would eventually die. It can be one of the most difficult and challenging diseases to correctly diagnose and treat. *Remember, feather picking is not a diagnosis but, rather, a sign of, or result of, some other problem.*

SIGNS TO WATCH FOR: Actual "picking" of feathers; the feathers will appear broken, twisted, crushed or deformed. Some birds will pick only when bored (e.g., when left alone or during the night). Birds will often not pick when their owners are present. The degree of picking and its location on the body varies with each bird, but the chest, abdomen, inside of wings and upper legs are common sites. The head and neck feathers, however, will appear perfectly normal; the bird cannot reach these feathers with its beak.

DIAGNOSIS: There are many different causes for feather picking, falling into two general categories; medical and nonmedical (behavioral). Since birds cannot communicate with us, determining which one, or both, is involved can be difficult. Once again, the workup approach (see page 201) is necessary.

NONMEDICAL *(behavioral/psychological)* CAUSES: The feathers on the head and upper neck will appear perfectly normal. Boredom, nervousness, insecurity, sexual frustration and other causes of stress are all possibilities. "Picking" associated with the breeding season (i.e., reproductive cycle) may be the result of an excessive display of courtship behavior. If two or more birds are caged together, always consider the possibility of one bird "picking" on another.

MEDICAL CAUSES: A variety of medical problems can result in feather picking. With some diseases, the feathers can become damaged, but not due to "picking." If the feathers on the head and upper neck are involved, a medical cause should be suspected. These could include infections of the skin and feathers (bacterial, viral and fungal diseases), parasites on the skin (very rare) or inside the body (e.g., *Giardia*), internal diseases, hormone (e.g., thyroid, progesterone or testosterone) imbalances, infections liver disease. Inadequate nutrition

AVIAN VETERINARY CARE: There are many different treatments for feather pickers. No one treatment consistently works—even when the diagnosis is known. However, the highest cure rate will *always* be achieved when the underlying cause can be identified.

Whenever possible, the underlying problem should always be corrected

Feather pickers. (A) Some birds pick only small areas of their body, such as the leg on this macaw. (B) Other birds will pick large areas of their body. Note that this Goffin's cockatoo has normal feathering on the head and neck.

first. However, at the same time, the "chewing frenzy" must be stopped. Regardless of the cause, the longer the picking is allowed to continue, the more difficult it will be to control. In some instances, even when the original cause is long gone, the picking still continues. It simply becomes a bad habit.

Avian veterinarians have in their "arsenal" a variety of treatment options. Drugs such as sedatives, behavior modifiers and hormones are sometimes used. Restraint collars and bandages may be used to physically prevent picking. Additionally, foul-tasting sprays, upper beak grinding and even acupuncture are other options. When it comes to feather picking, there is no "quick fix!"

HOME CARE FOR NONMEDICAL CAUSES OF FEATHER PICKING: Once medical causes for feather picking have been ruled out, it's time to examine the possibility that a behavior problem may be the culprit. Like humans who bite their fingernails, the "feather picker" will usually find the behavior rewarding, relaxing or enjoyable. If not controlled in its early stages, picking can become a deeply ingrained habit that is difficult to stop.

Since the causes for most nonmedical-related feather picking are associated with stresses of some kind, the approach to treatment is similar in all cases. Chris Davis, noted avian behaviorist and author of the chapter "The Well-Mannered Parrot" in this book, has made many of the valuable suggestions that will be discussed.

The common thread in *all* of these ideas will be *change*. Remember, maintaining the status quo hasn't worked. Something in the bird's environment may have created the picking. It could have been too much of something or perhaps too little. Therefore, look over the bird's environment and try and determine what may have started it in the first place. Once this has been done, make changes! Utilize these suggestions as ideas for change.

There are no two birds alike. What approach may work with one bird is not necessarily going to work with another. Unfortunately, in some cases, no matter how much effort has gone into trying to stop this problem, the bird may not be curable. In others, simply trying *one* of the following suggestions has helped. Many times the secret to success is persistence and creativity. If at first you don't succeed, try, try again!

Changes in Food: In the wild, birds spend their daytime hours with companions, searching for food and preening each other. There are many interesting things to do in the jungle, including tearing up a seemingly endless supply of leaves, wood and bark.

On the other hand, life in a cage is not very exciting. Therefore, it is important to provide a lot of different activities. Among these activities, food can play an important role. Since the act of shredding is an enjoyable pastime, food can be used for this purpose.

The importance of a well-balanced diet has already been discussed (in chapter 4). It is also known that inadequate nutrition can be a cause of feather picking as well. In addition, feather picking puts added nutritional stress on a bird.

To help alleviate the boredom that may be associated with picking, try offering easily shreddable foods for the bird to play with. Try any or all of the following:

Carrot sticks	Apples
Green beans	Breadsticks
Spinach leaves	Zucchini sticks
Peas in the pod	Miniature bagels
Corn on the cob (cut into disks)	Miniature rice cakes

Although some birds may show fear or limited interest in the new foods, continue to offer them.

Changes in Caging: Since each situation is different, the owner must evaluate the effect caging might be having on the "picker." The following ideas are only some of the possible changes that could help:

- If the cage is too small, try a larger one.
- Cover the cage or uncover the cage more.
- Move the cage to another area of the house.
- Provide a privacy box in the cage for a place to "hide."
- Provide more toys—but don't overcrowd the cage.

Inexpensive, easily shredded toys can help redirect the feather picker's attention and include:

Rope	Wood
Straws	Pine cones
Cardboard	Wooden craft sticks
Toothbrushes (new)	Complexion brushes (new)
Toys catering specifically to feather pickers	Paper towels (twisted and knotted)

All these items should be clean and of a nontoxic material. If there is doubt as to the safety of any of the items, *do not use them.*

Changes in the Home: Birds become extremely dependent upon other "flock" members, human or animal. Birds that are accustomed to a set routine may not easily tolerate disruptions. In regard to humans, any changes in time spent with the bird or "new faces" could be stressful. If another animal has appeared or disappeared from the scene, this too is a disruption in routine. If any of these changes sound familiar and correspond to the onset of picking, consider them a likely culprit. Then work to correct the situation.

These suggestions may help to alleviate some of the stress:

- Provide lots of direct attention.
- Leave the radio on when no one is at home.
- Increase periods of sleep.
- Obtain a companion bird, a cagemate. However, know in advance that this frequently does not help. Also, your bird will usually become bonded with its mate. As a result, less attention will be paid to its owner and the picking could still continue.

Have You Considered . . . That, unfortunately, people often scold their birds, glare at them, or pick up and cuddle them when they see feather picking. This only serves to reward the behavior. Even if the bird is being scolded, it will still have the undivided attention it craves. The behavior will continue at a later time in order to be "rewarded" with the same results!

However, do make sure good behavior is rewarded. It is important to reward the bird with a look, a compliment or a tickle when it is playing with its toys, or shredding its food. This is the only way it will understand what is desired by its owner.

Psittacine Beak and Feather Disease Syndrome (PBFDS; Formerly Cockatoo Syndrome): The name of this disease was changed when it was learned that *many* species, not just cockatoos, are susceptible. Dr. Branson Ritchie and his team at the University of Georgia pioneered most of the work on this disease, and his research forms the basis for this discussion. A great deal of time, energy and resources went into positively identifying a virus as the cause of psittacine beak and feather disease syndrome. PBFDS is most common in birds less than three years old. However, even birds over ten years of age occasionally develop this problem.

TRANSMISSION: This is a highly contagious disease, especially to young

An advanced case of psittacine beak and feather disease syndrome (PBFDS).

(A) Normal feathers. (B) Abnormal feathers associated with PBFDS. Note the pinched and deformed quills.

birds. It is most likely spread by preening activities or ingestion of contaminated feather dust. Infected droppings may be another source of transmission. It *may* also be possible for an apparently normal parent to transmit this disease to its offspring. Since the virus is long lived outside the body and resistant to many of the common disinfectants, environmental contamination is still another possibility.

Signs to Watch For: The *acute form* (rapid onset) is generally recognized in very young birds. It is characterized by depression, diarrhea, crop problems, weight loss and often death. In this form, there are only minimal feather abnormalities. The *chronic form* (gradual onset) exhibits "classic" feather lesions. These include retained feather sheaths, blood within the feather shaft, short "clubbed" or "pinched" feather tips and deformed, curled feathers. The powder down feathers are usually affected first. There is an obvious loss of the normal "powder" these feathers produce. As the disease progresses, the contour feathers on the wings and tail become involved. On close examination, the feathers appear to have a near translucent appearance.

Beak lesions may also occur, but usually *after* there is severe feather involvement. The beak changes include overgrowth, fractures and decay. Ulcers are sometimes present in the mouth.

Diagnosis: In advanced cases, a bird displaying many of the "classic" signs as described above would be highly suspect. There is a blood test available to diagnose PBFDS.

Avian Veterinary Care: Unfortunately, there is no effective therapy. The disease is considered fatal. Most birds with "classic" signs do not survive longer than six to twelve months.

Prevention: A vaccine has been found to be effective in preventing PBFDS. However, due to lack of funding for research and development, this vaccine is not yet commercially available.

KIDNEY DISEASE

The kidneys filter the blood, remove poisonous waste products and regulate the electrolyte balance in the body. As a result, the kidneys are susceptible to a variety of diseases.

SIGNS TO WATCH FOR: General signs of a sick bird; there are *no* specific signs.

DIAGNOSIS: In mammals, kidney disease can be diagnosed from routine blood tests and urine analysis. However, in birds, blood and urine tests for kidney disease have not proven to be consistently reliable. Therefore, diagnosis is difficult. X rays can indicate a change in kidney size and appearance, but still do not provide a clear diagnosis. Kidney biopsy, although not routinely performed, is the best method of diagnosis at this time.

AVIAN VETERINARY CARE: General supportive care, dietary changes and antibiotics. If a biopsy is performed and the *exact* cause for the kidney disease is known, there is a chance treatment could be more specific.

NEUROMUSCULAR (NERVE AND MUSCLE) DISORDERS

Brain, spinal cord, nerve and muscle disorders are a very complex branch of medicine, and expensive and advanced technological medical instruments are usually necessary to properly diagnose them. Veterinary medicine in general does not have these options readily available. Although presenting signs and routine diagnostic tests will usually suggest an abnormality in this area, a more accurate diagnosis is usually not possible. Infections, trauma, cancer, metabolic problems, poisons, dietary deficiencies and hereditary factors can all affect these particular areas.

Hypocalcemia (Low Blood Calcium): Calcium is a well-known necessity for "strong bones." However, it also plays critical roles in nerve transmission and muscle contraction. A syndrome of low blood calcium is known to occur, especially in African Greys. Its cause is unknown.

SIGNS TO WATCH FOR: Intermittent tremors or convulsions (see page 149).

DIAGNOSIS: Blood test for calcium level.

AVIAN VETERINARY CARE: Calcium supplements and antiseizure medications as needed.

HOME CARE: Extra calcium in diet using foods high in calcium (i.e., low-fat cheese, yogurt) and balanced mineral supplements; On the recommendation of a veterinarian, supplemental calcium can be added to the food or drinking water.

Epilepsy: Refer to convulsions in Chapter 11.

Vitamin E/Selenium Responsive Syndrome: This disease is also called cockatiel paralysis syndrome because it is most commonly observed in this species. A vitamin E deficiency is probably the underlying cause. The lack of vitamin E can result from a dietary deficiency, a digestive tract absorbtion problem or oversupplementation with oily substances.

Hypocalcemia in this African Grey caused this abnormal posture.

SIGNS TO WATCH FOR: Weakness, often leading to paralysis of jaw, wings or legs; difficulty with grasping perch, mouth "hanging open."

DIAGNOSIS: No specific tests available; however, it is important to perform blood tests and X rays to rule out other possible causes.

AVIAN VETERINARY CARE: Injection of vitamin E/selenium can often show immediate improvement; oral supplementation is also available.

HOME CARE: Good sources of vitamin E include green leafy vegetables, corn, soy, seed oils and eggs. Do not supplement diet with other oils (e.g., vegetable and fish oils) unless recommended by a veterinarian.

Newcastle Disease (Velogenic Viscerotropic Newcastle Disease, VVND): Newcastle disease is a very serious viral disease found in all domestic and wild birds throughout the world. It has a near 100 percent death rate in affected birds. Very importantly, this disease can spread quickly to poultry and cause enormous losses. Imported pet birds, especially young ones, have been incriminated as one of the more common sources of VVND. It is for this reason, and this reason only, that *all* imported exotic birds must be quarantined prior to entering the United States. There are government regulations involving the prevention, control and elimination of Newcastle disease. *All* suspected cases must be reported to the United States Department of Agriculture (USDA).

TRANSMISSION: It is highly contagious, and infected birds spread it via their droppings, respiratory discharges and even by contaminated food, water and caging.

SIGNS TO WATCH FOR: As the disease progresses nervous system signs develop, including paralysis of wings and/or legs, muscle twitching, head and eye twitching, convulsions. Severe respiratory infections and bloody diarrhea may also occur. Sudden death may be the only sign.

DIAGNOSIS: Isolation of the virus from feces in live birds, or from organs of dead birds; these tests must be performed in government-approved laboratories.

AVIAN VETERINARY CARE: None; all sick and exposed birds are euthanized once diagnosis is confirmed.

Finally, the following is an important disease that usually involves multiple organ systems:

POLYOMA VIRUS

In past years this very serious disease has been called budgerigar fledgling disease or papovavirus infection. It affects primarily very young birds and it is only occasionally diagnosed in adult birds. For this reason, aviaries raising young birds are at a much higher risk of a polyoma outbreak than homes with individually kept pet birds.

TRANSMISSION: Adult birds are usually carriers. These birds, having recovered from the disease, generally appear very healthy but shed the virus to young, susceptible birds. It is thought the disease is spread through the droppings and possibly in the air and even from parent to offspring through the egg.

SIGNS TO WATCH FOR: The classic presentation is the sudden death of a previously very healthy young bird around weaning age. Signs could include: weakness, appetite loss, abdominal enlargement, bleeding underneath the skin, tremors, paralysis, diarrhea, regurgitation and sometimes feather abnormalities.

DIAGNOSIS: A specific test is available. Samples are very simply collected from a swab of the cloaca.

AVIAN VETERINARY CARE: Unfortunately, there is no treatment available. However, other diseases can appear to be very similar and therefore all sick birds should be examined immediately.

PREVENTION: Any new bird being introduced into a home with other birds, especially young ones, should be tested and found negative for the polyoma virus *before* coming into contact with other birds. After an outbreak, the environment (i.e., walls, floors, airducts, cages) can even be tested to be sure that cleaning and disinfecting has been effective in eliminating the virus.

A vaccine should be also available in the near future to prevent polyoma virus disease in birds.

13

Veterinary Care

"Bird Doctors," Diagnostic Testing and Therapeutics

LONG GONE are the days when a "sick bird was a dead bird." Today, a sick bird is a much luckier bird than ever before. The advances in avian medicine have enabled veterinarians to provide health care for birds in ways never before known. Avian medicine is the fastest-growing branch in all of veterinary medicine. More and more veterinarians are developing the knowledge and skills necessary to provide good veterinary care for pet birds. The nation's veterinary colleges have recognized the dramatic increase in birds as household pets and the need for well-trained avian veterinarians. The Association of Avian Veterinarians now boasts over two thousand members throughout all fifty states and the world. These doctors all share a common interest—birds! They also fund research on avian diseases, reproduction, conservation and education.

As a pet owner, sooner or later the need for veterinary care will occur. With birds, often this need arises very quickly. Therefore, plan ahead, establish a relationship with a veterinarian knowledgeable in avian medicine *prior* to a medical problem or emergency.

This chapter includes a discussion on a wide range of veterinary-related topics, including how to find a qualified avian veterinarian, what to look for while visiting the clinic, and a discussion of the latest in diagnostic and therapeutic medicine.

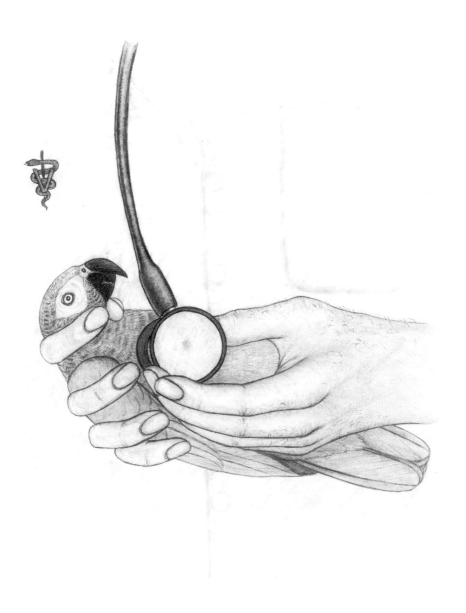

VETERINARIANS: WHEN TO SEEK PROFESSIONAL HELP

New Bird Checkups

It is always best to have a newly acquired pet bird examined by a veterinarian. This should be done immediately after purchase. A thorough exam is a good insurance policy for the long-term health of a bird (see pages 6–8). If any problems are found, the buyer, seller and veterinarian should discuss the available options.

New bird owners usually have many questions on nutrition, behavior and preventive medicine. They have already heard lots of conflicting do's and don'ts on pet bird care. The veterinarian and staff can help resolve any concerns and answer questions.

In Health . . .

The importance of prevention and early detection of medical problems is well known in all areas of medicine. Most dog and cat owners understand the value of yearly checkups and disease prevention through annual vaccinations. However, many bird owners still do not understand the importance of yearly exams for their birds.

Birds mask their illnesses until problems are usually well advanced. They also can't communicate how they're feeling. As a result, many birds are unnecessarily presented to veterinarians in a serious or life-threatening condition. Birds often carry potential disease-producing organisms, and when the conditions are right, these "bugs" can cause problems. Annual physical exams will not only help prevent disease but also minimize the seriousness when disease occurs.

Yearly exams also provide a way for owners to stay current as new information on pet bird care becomes available. This includes information on nutrition, behavior and preventive medicine. Vaccines are available to protect pet birds from certain diseases. New vaccines are also currently being developed. An annual examination by a qualified avian veterinarian is a valuable tool for the overall health and vitality of a pet bird.

. . . in Sickness

Time is critical in the treatment of sick birds, and the sooner the bird gets to a veterinarian the better. Whenever a bird shows any signs of sickness, a veterinarian should be consulted. Unfortunately, many birds are given home remedies first, before a veterinarian is contacted. This delay in medical treatment can complicate matters.

Obviously in an emergency, veterinary care should be sought immediately. In these instances it is best to have already done the research to find a veterinarian knowledgeable in bird care.

VETERINARIANS: HOW TO FIND ONE KNOWLEDGEABLE IN AVIAN MEDICINE

The best way to start looking for a "bird doctor" would be to ask local veterinarians, the veterinary association in your community or state, local pet stores and bird clubs. Usually, if enough "bird people" are asked, certain names will continue to be mentioned. Veterinarians with a bird interest become known and develop a reputation throughout the community. In virtually every large town and city there should be a veterinarian with a special interest in birds.

It is *not* recommended to rely solely on the yellow pages. Unfortunately, there are still many veterinarians who advertise that they treat birds but have not taken the time to learn the necessary basics of avian medicine.

All veterinarians with a serious interest in birds should be a member of the Association of Avian Veterinarians (AAV). This is well worth asking about. However, even being a member of AAV does not attest to their avian medical abilities. It is, however, a very good start.

In September 1993 the first avian medicine board certification test was offered. Veterinarians with a special interest in birds and who meet other demanding requirements can choose to take this test. Achieving board certification in avian medicine demonstrates a high level of proficiency in this field. It is a very demanding test, requiring months of preparation. Since this program is still in its infancy, as time goes on, more and more doctors will become "boarded". If there is a boarded avian specialist in your area, this doctor will obviously be well qualified to treat birds. However, it does not mean other veterinarians are not equally qualified. It may be they have simply not yet taken the test.

WHAT TO LOOK FOR WHEN VISITING AN AVIAN VETERINARIAN

A good "bedside manner" is important but does not necessarily indicate competence in medicine. Determining this is quite another matter. Most pet owners are really not capable of evaluating the quality of medicine practiced. This is the reason an avian veterinarian's reputation is so important. As recommended in the previous section, spend the time, do your "homework," and find a highly skilled avian veterinarian before you need one.

In addition to a good bird reputation, evaluate the doctor's hospital and staff. Here are a few suggestions to help you assess the overall quality of care provided.

- Is the hospital clean and inviting? Are there bird-related items in the reception area or exam room?
- Does the hospital seem equipped to treat birds? Some of the standard equipment needed should include a gram scale, incubators, a radiograph machine (X rays), laboratory facilities, isoforane gas anesthesia and a clean and organized surgery room. Ask for a tour of the hospital!

- Are the staff members friendly, professional and knowledgeable? Many clinics employ Animal Health Technicians (AHT), Registered Veterinary Technicians (RVT), or Certified Verterinary Technicians (CVT) who are licensed veterinary nurses. These highly trained professionals are an asset to any veterinarian and will help ensure that the animals receive high-quality medical care.

- Does your veterinarian fulfill Dr. James Harris's Three C's for a successful veterinarian: competency, communication and compassion? A complete history should be taken and "hands on" physical exam performed. Capture and restraint should be done gently, carefully and with minimal effort. The suspected cause or causes should be thoroughly explained, diagnostic and treatment options discussed in simple and understandable terms. All questions should be answered.

- Are fees openly discussed? Cost estimates, preferably in writing, should be given *before* any tests or treatments are begun. Remember, medicine is not an "exact science" and estimates are just an approximation of costs. However, if the health status changes and the estimate is no longer valid, it is customary to inform the pet's owner. If necessary, ask about billing policies. Small businesses may not be able to offer "loans," but the use of credit cards and other options usually exist.

- Is follow-up care provided? Your veterinarian should be available to answer any questions on cases *currently* under their treatment.

- Does the hospital provide after-hours emergency coverage? Inquire about their policy concerning emergencies outside regular office hours.

WHAT VETERINARIANS LOOK FOR IN CLIENTS

Health care is a team approach. Veterinarians are looking for clients who understand health care for their bird is a two-way street. A good client is a partner in this relationship, willing to do what it takes to achieve success. This requires good communication.

For example, the veterinarian is responsible for providing clear and exact home care instructions for the owner to follow. Veterinarians depend on clients to properly follow through with the home treatments. If medications are not given correctly, the animal may not recover. The veterinarian would be under the mistaken impression the medication failed, when in fact this was not the case. Clients need to comply with the instructions given them. If there are any questions, *always* ask. If at home, call the hospital for clarification.

In addition to following directions, bird owning clients should keep the following ideas in mind:

- Do not expect a veterinarian to make a diagnosis over the telephone. Even the best veterinarian cannot see or feel a bird over the phone. Remember, many different diseases and injuries appear very similar.

- Clients *must* have confidence in their veterinarian. If not, it would be better to find another doctor for your pet's health needs.
- A client must understand that a veterinarian can *never* guarantee the pet will recover, only that the very best effort will be made. Veterinarians care very much for the welfare of their patients, but they cannot save them all. A good client tries to understand this in spite of difficult circumstances.
- Excessive waiting time to see the doctor can be a cause of great frustration. In any hospital, unexpected and unplanned-for emergencies occur frequently. These cases must receive first priority. Clients need to remember that most doctors really try to do everything possible to minimize the wait.
- Clients should expect their veterinarian to offer alternatives for the treatment of their pet. This might include simply sending medication home versus performing diagnostic tests, or home treatment as opposed to hospitalization. The veterinarian's responsibility is to offer these options. However, if circumstances dictate that the ideal and most complete approach is not possible, clients need to understand the odds for recovery will be less. The veterinarian should not be held responsible.

GOING TO THE VETERINARIAN: THINGS TO REMEMBER

- Call ahead and make an appointment. If this is a first-time visit, arrive fifteen minutes early to fill out the necessary paperwork. For an *emergency*, still call ahead. Make sure the doctor is in and allow the staff time to prepare for your arrival.
- Birds should be carried into the hospital in some type of cage or container. It is best to bring the bird's own cage (do not clean it, so the actual environment, including the droppings can be observed). If the cage is too large to move, use a cardboard box, plastic transport carrier or smaller cage. There should be holes for ventilation. Be sure to bring along the paper from the cage floor and a sample of the food being eaten.
- Just before leaving, consider emptying water cups so they don't spill, lowering or removing perches if the bird is showing any instability or excessive weakness, removing any swings or toys that could injure the bird during the ride and possibly covering the cage, which may help some birds to relax more.
- Bring any medications or other supplements the bird has recently been given.
- Write down a list of any questions. In the exam room, clients frequently forget many of the questions they had wanted to ask.

THE EXAMINATION

The cornerstones of any examination are a thorough history and physical examination. When visiting the veterinarian, be prepared to answer these questions:

- Age and sex, if known.
- Length of ownership and where purchased (private breeder, pet shop, etc.).
- The main complaint. What are the signs and when did they first appear?
- Has the bird been exposed to other birds? Are any other birds sick? Are there any newly acquired birds in the house? Are any family members ill?
- Are there any previous medical problems? (If your bird has been treated by another veterinarian, have the records forwarded to the new doctor.)
- Reproductive history, if any?
- Diet? What has the bird been eating? Has the appetite changed?
- Has the activity level remained normal? Sleeping more? Talking less? Any new or strange behaviors?
- Any regurgitation or vomiting? Coughing or sneezing? Change in droppings?
- Have there been any changes noticed in the feathers? Molting? Feather picking?
- Have there been any recent changes in the bird's home environment?
- Is the bird allowed to fly around the house?
- Type of caging?
- Any chewing on strange objects in the cage or around the house?
- Has any home treatment been attempted? If so, what and for how long?

In Chapter 10, "Home Physicals," the basics of the "hands off" visual examination were discussed. In addition, there is the "hands on" physical examination. While it may be easy to teach someone the steps involved in conducting these exams, it is another thing to have acquired the knowledge and practical experience to determine what is normal and what is abnormal. Also, differentiating one problem from another similar-appearing one requires a great deal of skill. It takes years of study and practice to interpret the findings and make recommendations as to the best course of action. This is the job of the avian veterinarian.

In cases of a severe respiratory disease or shock, a veterinarian might choose to avoid the physical exam completely until the bird can be stabilized. Good medical judgment is important so as not to compromise the patient any more than it already is.

Example of an examination checklist used by avian veterinarians.
(Courtesy Association of Avian Veterinarians)

Association of Avian Veterinarians

Advancing and Promoting Avian Medicine and Stewardship

Reference # _____

ASSOCIATION OF AVIAN VETERINARIANS
CERTIFICATE OF VETERINARY EXAMINATION
Caged or Aviary Bird

Owner: _____ Date: _____

Address: _____ Telephone: _____

_____ Bird's Name: _____

IDENTIFICATION

Species _____ (Tattoo, Band, Microchip Number) _____

Age _____ Sex _____ Weight (in grams) _____

HISTORY

Origin of bird: ☐ Wild-caught ☐ Captive-bred (Name of Breeder _____) ☐ Hand-fed ☐ Unknown

Diet _____

Medical History _____

PHYSICAL EXAM	Normal	Abnormal	Not Examined	Notes
General appearance	☐	☐	☐	
Integument	☐	☐	☐	
Feather condition	☐	☐	☐	
Beak	☐	☐	☐	
Nares	☐	☐	☐	
Eyes	☐	☐	☐	
Feet	☐	☐	☐	
Pharynx/choana	☐	☐	☐	
Vent /cloaca	☐	☐	☐	
Musculoskeletal	☐	☐	☐	
Respiratory system	☐	☐	☐	
Cardiovascular	☐	☐	☐	
Neurological system	☐	☐	☐	
Urine/urates	☐	☐	☐	
Feces	☐	☐	☐	
Other				

RADIOGRAPHIC FINDINGS _____

_____

LABORATORY TESTS AND DIAGNOSTICS

Test	Date run	Lab/method	Normal	Abnormal	
			☐	☐	_____
			☐	☐	_____
			☐	☐	_____
			☐	☐	_____
			☐	☐	_____

Clinic _____ Examined By _____

Address _____ Phone _____

City _____ State _____ Zip _____ *This form is not a guarantee of good health. Rather, it is intended for clients to monitor the progress of their avian pets.*

DIAGNOSTICS

Veterinarians perform laboratory tests to help them arrive at an accurate diagnosis. This is the key to an effective treatment and a rapid recovery. There are numerous tests available. No one test will consistently yield the diagnosis. Frequently, it will become necessary to perform a few different tests in order to accurately piece the puzzle together.

The various diagnostic tests, including how they are collected and how they are interpreted, are briefly described.

Blood Tests

Recent advances in laboratory medicine now allow a battery of tests to be performed on minute amounts of blood. The sample is collected from a cut toenail or directly from a vein in the neck, wing or leg.

Many times blood tests can detect disease before any outward signs become apparent. They assist with establishing a diagnosis and a future outcome (prognosis), and allow a patient's condition to be more closely monitored than depending solely on visible responses.

One area of a modern avian diagnostic laboratory.
(Courtesy Avian and Exotic Clinical Pathology Laboratory)

Blood collection from the toenail.

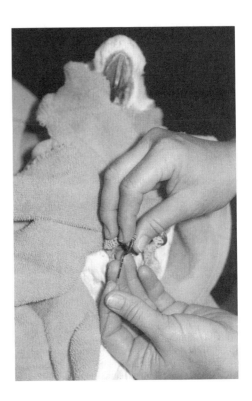

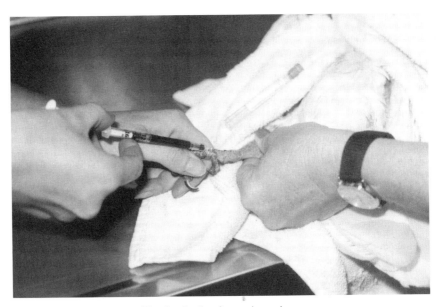

Blood collection from a leg vein.

Complete Blood Count: This test counts the various white cells, red cells and platelets. It provides very valuable information. It can determine whether an infection or decrease in red blood cells (anemia) is present, the severity and some idea of how long the body has been affected. Blood protein level is also measured.

Blood Chemistry Profile: Diseases change the way certain organs function. This affects the amount of chemicals, including enzymes and electrolytes, and cells found in the blood. These chemicals can be measured and any changes in normal levels can indicate a problem.

Some specific diseases that can also be diagnosed through blood tests include psittacosis, psittacine beak and feather disease, thyroid gland disorders, aspergillosis and sometimes lead poisoning.

Radiology (X ray)

Taking X rays of birds involves a few "tricks of the trade." These include specially designed restraint boards that lessen the stress of handling and are safe to use. For highly stressed or large birds, sometimes anesthesia is the best and safest method of restaint.

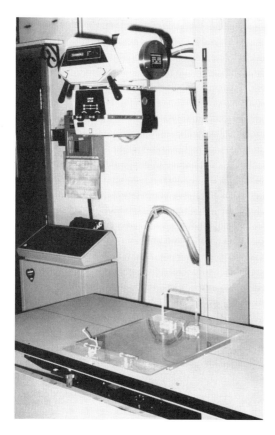

An X-ray machine, showing the Plexiglas avian restraint board.

A cockatoo being safely restrained for an X ray.

The ability to "see" inside the body is one of the most valuable diagnostic tools for birds. The system of air sacs surrounding internal organs make birds ideal X-ray subjects. As a result, visualization of the internal organs is better than in mammals. Changes in the shape and size of organs, presence of foreign objects and bone abnormalities such as fractures and dislocations are some of the important information gained from radiographs.

Bacteriologic Exams

A sterile cotton swab is used to collect samples. Any site on the body can be used, but most common are the mouth, cloaca, eyes, nostrils, skin and feather follicles.

Since infections are the most common problem in pet birds. this is a very useful test. It "looks for" the presence of bacteria, fungi and yeast.

Gram Stain: A very simple and quick screening test for the presence of bacteria and yeast. The name of the test is derived from the type of stain used to microscopically examine the sample. It measures the amount of organisms present and distinguishes between two different classifications of bacteria. This is important, because in birds the ratio of the two catagories must remain within a narrow range. Most of the bacterial problems seen occur when the range of one of these categories, called Gram-negative bacteria, increases.

Culture and Sensitivity: This test identifies the organisms causing disease (culture) and then tests for which antibiotics will be most effective in eliminating them (sensitivity). This is important because it helps minimize the guesswork involved in selecting the most effective antibiotic.

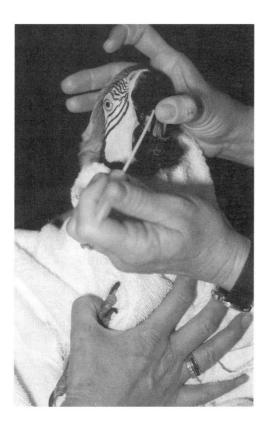

A sterile swab is used to collect a sample from the throat for a micro-biological examination. Note that the upper beak has been placed inside the lower beak so that the bird cannot chew on the swab.

Fecal (Stool) Analysis

Feces are collected from cage paper. Samples can also be collected directly from the cloaca using a cotton swab.

A fecal analysis is a microscopic exam of the stool to detect intestinal parasites ("worms") and abnormal amounts of yeast and bacteria.

Urine Analysis

Urine is collected directly from the droppings. Wax paper lining the cage floor will help to separate the urine portion from the feces.

Urine analysis is not commonly performed in birds. It can, however, be helpful when problems such as urinary tract infections, kidney disease and diabetes are suspected.

Biopsy

A small piece of tissue is removed surgically from any "suspect" area. Another method is to use a special hollow-core needle and syringe. The needle is inserted into an organ or tumor and a sample is withdrawn. There is very little discomfort to the patient.

235

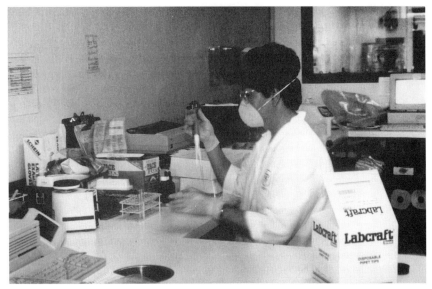

Laboratory technician preparing samples for psittacosis testing.
(Courtesy Alan M. Fudge, D.V.M., California Avian Laboratory)

The tissue collected is microscopically examined. It is primarily a means of diagnosing cancer, but it will also identify infections, inflamations and parasites within tissues.

Endoscopy

An endoscope is a very-small-diameter instrument providing light and magnification to view the interior of the body.

In birds, endoscopy is most commonly used to view the internal organs. Under anesthesia, a tiny skin incision is made on the side of the abdomen and the endoscope inserted. It provides a firsthand look at the shape and size of organs. In larger birds, endoscopy is also used to view the inside of the trachea. Surgical sexing is performed with an endoscope.

Electrocardiogram (ECG)

An ECG is a recording of the electrical activity of the heart on a moving strip of paper. It is a safe and simple procedure to perform on birds.

Although not commonly performed on birds, it is helpful in the diagnosis of heart disease. In general, heart problems are not common in pet birds.

Ultrasound

Ultrasound uses very high frequency sound waves, similar to sonar, to visualize internal organs.

236

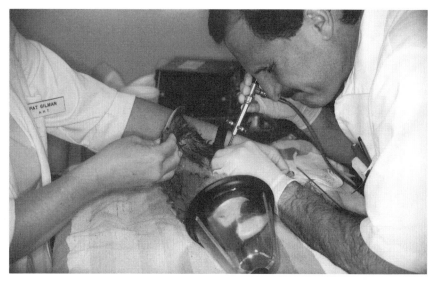

This anesthetized macaw is undergoing diagnostic endoscopy.

Due to the highly specialized nature of this test, it is not rountinely performed on birds. However, in the years to come it will probably become a more valuable diagnostic tool. Internal organs can be seen "in action," and abnormalities can quickly be seem.

Necropsy (Postmortem)

After death, this is the dissection and examination of a body to determine the cause of death. If a necropsy is going to be done, the body needs to be refrigerated, not frozen, and taken to the veterinarian as soon as possible. Wrap the body in newspaper and then in plastic.

Postmortems are routine in most avian practices. For the owner's benefit, determining the cause of death may help ease the pain of loss. Also, if other birds are owned, preventive measures could be taken to curb a potential disease outbreak. For the veterinarian's benefit, the knowledge gained will also improve the care of future patients.

SEX DETERMINATION

Or, "Gee, it laid an egg. I had always thought it was a boy!" Most pet birds do not show any external sexual characteristics. In other words, the "boys" and the "girls" all look alike: i.e., they have same size, color, shape and behaviors. Special testing methods are required to differentiate a male from a female bird.

For aviculture, having the correct sexes "paired up," is obviously essential for a successful breeding program. For pet birds, remember, the bird know its

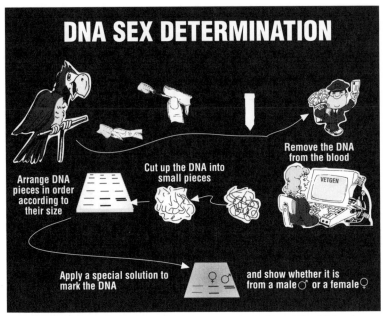

A bird's sex can be determined at any age by looking at the DNA contained in a single drop of blood. *(Zoogen)*

sex and this is all that really matters. However, for those owners who "just have to know," there are now simple and safe methods available for sex determination.

Observation: Unless an egg is laid, this method is not reliable for pet birds. Do not attempt to identify sexes based on behaviors observed. There are *no* actions, attitudes, habits or tendencies that are consistent with one sex or another. Females can spontaneously lay infertile eggs with no male bird around.

DNA Sexing: This technique involves analyzing the red blood cells to determine the presence of male or female chromosomes. It is a reliable, convenient and reasonably-priced test that can be performed on *any* age bird. Only one drop of blood is required, samples are mailed to the lab and results take about three weeks. "DNA-fingerprinting" for positive individual bird identification is also available.

Surgical Sexing: Of all modern methods, this is the oldest and quickest way to determine sex. An endoscope is passed into the body cavity of an anesthetized bird, and a view of an ovary or testicle is seen. Although this technique involves both anesthesia and minor surgery, an experienced avian veterinarian can perform it with *very* minimal risk.

Fecal Steroid Analysis: A small sample of stool is analyzed for the presence of reproductive hormones. The sample is collected from the cage floor and mailed to a laboratory. Birds must be sexually mature for this technique to be conclusive.

Feather Sexing: The feather pulp from a young, growing feather ("blood feather") is analyzed for the presence of male or female chromosomes. The sample must be sent to the lab on an ice pack by overnight mail.

For the method best suited to your specific needs, consult an avian veterinarian. Each of these methods has advantages and disadvantages.

VACCINATIONS

Vaccines are used to immunize or protect the body from specific diseases. They stimulate the body's immune system to produce antibodies against the organism causing the disease. These vaccines have been modified in such a way to insure *only* protection. They cannot cause the disease.

The vaccines currently available for pet birds include Pacheco's disease and pox virus. For individually kept pet birds, the risk of contracting either of these diseases is low. Some vaccine reactions have been reported, and therefore the question of whether to vaccinate should be discussed with an avian veterinarian.

A vaccine for psittacine beak and feather disease is currently being developed. Hopefully, this is just the beginning. Vaccines are one of the true medical wonders of our century.

THERAPEUTICS: THE ART AND SCIENCE OF HEALING

Primum non nocere ("First do no harm"). This ancient physician's oath is one of the guiding principles permeating all branches of medicine. However, nowhere does it take on more importance than in the field of therapeutics. The science, and especially the art, of medicine helps decide which weapons from the vast arsenal of treatments will be safest and most effective. Veterinarians spend many years in school and in practice learning, developing and polishing their skills in this area.

There are many options available for the treatment of sick birds. No one approach is always going to be effective. Many factors *must* be weighed when selecting the best treatment regimen. These include:

- Age and species
- History and physical examination findings
- Unique anatomy and physiological characteristics
- Unique nutritional and environmental requirements
- General health
- Diagnostic tests results
- Severity of disease or injury
- In-hospital or home care
- Owner's ability to restrain and handle patient
- Combined effects of all drugs and other treatments given
- Finances

This section will briefly discuss many of the treatment options available in avian medicine. This list continues to increase as research and technology evolves.

In-Hospital Care versus Home Care

Sometimes the decision as to whether or not to hospitalize a sick bird is very easy and sometimes it's not. A severely ill bird requiring special treatments such as surgery, oxygen, "force" feeding and close monitoring (i.e., for shock, seizuring, poisoning, severe breathing difficulties) will need to be hospitalized. Also, especially with the larger birds, owners are simply unable to handle and medicate their birds. In these instances, the bird will have to be hospitalized or will require daily visits to the hospital.

The vast majority of birds, on the other hand, will *not* require hospitalization. These birds can be treated adequately and effectively at home. Home care has the distinct advantage of providing a familiar and stress-free environment. It is also considerably less expensive.

The ultimate decision should be made in the partnership between veterinarian and owner. There are many factors to consider, and each case must be handled individually.

Hospitalized birds should be kept in an incubator. This is an enclosed container with settings for proper temperature and humidity. It also has "see-through" sides for easy viewing and monitoring of the patient. An oxygen-enriched environment can be set up when breathing difficulties are a problem.

Medications/Drugs

Drugs are any substance used to aid in the diagnosis, treatment or prevention of diseases and other problems. They can relieve pain and promote healing. When used correctly, drugs are an aid to the ultimate healer—Mother Nature.

Selecting the most effective drugs and using them correctly are essential. Birds can react unfavorably to any medication. *Drugs safe in humans, dogs, cats and other animals may not be safe in birds.* Also, since birds are relatively tiny creatures, drugs must be used at their *correct* dosage. The choice of drugs must be based on the above list of factors to be weighed. Only veterinarians, and specifically avian veterinarians, have the specialized knowledge necessary to make these decisions.

Once the choice to use a drug is made, still more decisions are necessary. These include:

- Dosage (amount of drug to be given; many drug dosages vary within specified limits)
- Frequency (How many times daily? Once, twice, three times or more?)
- Duration of therapy (How many days is medication to be given?)
- Route (oral, injection—i.e, intramuscular, subcutaneous, intravenous—and topically are the most common methods)
- Form (liquid, injectable, powder, "crushed-up" pill, capsule—many drugs come in a variety of forms)
- Possible side effects
- Cost

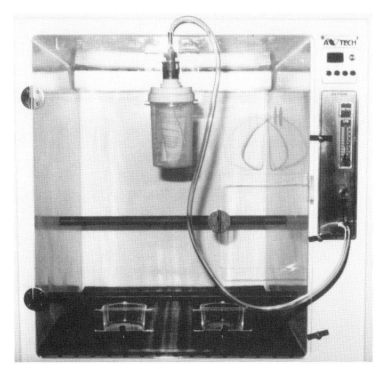

Incubators for birds.

Method of Administration

ORAL (by mouth)

Directly into the Mouth: This is a very good method for small birds and birds very easy to handle. For larger birds, medication given by mouth may be difficult. Towel restraint is necessary; the head has to be held steady and accurate dosing can be a problem. Do not use a glass eyedropper to administer medication. Some drugs are not available in an oral form.

Medicating the Water: This is the least effective method. Sick birds usually drink less water, and therefore accurate dosing is not possible. Many medications do not evenly dissolve in water or will give it an unpleasant taste. Medicating the water is best used in healthier birds when medications are given long term or when treating a large group of birds.

Medicating the Food: There are commercially formulated diets that contain antibiotics. These generally work well, especially when long-term treatment is necessary or with difficult-to-handle birds. Problems can arise because birds must be converted to these diets as their only source of food.

Another method is to "bury" medication in soft foods. When using this option, be sure the bird eats all the medicated food.

INJECTABLE (by injection)

This is the *most* accurate method of administering medications. Once owners have been properly instructed in the technique, it can safely be done at home. It is rapid, painless, very low risk and is also less stressful on the bird than giving medications directly into the mouth. Owners are predictably very fearful at first, but quickly learn the method is really quite easy. The most difficult part is the restraint.

Intravenous (into a vein): Used by veterinarians to gain rapid effects of life-saving drugs.

Intramuscular (into a muscle): This is the preferred method for most injectable drugs. It is also the most common route used by owners for administering antibiotics at home.

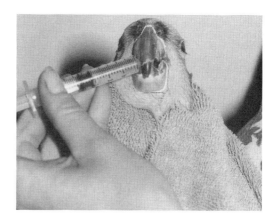

A properly restrained bird receiving oral medication. A syringe without the needle allows for accurate dosing.

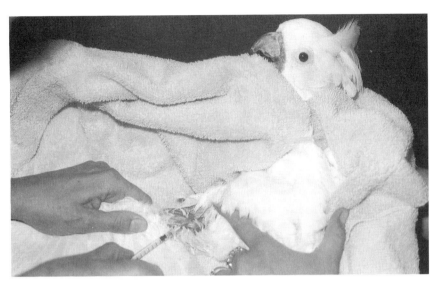

(A) A cockatoo receiving an intravenous injection into the wing vein. (B) Close-up of the injection site.

Subcutaneous (beneath the skin): Used most frequently by veterinarians for giving fluids to dehydrated birds.

Intraosseous (within the bone): Veterinary-administered medications, usually fluids, given through a needle placed directly into the marrow cavity. This method is generally reserved for very sick birds.

TOPICAL (applied directly to area being treated)

243

An intramuscular injection into the pectoral muscles.

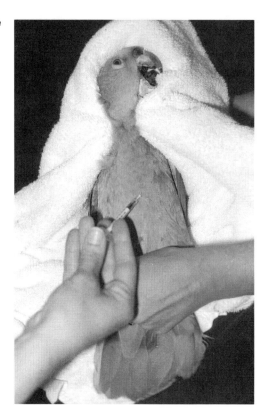

Dermatological (for skin and feathers): Topical skin and feather medications have limited use. Avoid oil or "greasy" compounds, as they will damage feathers.

Intraocular (into eye): Commonly used for eye infections or other eye problems. Use only medications specifically labeled for eye use.

Intranasal (into nares): Medications can be flushed or instilled into the nose for severe sinus infections.

Intrasinus (into sinuses): Used by veterinarians for sinus infections. Helps to clean and treat infected sinuses.

FLUID THERAPY

Many sick birds will not drink enough water, and as a result become dehydrated and weak. Providing additional fluids can sometimes be the most important part of the treatment. Fluids are usually given by injection or, sometimes, orally with tube feeding. Birds in shock usually receive fluids directly into a vein or a bone. Subcutaneous fluids are used in birds that are stable and only slightly dehydrated. For long-term fluid administration, fluids can be given through a catheter and dripped into a vein or the bone marrow.

INHALATION THERAPY (breathing medication into lungs)

Vaporization or Nebulization: Medication is suspended in a very fine liquid mist. These microscopic droplets are inhaled deep into the respiratory tract. They soothe and moisturize inflamed linings. It is an especially beneficial method for birds with air sac infections or obvious breathing difficulty.

NUTRITIONAL SUPPORT

Tube Feeding: If sick birds are not eating well, they will often require "force feeding." Tube feeding can sustain a bird nutritionally until it is well enough to eat on its own. Tube feeding is done with a tube attached to a syringe and using specially prepared food. The tube is inserted through the mouth directly into the crop, where an appropriate amount of food is given. Fluids and medications can also be given through the tube and with the food. In inexperienced hands, tube feeding could severely injure a bird. Therefore, it is *not* recommended as a home treatment.

Type of Medications

Antibiotics: These drugs have saved many lives that otherwise would have been lost. Antibiotics kill or inhibit bacteria. They are not effective against viruses. They can be used in a viral infection to prevent bacteria from causing more problems. There are many different antibiotics in use. This is because all antibiotics are not effective against all the various types of bacteria. Selection is

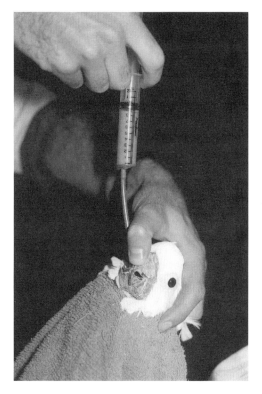

Tube feeding. The bird cannot chew on the tube because the upper beak has been carefully placed inside the lower beak.

based on many of the factors already discussed and, in addition, the results of a culture and sensitivity test when available.

Antiyeast/Antifungal: Just as their name states, these drugs kill or inhibit the growth of yeast and fungi. These organisms commonly cause infections in pet birds.

Antiinflammatory: These medications suppress inflammation. They can help control pain and are used to treat shock, some cancers, joint problems, allergies, and sometimes skin problems in birds.

Anthelmentic (ANT-hel-MIN-tik): This is the medical name for drugs used to kill parasites.

In addition to this very brief list of drugs, there are a myriad of other drugs used in avian medicine. These include hormones, antiseizure, antiviral, vitamins, minerals, sedatives, anesthetics, respiratory and heart stimulants, behavior modifiers, appetite stimulants and still more! Most importantly, drugs are a wonderful addition to the fight against disease. They *must* be used correctly and under the supervision of a veterinarian. If used incorrectly, drugs can do much harm.

Surgery

In recent years, avian surgery has become more highly developed, and the most important advancement has been in the field of anesthesia. General anesthesia eliminates the patient's feeling of pain while totally unconscious. An anesthetic called isoflurane is the safest anesthetic used in birds. As a direct result of isoflurane, complicated surgeries can be performed with very little anesthetic risk.

Surgery may be necessary for tumors, broken bones, abscesses, lacerations, retrieval of foreign bodies, obstructions, prolapses and sometimes for egg binding.

The actual surgical procedure is very similar to that used in other animals:

- Prior to anesthesia, radiographs and blood tests may be needed. This is not only to gain more information about the problem, but also to check for other factors that could increase the risk of anesthesia and surgery.
- The patient should be as relaxed as possible prior to surgery. Therefore, the bird should be in the hospital a few hours, or even the night, before.
- Isoflurane should be used for anesthesia.
- Once the bird has been anesthetized, the feathers around the surgical site will be removed and the skin thoroughly cleaned.
- The patient's heart rate, breathing rate and other vital signs will be closely monitored to evaluate the depth of anesthesia and for unexpected problems that could occur.
- The surgery should be performed under generally accepted sterile conditions. Surgical instruments designed for human eye surgery are often used because of their small size, and suture material of very small diameter is used to close incisions and wounds both inside the body and on the skin. Blood loss must be kept to an absolute minimum.

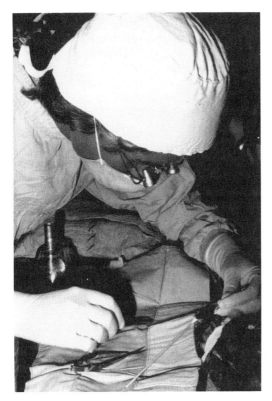

Surgery on the eye of a bird.

- Recovery from anesthesia usually takes only minutes when isoflurane is used. Ask to be called immediately after your bird recovers from anesthesia.

Bandages, Splints and Collars

The application of bandages, splints and collars is frequently necessary. Properly applied, they support and protect a muscle, ligament or tendon injury, or broken bone. They also protect cuts and bruises and will keep a bird from picking at the area. It requires considerable skill and experience to properly apply one of these devices. If they are improperly applied, they can cause serious injury to a bird. It is recommended that only veterinarians apply a bandage, splint or collar to a bird.

Restraint collars used to be applied routinely for feather-picking birds. They are still used, but usually only in severe cases where birds are actually traumatizing their skin. Collars are usually made from plastic or leather. They encircle the neck of the bird and prevent the beak from reaching its skin and feathers.

Upon the application of a collar, a bird can become very stressed, and at first may ''fight'' the collar and stop eating. It *must* be watched closely for the first several hours after the collar has been applied. Within a short time most

247

Bandaging: (A) Lower leg bandage. (B) Wing bandage.

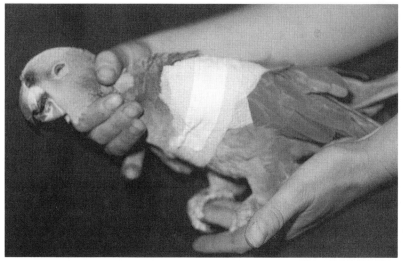

birds will accept the collar. Depending on the problem, collars can be left on for days, weeks and sometimes even months.

IMPORTANT POINTS TO REMEMBER WITH BANDAGES AND SPLINTS

- Keep it dry! A wet splint or bandage can cause infection and delay healing.
- Watch for picking. Light "preening" of the bandage is normal, but digging and tearing at it are not.
- If part of the bandage comes off or slips down, the entire bandage will probably need to be changed.

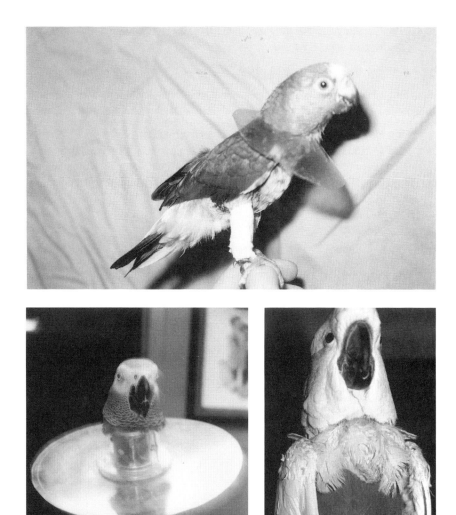

Different types of restraint collars, from the very simple X-ray film collar to the molded plastic version to the custom-fitted leather breast plate.

- If toes or a wing tip are exposed below the bandage, check them daily for swelling. If swelling is noted, the bandage could be too tight and will need to be changed.

If any of these problems develop, call your veterinarian immediately.

Alternative Forms of Avian Therapy

Holistic medicine, practiced by some veterinarians, offers still another alternative to healing. It involves a more natural and philosophical approach to treating the entire body, not just the affected part. Treatments include acupuncture, homeopathy, herbs, special nutritional supplements and other nonconventional methods.

14

Home Care for the Sick Bird

Basic First-Aid Measures

HOME CARE for a sick bird involves basic first-aid measures and good nursing care. First aid is the simple procedures owners can use in an emergency, *before* veterinary care can be obtained. These recommendations are general in nature, and can be used regardless of the problem. The sooner these suggestions can be put into use, the better will be the chances for recovery. However, remember—*these home care procedures are not meant as a substitute for veterinary care*. In fact, the home hospital should actually be run as a partnership, with bird owner and veterinarian working together.

These same home care suggestions can also be followed when bringing a sick bird home from the hospital. However, when your veterinarian's advice is contrary to what is given in this book, *always* follow his/her instructions. Your veterinarian will be able to take into account the special needs of your bird.

THINGS TO DO BEFORE AN EMERGENCY ARISES

1. Be prepared! Have all necessary supplies ready to go (see the information in a first-aid kit later in this chapter) and know how to use them. Being able to start treatment right away could mean the difference between life and death.
2. Learn how to safely and properly restrain your bird (Chapter 7). Administering medications or treating injuries such as bleeding require proper restraint. Practice basic restraint periodically with your bird.
3. Keep this book handy for quick reference.

BASIC REQUIREMENTS FOR SICK BIRDS

Warmth

The importance of extra heat cannot be overemphasized. It allows the body to concentrate more of its energy on "repair and recovery" and less on maintaining normal body temperature. *Sick birds should be maintained in an enclosed environment of 80° to 90°F.*

Below are a few suggested methods for providing the increased warmth:

- For small cages, place a heating pad beneath the cage or alongside it. Use a low setting. Do not allow the bird to chew on the heating pad. To prevent heat loss, cover the cage on top and three sides with a towel.
- For large cages, an electric blanket, on a low setting, could be suspended or "tented" over the cage. Be very careful; large birds are very inquisitive and could chew on the blanket.
- A small aquarium with a screen- or towel-covered roof can be placed on top of a heating pad. This makes an excellent home hospital cage. If the floor gets too hot, check the setting on the heating pad. If necessary, line the aquarium with newspaper.
- Use a red/amber infrared 250-watt heat lamp (sometimes called a brooder lamp). Use a special fixture with a porcelain socket and clamp set-up. Place it two to four feet away from the cage.

A *thermometer* to measure temperature is strongly recommended. Remember, hot air rises. Therefore, for the most accurate reading, try to place the thermometer down near the floor of the cage. Do not let larger birds chew on it.

Use of an infrared 250-watt heat lamp for home care of a sick bird.

For cages, hang the thermometer outside the cage and near the floor of the cage. For aquariums, a thin wall-mounted aquarium thermometer works well.

A standard light bulb is *not* recommended. The bright light can be stressful and disrupt the bird's normal sleeping patterns.

Regardless of the heat source, try to focus the heat more toward one side of the cage than the other. In this way, the bird can move around and find its most comfortable temperature. To be sure the bird is being kept at the proper temperature, watch its appearance and behavior. If a bird becomes too warm, it will hold its wings away from the body and pant. If too cold, it will sit in a huddled position with feathers fluffed.

Food and Water

Food: Every effort must be made to make sure a sick bird continues to eat. Unfortunately, sick birds usually lose their appetites, in spite of their increased nutritional needs. If birds do not eat enough, they become weakened and less able to fight off disease. Birds have a fast metabolic rate and will lose weight rapidly when they stop eating or eat less than their normal daily requirements.

Rule #1: Make sure the food is easily accessible. Whether the bird is perching or sitting on the cage floor, make certain the food is conveniently located. For example, if the bird is on the cage floor, place the food and water cups on the floor nearby or even sprinkle the food around on the floor. This is no time to worry about proper hygiene. The less energy expended on searching or reaching for food, the better.

Rule #2: Don't worry about a balanced diet. Whatever a sick bird wants, feed it! However, a nutritious and fresh assortment of foods is always preferable.

Rule #3: Spend time trying to stimulate the appetite.

- Offer favorite foods.
- Try warming home-cooked foods.
- Soak seeds to soften and make them easier to eat, even hull them if necessary.
- Sweeten foods slightly, with fruit juice or tiny amounts of honey or Karo syrup.
- Hand feed.

Hand-feeding is a good approach for a tame bird or a baby bird that isn't eating from a food dish. It is not practical for giving large amounts of food. Follow the same recommendations given for feeding baby birds (see Chapter 5). In addition to a spoon, a plastic medicine dropper, syringe or even a small piece of cardboard can be used to place the food right next to the beak or directly into the mouth. Give only small amounts at a time, and be sure it's being swallowed

Author's Note: Tube-feeding (see page 245) is an excellent way to force-feed a bird. However, in inexperienced hands a bird could become severely injured. If tube-feeding is going to be done at home, it *must* be done under the supervision of a veterinarian. Follow the doctor's guidelines very carefully.

This is an example of a gram scale. Many different types are available. *(Bonnie Jay)*

Rule #4: Monitor weight daily. Sick birds should be weighed on a daily basis. A scale showing weight in grams is preferred because it is more accurate and can detect very slight losses. Weight losses of more than 10 percent may require force-feeding.

Grit, if being used, should be removed. Sick birds are more apt to overeat it and could develop serious intestinal problems.

Water: Sick birds frequently do not drink enough water or other fluids. In addition, their droppings usually contain increased amounts of urine. As a result, dehydration occurs and causes even more serious problems. Attempts need to be made to provide additional fluids on a regular basis.

Fluids can be supplied in a number of different ways.

IF THE BIRD IS STILL DRINKING WATER: Try adding fruit juice, Gatorade, or Pedialyte. Use these full strength or diluted with water. Pedialyte is an infant fluid and electrolyte replacement solution available at most drugstores. Also, Karo syrup or honey can be added to drinking water at a dilution of one teaspoon per cup of water. These are all good "quick" energy sources.

IF THE BIRD IS STILL EATING: Add more fruits to the diet. They will provide a good source of quick energy. In addition, moistened cereals or other foods, including warm soups, can be tried.

IF THE BIRD IS NOT DRINKING SUFFICIENT AMOUNTS: A plastic eye dropper, turkey baster, syringe or straw with finger kept over one end can be used to offer fluids directly into the mouth. Be careful not to give too much of the fluid at one time. The same fluids already discussed in this section can be used.

AMOUNT OF FLUIDS TO GIVE*

Finches/canaries	4–5 drops
"Budgies"	6–10 drops
Cockatiels	¼ teaspoon
Amazon parrots	1–3 teaspoons
Large cockatoos/macaws	1½–3 tablespoons

Rest and Relaxation

Less stress means more energy conservation.

- Place the sick bird in a dimly lit and quiet room.
- Each day, provide twelve hours of darkness for sleeping and twelve hours of light to encourage eating.
- Avoid unnecessary handling.
- Keep other pets and children away.

Medication as Directed (if Needed)

If the sick bird has been examined by a veterinarian, medication will probably be prescribed. It is *very* important that directions be followed closely. This includes the proper dosage, correct number of times each day and for the total number of days prescribed. While still at the veterinary hospital, be sure *all* instructions are clearly explained. If you have any concerns, *ask questions*!

Medications prescribed could be in the form of oral liquids, injectables, topical sprays, powders, drops or ointments, and food or water additives. With a little practice, all of these medications are easy to give. Proper restraint (see Chapter 7) is usually the most difficult part. The veterinarian or a staff member should offer to demonstrate the correct method of restraint and medication administration.

Owner with an "Observant Eye"

While a bird is sick, owners need to look, listen and pay special attention to their patient. In other words, is the "little guy" getting better or worse?

DROPPINGS: Continue to observe their number, volume, color and consis-

---

*These amounts are only approximations. If the fluids are difficult to give, divide the amount and give some every fifteen to twenty minutes. The total amount should be given several times throughout the day as needed.

tency. They provide an excellent indicator of how things are going inside the body.

BREATHING: Look and listen to the pattern and rhythm of respiration. Is it smooth or forced? Is it getting better or worse?

FOOD AND WATER CONSUMPTION: Has it changed? Is more or less being consumed?

BODY WEIGHT: Is it increasing or decreasing?

BODY TEMPERATURE: Does the bird appear too hot, too cold or just right?

GENERAL APPEARANCE: More alert and responsive? Standing up straight or hunched over? Feathers being groomed?

FIRST AID

First Aid "Don't's"

Birds are more sensitive to medications than other animals and humans, so:

- *Do not* give your bird human medications or medications prescribed for another animal, unless directed by a veterinarian.
- *Do not* give your bird medications suggested by a friend, store employee or human physician.
- *Do not* give your bird any alcohol or laxatives.
- *Do not* apply any ointments or oils, *unless* directed by a veterinarian.
- *Do not* bathe a sick bird.

THE WELL-STOCKED FIRST-AID KIT

Emergency care instructions (Keep a copy of this book handy, or make copies of the chapters on restraint, emergencies, diseases and home care for the sick bird.)

Important telephone numbers (e.g., veterinarian)

Small writing pad and pencil

Heat source (e.g., heating pad or heat lamp and clamp setup, extension cord)

Quick energy supplements (e.g., powdered Gatorade, or other fluid/electrolyte solution, plus a few plastic eye droppers, turkey baster, etc.)

Restraint supplies (e.g., appropriate-sized towels)

Penlight (for the exam or for catching the bird in a darkened room)

Blood "stoppers" (styptic powder, silver nitrate stick)

Scissors (manicure-type for wing trimming, possibly child's blunt type for bandage materials)

Bandage materials (½-inch masking tape, gauze roll)

Assorted Q-tips, cotton balls, gauze squares, plastic zip-lock bags, paper towels or tissue

Small and/or large nail clipper and blunt-end nail file

A first-aid kit for birds.

Small blunt tweezers or hemostats (forceps), needle-nose pliers
Antiseptic/disinfectant solution (e.g., betadyne, nolvasan, hydrogen peroxide in plastic bottles)
Eye irrigation solution (available from a regular pharmacy)

For convenience, keep all these items together in some kind of box or container, like a fishing tackle box. Take it along when traveling with your bird—vacations, bird shows.

15

The Loss of a Pet Bird
"When the Bond Is Broken"

" '*N*EATH THIS STONE *doth lie more love than could ever die.*" This beautiful tribute is carved in a granite headstone at a local pet cemetery. These words demonstrate the depth of emotion people feel for their pets. This chapter addresses the issues and feelings involved when a pet death occurs and some of the ways to cope.

THE LOSS . . .

Sooner or later, most pet owners will face the loss of a beloved pet. Whether due to natural causes, accidents, old age or for whatever reason, the fact is they're gone, and you're left with the emptiness. Mental health care professionals have only recently realized the impact that losing a pet can have on people. Many books are now available to help people more effectively deal with this difficult problem; see the Bibliography.

The agony suffered when a pet is lost can seem unbearable. The grief process can linger for months, even years, unless a certain progression of emotions occur. In research done by Elisabeth Kübler-Ross, a front-runner in grief acknowledgment, she found the grieving process was divided into five distinct areas. These are anger, denial, sadness/depression, bargaining and acceptance. She also discovered that, unless each of these areas is resolved, an individual can remain "stuck" in the grieving process. It is important to completely work through each of these phases. This discovery confirms the normalcy of the emotions, pain and thoughts suffered when someone dear to us has been lost.

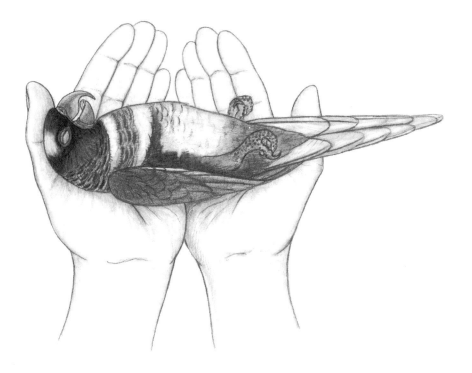

Pet lovers have been told by well-meaning people, "It's only an animal." For years, many pet owners would not allow themselves to grieve over the loss of a pet. They could not find the acceptance and support of friends who understood what they were going through. Strong support of close family and friends can be critical in allowing the grieving process to become complete.

Following are some important concepts about pet loss. These subjects range from euthanasia, to options for the body, to books and support groups.

Euthanasia

Fortunately for many bird owners, the decision regarding euthanasia (humane death) may never have to be made. Birds can often die so quickly, they take this difficult decision away. However, if faced with a situation where your pet is suffering, and all hope has been exhausted, the decision for euthanasia may have to be confronted.

It is important to understand what will actually happen during the euthanasia and what method will be used. Usually a lethal injection is given into a vein. The drug is a potent anesthetic agent given in a concentrated form. The pet goes into a very deep anesthetic "sleep," and the drug stops the heart. It takes less than five seconds for death to occur. The only sensation is the needle prick. Gas anesthetic can be used as well. It is generally more costly and takes longer. However, some people perceive it to be less traumatic to their pet. Regardless of the option, it must be performed by a veterinarian.

Discuss the options your veterinarian can offer and listen to their opinion. Other considerations include where it will be done—in hospital or in the home? Do you want to be with the animal? Do you want to view the body afterward? There are no right or wrong answers. Each situation is different. Most owners do *not* want to be with the animal during euthanasia. Providing there is a trusting relationship with your veterinarian, this is usually best. Most owners want to remember their pet as they were in life, not in death. A caring and sensitive veterinary staff will understand everyone has different needs, and every attempt should be made to meet those needs.

Options for the Body

What options are there regarding care of the body, if a pet should die? Many people are not aware of the choices available to them.

Some owners want to bury the pet in their backyard. However, this is not legal in many areas. If it is legal in your community, make certain the grave is dug deep enough to prevent other animals from disturbing it.

Cremation is another very accepted option. Private pet crematoria, cemeteries, and some veterinary clinics have the ability to cremate an animal. The body is turned into "cremains" (not really ashes), by heat approaching 2,500°F. The term "cremains" is preferred because ashes are thought of as powdery. "Cremains" still have bone fragments in them and are a different consistency from ashes. The "cremains" can then be scattered, buried or placed in an urn for safekeeping. Pet cemeteries may even offer mausoleums where the "cremains" can be interred.

Burial at a pet cemetery is a third option. These areas are specifically zoned for burial of pets. They provide a quiet, beautiful surrounding to help ease the loss and emptiness. Since there are many options to chose from, costs vary widely. The process can be as simple or as elaborate as personal preferences dictate. Any choice made is perfectly acceptable. After visiting the cemetery, it will be readily apparent that you are not alone in your feelings for a pet.

Your final option is to leave the body at the veterinary hospital. This option is the one most frequently selected. Every clinic is a little different, but most will have a service pick up the bodies and cremate them. The animals are not cremated individually. The remains will be returned to the earth. It is okay to ask how the clinic handles this. The staff should also be prepared to discuss it.

Easing the Pain: Support Groups and Books

Talking about your pet, and the loss felt, can be the quickest way to lessen the hurt and "numbness." Choose appropriate people to talk with. No one wants to hear "It was only a pet!" Your veterinarian or their staff may be the best source to assist with this. Remember, these professionals also love animals or they wouldn't be in this field. They have dealt with this type of problem many times, both with their own animals and their clients'. As hard as it is to talk about the death of a pet, the more it is done, the easier it will be.

There are also pet loss support groups run by qualified individuals with psychology backgrounds. Many pet owners feel they could not have handled it on their own. Without the support group, they would have been lost. It is very comforting to know others have gone through similar circumstances. To locate such a group, contact your veterinarian or local veterinary association.

As previously mentioned, there are many great books on the subject of pet loss. Some of these are listed in the Bibliography. Reading can help to better understand and ease the hurt. This can be extremely important if children are involved. There are also wonderful books written especially for children. For them, these books can help make sense of what has happened to their pet.

As strange as it may seem, the final suggestion can sometimes be the best. Get a new pet. For some people it is better to work through the grieving process *before* a new pet is introduced. For others a new pet will help them to work through the process much more quickly.

There is *no* disrespect shown to your previous pet by getting a new family member. The intent is not to replace the "hole in your heart," just to fill up another one! Turning your mind to life and renewal can really help ease the emptiness. Think of this as a memorial to your "old friend," since the love and companionship it spoiled you with was so special.

Don't be surprised if other pets in the family react to the loss as well. There is plenty of evidence to suggest that animals mourn the loss of other animals.

Therefore, be a source of consolation for the other pets in the family. Spend time with them to help ease their loss too. Lack of appetite, incessant vocalization, poor ''potty'' habits and other abnormal behaviors may begin. Encourage interaction between family members and existing pets. It will make everyone feel better.

Despite the pain and sadness occurring ''when the bond is broken,'' the incredible joy that pets bring to our lives makes us willing to go through it again and again.

References

APPENDIX A

Everything You Always Wanted to Know About . . . : A Species Guide

by Betty Byers Schmidt

T HE FOLLOWING INFORMATION will provide a brief introduction to the background, basic requirements and personality of selected, popular pet birds.

The species are arranged according to their origin in their native habitat.

Parrots of the Americas

Parrots of Africa and Asia

Parrots of the South Pacific

Other Pet Birds

Parrots of the Americas

THESE PARROTS vary in size from the largest Hyacinthine Macaw (*Anodorhynchus hycinthinus*) at approximately 40 inches long to the 4½ inch Spectacled Parrotlet (*Forpus conspicillatus*). Most parrots are various shades of green, blue, red, yellow, and orange. Approximately 470 species of parrots live in the Americas.

The only native North American parrot, the Carolina Parakeet (*Conuropsis Carolinensis*) became extinct in 1918 because of the feather trade, farmers and colonization that diminished their native habitat. Numerous other parrots of the Americas are becoming endangered through trapping and habitat destruction.

MACAWS

Common name:	Macaw
Scientific names:	*Ara, Anodorhynchus, cyanopsitta*
Native habitat:	Mexico, Central and South America
Coloration:	Varies with the different species
Length:	12 inches to 40 inches from head to tip of tail.
Life span:	25 to 50 years or more.
Age at maturity:	Approximately 2 years for smaller macaws, about 5 years for larger species
Sex determination:	No visible characteristics

Cage requirements:	18″L × 24″H × 18″W for the small macaws, 5′L × 5′H × 3′W for the larger macaws; Cages should be constructed of strong material such as wrought iron or heavy gauge wire.
Nutritional requirements:	Food offered should be similar to that of other parrots

The best known and most often photographed varieties are the scarlet, blue and gold, and military macaws. These large birds do require extra attention, but at the same time give back tremendous amounts of affection. Their vocabulary can become extensive, and tricks are often easily learned. Because of their bulk and large stature, they seem to prefer to climb and walk, rather than fly around in small areas. Their powerful beaks can easily crack a macadamia or Brazil nut. The smaller macaws require less attention, make good pets and can also learn to talk and do tricks. All macaws like to chew, so supply them with plenty of wood and natural branches. Most macaws characteristically have a large, sometimes featherless skin patch around their eyes extending to their upper beak.

Macaw Varieties

Scarlet: *(Ara macao)*	These intelligent, beautiful birds can be affectionate to their owners. They can also be unpredictable in their behavior at times. DESCRIPTION: They are a brilliant scarlet at the head, chest and wing areas. Blue, yellow, green and orange are the other colors on the wings. Some of their red tail feathers can be as long as 30 inches. The upper beak is horn-colored, and the lower beak is almost black. Length from head to the tip of the tail can be up to 36 inches. Their weight can be over 2 pounds.
Blue-and-gold: *(A. ararauna)* 	These birds, like the scarlet macaw, are intelligent and can be very affectionate. They are also known to be mischievous. DESCRIPTION: The forehead is green while the upper part of the body, wings and tail are a rich blue. From the side of the neck down to the front of the lower body, the feathers are a golden yellow. There is a black ''bib'' of feathers just below the lower beak. Both the upper and lower beak is black. They can be 34 inches long and weigh about 2 pounds.

270

Green-winged:
(A. chloroptera)

They have a pleasing and gentle personality.
DESCRIPTION: These birds are similar to the scarlet macaw, except they are stockier and have a larger head and beak. There are lines of red feathers circling both eyes and green feathers on the middle portion of the wing.

Hyacinth:
(A. hyacinthinus)

These macaws are not commonly found as pets because they are difficult to obtain and expensive. They can be very affectionate and gentle.
DESCRIPTION: They have an oversized and powerful black beak and a beautiful cobalt blue body, wings and tail. There is some yellow skin surrounding the eyes and lower beak. Their overall length is 40 inches and weight can be close to 3 pounds.

Noble:
(A. nobilis)

They are the smallest and least colorful of all the macaws. However, they have wonderful personalities. They can learn words and phrases in a short time. The noble can be a loving and gentle bird.
DESCRIPTION: These macaws are almost all green, with some blue in the crown and some red at the bend of the wing. Some will have an all black beak, while other subspecies will have a silvery horn-colored upper beak. They have dark gray feet and can be 12 inches long and weigh around 6 ounces.

Other Varieties: There are other types of macaws that make very good pets. They are the the mid-size military (*A. militaris*), yellow-collared (*A. auriocollis*) and the small severe (*A. severa*).

CONURES

Common name:	Conure
Scientific names:	*Aratinga, Pyrrhura*, etc.
Native habitat:	Central and South America
Coloration:	Most are green, with various shades of blue, red, orange, yellow, and black.
Length:	9 to 21 inches from head to tip of tail

Life span:	10 to 35 years or more
Age at maturity:	Depending on variety, from 1 to 3 years
Sex determination:	No visible characteristics
Cage requirements:	18″L × 18″H × 18″W, depending on size of bird
Nutritional requirements:	Food offered should be similar to that of other parrots.

Conures are intelligent birds, with a reputation for being noisy and destructive. However, this does not apply to all individuals. Both sexes are known to talk and perform tricks, and are loving companions when acquired at a young age or if they were hand-fed. Conures are known as "miniature macaws" because of their strong resemblance to these larger birds.

Conure Varieties

Janday:
(A. jandaya)

These birds can be noisy, but they are also extremely affectionate. When gently scratched, their feathers fluff up to make them resemble little "fluff balls."
DESCRIPTION: This bird has a yellow neck, head, and chest. There can be some orange in the yellow. Some flight and tail feathers are blue, while the chest feathers are orange. The rest of the body is green. They are about 10 inches long from the top of the head to the tip of the tail.

Nanday:
(N. nendayus)

This variety is easy to obtain and inexpensive. Although they are not known for their talking ability, their personality is similar to the janday. They can be noisy.
DESCRIPTION: The beak and head is black while the upper chest is blue. Some parts of the wing and tail feathers are blue with some green. The body is green with red thighs.

Halfmoon:
(A. canicularis)

This little conure is smart, will talk and do some tricks. It is sometimes called a "dwarf parrot" and is not usually expensive. It can be affectionate but noisy at times.
DESCRIPTION: They are about 9 inches long and mostly green in color. There is a small amount of orange feathering above the nose. The upper part of the beak is a horn color while the lower beak is black.

Cherry head: *(A. erythrogenus)*	If obtained at an early age it can make a charming pet. Both male and female can talk and learn a few tricks. These birds are not usually expensive, but they are also not always available. DESCRIPTION: With an oversized, horn-colored beak, a large almost all-red head, a green bulky body and slender tail, this conure appears top heavy. It measures about 13 inches long from the head to the tip of the tail. Immature birds have no red on the head.

Other Conure Varieties

There are numerous varieties of medium-to small-size conures from the Americas. Some of the more common varieties include:

Pyrrhura family:	Most of these birds are 9 inches to 12 inches long, such as the red-bellied conure (*P. frontalis*), pearly conure (*P. lepida*), and green-cheeked conure (*P. molinae*). They make good pets, and are not known for their talking ability.
Enicognathus family:	These birds range in size from 12 to 16 inches long. They can become good talkers and can be noisy at times. The two species of birds in this family are the austral conure (*E. ferruginea*) and the slender-billed conure (*E. leptorhynchus*).
Cyanoliseus:	This large (17- to 20-inch) course is commonly called the Patagonian conure (*C. patagonus*). They can learn to talk and can be noisy at times.

AMAZONS

Common name:	Amazon
Scientific name:	*Amazona*
Native habitat:	From Mexico, south through Central and South America
Coloration:	Almost all are green with various shades of red, orange, yellow, blue and sometimes white.

273

Length:	From 10 inches to 18 inches long
Life span:	25 to 50 years or more
Age at maturity:	2 years or more, depending on variety.
Sex determination:	Most have no visible characteristics.
Cage requirements:	18″L × 24″H × 18″W (minimum)
Nutritional requirements:	Food offered should be similar to that of other parrots.

Amazons are the most popular of the larger pet birds. They are usually very friendly and loving, especially if purchased young. Older Amazons can be difficult to tame. Amazons can be playful, so be sure to supply lots of toys for their enjoyment. Unfortunately, some Amazons can be noisy during the early morning and evening hours

Amazon Varieties

Yellow nape:
(A. auropalliata)

This bird is capable of learning a large vocabulary and is usually curious and playful. During the breeding season, some males are known to become moody and may not talk even though there is no female present.
DESCRIPTION: They are almost all green, except for some yellow feathers at the nape and maybe above the nostrils. The feet are dark gray and the beak is black. They may range in size from 12 inches to 15 inches long.

Double yellow head:
(A. ochrocephala)

The yellow head is the most common Amazon in the United States. They can be good talkers, playful and affectionate.
DESCRIPTION: The most striking feature of this bird is the amount of yellow on its head at maturity. There are varying amounts of yellow and red-orange at the bend of the wing, and the thighs can have some amounts of yellow. The rest of this 13- to 15-inch body and tail is green. There are many varieties or subspecies.

Blue-fronted:
(A. aestiva)

The blue-fronted Amazon can acquire an extensive vocabulary. It can be playful, but noisy at times.
DESCRIPTION: The species has a blue forehead and lores. Parts of the cheeks, crown and sometimes the upper breast are yellow.

The thighs are yellow and the bend of the wings have yellow and red. The rest of the 13- to 15-inch body and tail is green.

Spectacled:
(A. albifrons)

Although this is the smallest Amazon, it can be playful and affectionate and can talk. It does not develop an extensive vocabulary. DESCRIPTION: This species has a red, white and blue head coloration. Males will have red in their flight feathers, while the females may have little or no red at all. The rest of this 10-inch bird is green.

Mexican red-head:
(A. viridigenalis)

This is another popular Amazon species. Although they are not known as good talkers, they are affectionate and playful. DESCRIPTION: The color of the lores, crown and forehead is a deep scarlet. There is some blue-lilac behind the eyes, and the cheek feathers are an iridescent light green. The rest of the body is green, and the beak is horn colored. This Amazon is about 13 inches long from the head to the tip of the tail.

Other Varieties:

The lilac-crowned Amazon *(A. finschi)*, orange-winged Amazon *(A. amazonica)* and the red-lored Amazon *(A. a. autumalis)* will also make wonderful pets. They can learn to talk, and at times can be noisy.

PIONUS

Common name:	Pionus
Scientific name:	*Pionus*
Native habitat:	Central through South America.
Coloration:	Almost all are green, with various shades of yellow, blue, white, pink and brown. All have red tail feathers near vent.
Length:	9 to 12 inches long
Life span:	25 to 50 years
Age at maturity:	18 months to 3 years
Sex determination:	No visible characteristics.
Cage requirements:	18"L × 18"H × 18"W (minimum).

> *Nutritional requirements:* Food offered should be similar to that of other parrots.

The *Pionus* family of birds is usually quiet and inquisitive. They can have an extensive vocabulary. These birds are the "perfect" apartment bird.

Pionus Varieties

Maximilian: *(P. maximiliani)*	These birds seem to have one of the nicest personalities and some will talk some. DESCRIPTION: They have a dull purple bib around the neck area. There is a slight blue above the nose, and the rest of the bird is mostly dull green with some brown areas. They are about 11 inches long.
Blue-headed: *(P. menstruus)*	This variety is probably the most common. They make wonderful pets and can learn to talk. DESCRIPTION: This 11-inch-long bird has a dark gray beak with small reddish patches on both sides of the upper beak. The head, neck and upper chest are a beautiful color of blue. There is a small reddish patch at the throat area. Green is the dominant color of the body, with some brown tinting and, of course, red tail feathers at the vent area.

Other South American Varieties

The following birds are popular and less expensive, will talk or mimic and do some tricks.

Gray-cheeked parakeet: *(Brotogeris pyrrhopterus)*	These small, inexpensive birds are extremely popular. Although they are not known for their talking ability, they do mimic sounds of other birds. They are solidly built, 8-inch birds that weigh about 2 ounces.
Canary-winged parakeet: *(B. v. chiriri)*	This bird is often called a "pocket parrot" because of its length (8 inches). They are generally poor talkers but can learn to perform tricks.
Spectacled parrotlet: *(Forpus conspicillatus)*	This tiny (5-inch) bird is very intelligent. The male will have some blue feathering around the eye and a gray-blue feathering at the chest. The female is all green.

Black-headed caique:
(Pionite melanocephala)

These birds are true clowns and can talk. They will provide hours of pleasure. The head is black, the throat, nape and thighs are orange and the chest and lower belly and white, while the wings are green.

Parrots of Africa
and Asia

T HE FIRST WRITTEN RECORD of parrots was in 327 B.C. by the Greek sailor Oneskritos. Alexander the Great had marched his army toward India, and on their return home, a few "Indian ringnecked" parakeets were brought back with them. Hence, the name Alexandrine parakeet *(Psittacula eupatria)*. Of the approximate 117 species in this category, the dull-gray-colored greater vasa *(Coracopsis vasa)* from Africa is the largest at 20 inches long. The smallest is the orange-fronted parakeet *(Loriculus aurantifrons)* at 4 inches from New Guinea.

AFRICAN GREYS

Common name:	African Grey
Scientific name:	*Psittacus erithacus*
Native habitat:	Various countries in central Africa (such as Kenya, Uganda, Liberia and some islands off west coast of Africa)
Coloration:	Various shades of pastel gray feathers cover body; beak and feet are black, tail feathers bright red or maroon.
Length:	11 inches to 13½ inches from head to tip of tail

Life span:	40 years or more
Age at maturity:	About 3 years
Sex determination:	No visible characteristics
Cage requirements:	18″L × 24″H × 18″W (minimum)
Nutritional requirements:	Food offered should be similar to that of other parrots.

According to the *Guiness Book of World Records*, ''Prudle,'' a male African Grey, was reported to have a vocabulary of nearly a thousand words. These birds are generally considered to be the best talking parrots. They also have the unique ability to mimic such sounds as the doorbell, telephone, microwave, beepers, dripping faucet or animal sounds. Hand-raised Greys can begin to talk as young as 7 months old. Sometimes these birds prefer only one person. They make an enjoyable ''jungle sound'' when relaxed. When frightened, they produce a relentless ''growl.'' Both the maroon-tailed and the red-tailed are equal in their ability to be good pets and talkers.

African Grey Varieties

Red-tailed Grey:
(P. erithacus,
P. princeps)

DESCRIPTION: They will vary in shades of gray and in size from 12 inches to 14 inches long. Mature birds have a bright red tail, while the young birds have a blackish-red tail. Both the upper and lower beak is black, and the feet can be dark charcoal.

Timneh:
(P. timneh)

DESCRIPTION: It is about 12 inches long, with a maroon-colored tail and a fleshy-pink color on the upper beak.

LOVEBIRDS

Common name:	Lovebird
Scientific name:	*Agapornis*
Native habitat:	All species are from countries extending from central through southern Africa and some islands off its western coast.

279

Coloration:	Color varies with species. All have green feathering with various shades of red, blue, black, yellow, or gray in the head or tail areas.
Length:	5 inches to 7 inches long from head to tip of tail
Life span:	Approximately 10 to 15 years
Age at maturity:	8 to 12 months
Sex determination:	No visible characteristics
Cage requirements:	12″L × 12″H × 12″W (minimum)
Nutritional requirements:	Food offered should be similar to that of other smaller parrots

Although lovebirds can be active and mischievous, they can also be loving pets. Some like to chew on the cage paper and even hide under it. They are hardy, inexpensive birds, and some have been known to talk. It is not uncommon to teach the pet lovebird a few tricks, such as pushing a miniature baby carriage, jumping through hoops, lying on its back or standing on its head. It is not necessary to keep lovebirds in pairs. Single birds will be more affectionate and less noisy.

Lovebird Varieties

Peach-face:
(A. rosieicollis)

This bird is probably the most popular and most quarrelsome of all the lovebirds. They are smart and will learn tricks easily.
DESCRIPTION: They are one of the largest of the lovebirds at 6½ inches long. The face and upper breast are rose-pink, the rump a bright blue, the tail banded with orange and black; the rest of the body is green.

Masked:
(A. personata)

This bird is pleasing to look at and has a gentle personality.
DESCRIPTION: As the name indicates, it has a brownish-black head, a bright red beak and a white ring of bare skin around the eyes. There is some blue in the tail and flight feathers, while the rest of the body is yellow-green.

Fischer:
(A. fischeri)

These birds generally have a pleasing personality. They are usually not aggressive and learn to do tricks easily.

DESCRIPTION: They are mostly green, with some yellow on the underparts. The Fischers have a bright red beak with an orange head. The rump is a dusky blue, and there is some blue in the flight and tail feathers. Total length is about 5½ inches long.

Other African Varieties

The following birds have some characteristics that make them an ideal pet. They are small, can talk, are not usually noisy and can learn to perform tricks. Only recently has there been an active interest in breeding these birds. They are now more readily available and less expensive than many of the other more popular pet birds.

Senegal: *(P. senegalus)*	These 9-inch birds have a brown head, some green starting at the throat area and extending down to their chest area. Below this the color becomes an orange-yellow. The wings and back areas are green. They have an almost black beak and black feet.
Meyer's: *(P. meyeri)*	This bird is primarily brown with a bluish-green lower chest, and some yellow at the bend of the wing and top of the head.
Red-bellied: *(P. rufiventris)*	The sexes are differently colored. The male's chest is orange with a small orange band on the forehead. The thighs are green, while the rest of the bird is brown. The female has a greenish chest. They are 9 inches long.
Brown-headed: *(P. cyptoxanthus)*	As the name indicates, this 9-inch bird has a brown head and the rest of the body is mostly green.

INDIAN RING-NECK PARAKEETS

Common names:	Alexandrine, Indian ring-neck, Slaty-headed parakeet, blossom-head, plum-head, moustache, and others
Scientific name:	*Psittacula*
Native habitat:	India, Afghanistan, Burma, Thailand, Indochina, Java, Bali, etc.
Coloration:	Almost all are green, with different colors at head, neck and beak areas.

Length:	11½ inches to 23 inches long from head to tip of tail
Life span:	15 to 30 years or more
Age at maturity:	18 months and more
Sex determination:	For most of these species of birds, sexes can be determined by coloration at 18 months of age and older. Males will have more coloration in head and neck areas.
Cage requirements:	Will vary with size of bird because of their long tails; 18"L × 18"W × 18"H for the smaller ones.
Nutritional requirements:	Food offered should be similar to that of other parrots.

Ring-necks are intelligent birds. They can learn to talk and perform a few tricks. These birds are hardy and can survive rather harsh weather conditions when kept in an outdoor cage. Some beautiful color mutations have been seen in the Indian-ringneck variety, such as the yellow lutino, blue, turquoise and albino.

Alexandrine: *(P. eupatria)*	They are very intelligent and have been known to make good pets for 25 years or more. DESCRIPTION: At 24 inches long, this bird appears to have an oversized red beak. These birds are mostly green with a red patch on the wing. Mature males will have a black and pink band surrounding the neck area.
Indian-ringneck: *(P. manillensis)*	These birds can learn to talk and perform tricks. They are fond of playing with toys. DESCRIPTION: They are all green except for the beak, which is red. Mature males will have a pink and black ring around the neck, usually starting at 18 months of age. These birds are approximately 18 inches long. There is another variety called the African Ringneck (*P. k. kremeri*) that is smaller at 15 inches long and has a black lower beak.
Moustache: *(P. alexandri)*	Some learn to talk and learn to perform tricks. DESCRIPTION: This almost all green bird has a pinkish upper chest, a blue-gray head, and a thick band of black extending from the lower beak to just under the ear. Some of

the varieties have a pink upper beak and a lower beak black, while some others have a red upper and lower back.

Plum-headed:
(P. cyanocephala)

This variety is less common than the others. They can learn to talk and perform tricks. DESCRIPTION: At 13 inches long, this almost all green bird has a bluish-purple head, narrow black color around the neck, an orange upper beak and black lower beak. Females usually have a duller head color.

Parrots of the
South Pacific

T HE SOUTH PACIFIC has about 189 species of parrots. It is also home to the greatest variety of birds. One parrot from New Zealand, the kakapo (*Strigops habroptilus*) and the shy ground parrot (*Geopsittacus occidentalis*) from Australia are nocturnal and do not fly. The Papuan lory (*Charmosyna papou*) makes its home at over 11,000 feet in altitude, while the kea (*Nestor notabilis*) can be seen playing in the snow in New Zealand. Most of the lory and lorikeet family eat nectar, fruits and pollen, while the glossy black cockatoo (*Calyptorhynchus latami*) from southeastern Australia usually eats only small seeds from the cones of a tree called casuarina.

COCKATOOS

Common name:	Cockatoo
Scientific names:	*Cacatua, Probasciger, Calyptorhynchus, Callocephalon* and *Eolophus*
Native habitat:	Australia, New Guinea, Indonesia, Moluccas and Phillipines
Coloration:	Best-known cockatoos are white, with various shades of yellow, pink or orange, usually in the crest. Other less common birds can be various shades of black and gray,

with colors of pink, red, yellow and white either in body, head, or tail feathers.

Length:	12 inches to 28 inches from head to tip of tail
Life span:	30 years and longer.*
Age at maturity:	2 years or more.
Sex determination:	Eye color has been used for sex determination; however, it is not always accurate. Other methods must be used.
Cage requirements:	2'L × 3'H × 2'W (minimum).
Nutritional requirements:	Food offered should be similar to that of other parrots.

If obtained either very young or if they were hand-fed, these birds make exceptionally loving pets. Some males can be noisy, especially during the early morning and evening hours. Almost all cockatoos are natural chewers; therefore, they should be given branches or strips of wood to satisfy this habit. Some birds can become attached to one member of the family and no other. They can be mischievous one minute and sedate the next. All cockatoos are good fliers, so clipping their flight feathers is a good idea. The white cockatoos produce a fine powdery dust to which some people may be allergic. Frequent misting of the feathers on warm days will help keep this dust to a minimum. The uplifting of their crest feathers is a behavioral display used when frightened, happy or just seeking a little attention. Most of the cockatoos can be moderate talkers.

Greater sulphur-crested: *(C. galerita)*	The TV show "Baretta" with Fred the Cockatoo (a *Triton C. g. triton* subspecies) popularized this type of bird. They have a warm, friendly nature. Although they can be noisy at times, this is usually overshadowed by the devotion they show to their owners.
	DESCRIPTION: At 19 inches long, these are one of the largest white cockatoos. The yellow crest feathers go up and forward when raised. There is some yellow in the cheek patches, under the tail and wing. The skin around the eyes is white, but pale blue in the triton. The beak is black while the feet are dark gray.

---

*According to Forshaw in *Parrots of the World*, a little corella (*Cacatua sanguinea*) was banded as an adult on February 16, 1901, and died accidentally on January 12, 1972.

Umbrella:
(C. alba)

The umbrella can learn to talk, but can be noisy at times. Some are more playful and affectionate, while others are sedate.

DESCRIPTION: They have long, broad white crest feathers that when raised resemble an umbrella, and the feathers pointing backward. Almost all of the body is white with some dull yellow on the undersides of the tail and wings. *C. alba* has a black beak and dark gray feet.

Moluccan:
(C. moluccensis)

Although this bird can be noisy, it is usually gentle and loving. It can learn to talk, and perform a few tricks. This is probably the most beautiful of the white cockatoos.

DESCRIPTION: The crest is similar to the umbrella, except the feathers are salmon pink in color. The undersides of the tail feathers are pale orange, while the undersides of the wings are salmon. Various shades of pink-white to a deeper pink are on the chest and belly areas. The beak and feet are almost black on this 20-inch-long bird.

Bare-eyed:
(C. sanguinea)

This is a hardy, playful and very active cockatoo. They can develop a moderate vocabulary and even learn a few tricks.

DESCRIPTION: This 16 inch bird is almost all white, except for the undersides of the tail and wings, which are yellow. There is a slight salmon-pink color between the eyes and the horn-colored beak. The feet are dark gray. A blue-gray skin patch surrounds the eye. The patch below the eye may seem "puffy," but this is normal.

LORIES AND LORIKEETS

Common names:

Lory, Lorikeet

Scientific names:

Chalcopsitta, Pseudoes, Lorius trichoglossus, Lorius, Vini, Phigys, Glossopsitta, Charmosyna, Eos oreopsittacus, Neopsittacus

Native habitat:

Australia, New Guinea, Solomon Islands, Indonesia, Celebes and other parts of the South Pacific

Coloration:	Varies with each species
Length:	Lories can be from 9½ to 13 inches long, while lorikeets can be from 6 inches to 11 inches long
Life span:	15 or more years, depending on variety
Age at maturity:	1 to 2 years
Sex determination:	No visible characteristics
Nutritional requirements:	Diet very specialized

Lories have rounded tails, while lorikeets have pointed tails. They occur in a wide range of colors, and some species even appear iridescent. Because of their comical and playful behavior, they are considered by many as the "clowns" of the parrot world. They usually tame easily and seek the company of their owners. One of the major disadvantages of keeping these birds as pets is their tendency to squirt their droppings out of their cage and dirty their surrounding area. They have a brushlike tongue adapted for their natural diet of nectar, pollen, plant buds and insects. They frequently bathe and preen themselves.

Lory and Lorikeet Varieties

Blue Mountain lorikeet:
(T. moluccanus)

This is the most common of the lories. They can become very good companions because of their cheerful, comical and affectionate personality.

DESCRIPTION: The head is a rich violet-blue and the beak is a deep orange. The upper breast is scarlet with some red and yellow, while the lower body resembles the head. Usually, there is a small yellow-green collar on the front of the neck. The back, tail and wings are various shades of green. There are approximately twenty-one different subspecies in this family, each varying in coloration. They are about 12 inches long.

Blue-streaked lory:
(E. reticulata)

They make good pets because they are cheerful and playful.

DESCRIPTION: They have a purple-blue streak extending from the corner of the eye to the upper neck area. There is a small amount of black and red in the wings; the tail is black. The rest of the body is red, and the beak is red-orange. They are about 12 inches long.

COCKATIELS

Common name:	Cockatiel
Scientific name:	*Nymphicus hollandicus*
Native habitat:	Australia
Coloration:	In its natural habitat, the wild cockatiel is predominantly gray.
Length:	10 to 13 inches long from top of crest to tip of tail
Life span:	15 to 25 years
Age at maturity:	7 months to 1 year
Sex determination:	At maturity, there are usually color differences between sexes.
Cage requirements:	18″L × 18″H × 18″W (minimum)
Nutritional requirements:	Food offered should be similar to that of other parrots.

Cacatelho is a Portugese word meaning "little cockatoo." This is probably where the name "cockatiel" originated. In their native Australia, they are called quarrion and are nomadic. The cockatiel is a gentle and docile little bird. Males can become good talkers and whistlers but are more independent. Some females have been known to talk and are more loving and quiet. Both sexes make wonderful pets.

We may never see a blue or green cockatiel. To create various colors, most birds have two basic pigments: yellow and black. The yellow pigment produces shades of yellow through red. The black pigment produces dull shades of yellow through browns to black. The cockatiel differs from other birds in its feather pigments. It lacks the modifiers of black pigments to produce blue coloration and yellow pigments for green coloration. *All* varieties have the same personality and temperament.

Cockatiel Varieties

Normal gray:	Males are various shades of gray with orange cheek patches and some white on the wings. The head is yellow and white, including some of the crest feathers. Females tend to have gray heads but retain the orange cheek patches. The underside of their wings and tails have either a faint yellow spotting or creamy yellow barring. All youngsters look like the female until their first molt at about seven months of age.

Lutino:

These birds are all white; but some may have a yellow "wash." Both male and female have the orange cheek patches. The beaks and feet are horn colored and the eyes are a dark red. In a mature bird, the male will be all white on the underside of the wings and tail. The female will have a faint yellow barring on these areas.

Pearl:

The ends of almost all of the feathers are scalloped in white or yellow. Males will lose some of this scalloping after their first molt. By the time males are 18 months old they look like a normal gray cockatiel.

Pied:

These cockatiels are mottled with spots. Pieds with more white feathering are called heavy pieds while the ones with more gray feathers are called light pieds. These can be the hardest to sex because sometimes there is no difference in the coloring under the wing.

Cinnamon:

These birds are a light silvery-gray. Males usually have lighter facial areas.

Fallow:

These are the same as cinnamons, but with red eyes.

Charcoal:

They can also be called white faced, and are the newest variety to be developed. In both sexes the orange cheek patches are absent. The bird is a dull-colored charcoal with an all-white wing patch, since there are no yellow pigments. The males have an all-white face when mature.

BUDGERIGARS

Common name:

"Budgie" or parakeet

Scientific name:

Melopsitticus undulatus

Native habitat:	Australia
Coloration:	Originally green with black barrings on wings and back
Length:	7 inches from head to tip of tail
Life span:	8 to 15 years
Age at maturity:	6 to 8 months
Sex determination:	At about 4 months of age, cere becomes blue in male and brown or tan in hen.
Cage requirements:	12″L × 12″H × 14″W (minimum).
Nutritional requirements:	Food offered should be similar to that of other smaller parrots.

The "budgie" is the most common and least expensive pet bird. They are hardy, not noisy, and often will talk. Some males are known to have a large vocabulary and whistle short tunes. Occasionally, "English budgies" are available in pet stores. These birds are larger and also make very good pets. In their native Australia, "budgies" are a migratory species and are good fliers. There are many color variations from which to choose. It is believed that John Gould was the first to bring the "budgie" to England, in the 1800s.

The "budgie" was the first popular pet bird in the United States and remains a great favorite in America and the world over. *The Guinness Book of World Records* stated that in 1958 a "budgie" named Sparkie Williams won a talking contest in England. Before Sparkie died, he could say 531 words and 383 sentences.

Other South Pacific Parrots

Eclectus parrot: *(Eclectus roratus)*	At one time, many people thought this bird was two different species. This is because the males and females are colored differently. They can be good talkers. DESCRIPTION: Males are mostly all green, except the feathers on the chest area just under the wings are red and the upper beak is yellow-orange, while the lower beak is black. The females have a mostly bright red

head and chest area, some red on the wings, with a blue lower body and a black beak. These birds make wonderful, affectionate pets and will learn to talk. They are from 12 to 14 inches long.

Australian king parakeet: *(A. s. scapularis)*	These birds can make good pets and can even talk a little. DESCRIPTION: This bird does not acquire its adult plumage until its third year. The male's head, neck and chest areas are red. It has a blue rump, and most of the rest of the bird is green. The female's head, neck and chest areas are green.
Grass parakeets: *(Neophema)*	These 8- to 10-inch birds are colorful and quiet. They usually do not make good pets.
Rosellas: *(Platycercus)*	This colorful group of birds can be quiet, affectionate and also aggressive at times. They range in size from 10 inches to 13 inches long.

CANARIES

Common name:	Canary
Scientific name:	*Serinus canarius*
Native habitat:	Canary Islands, Madeira and the Azores
Coloration:	Originally, all green with some yellow-brown. Today, various shades or combinations of brown, orange, yellow, white, blue and red.
Length:	4½ to 7 inches long from head to tip of tail
Life span:	5 to 15 years.
Age at maturity:	1 year
Sex determination:	Males have a definite "song," and during breeding season, vent area in male becomes enlarged and prominent. Females rarely sing, and their vent area becomes only slightly prominent.
Cage requirements:	12″L × 12″H × 10″W (minimum).
Nutritional requirements:	Food offered should be similar to that of other small birds.

Canary Varieties

American singer:

As the name implies, this variety was developed here in the late 1930s. It is a cross between a *Roller* and a *border fancy*. The males are the most popular canary because of their soft, harmonious song.

DESCRIPTION: At 5½ inches long from beak to the tip of the tail, this variety has a compact, rounded appearance.

Border fancy:

The border canary is the ideal type for the beginning breeder. It probably originated in England in the early 1800s.

DESCRIPTION: This canary is compact, slender, and has a clean-cut look. They are 5½ inches long from the head to the tip of the tail. They can be all yellow, all brown, or a combination of the two.

Red factor:

This variety was originally obtained by crossing the wild canary with a brilliant vermillion Venezulean hooded siskin. In order to further enhance the red coloring, special diets can be fed.

DESCRIPTION: Since some are color-fed, there can be a variety of shades such as a frosted red, pastel pink, red-orange, rose-ivory, etc. They are about 6½ inches long from the head to the tip of the tail.

Norwich:

It is generally accepted that this type was established in the 1600s in Norwich, England. They have a sturdy build and are hardy. Among canary fanciers they have a reputation as being rather clumsy.

DESCRIPTION: Its larger size and girth have earned it the nickname "the John Bull of the canary world." They are 6½ inches long from head to the tip of the tail. Some can be color-fed, making numerous shades possible.

FINCHES

Common name: Finch

Scientific names: *Chloebia, Poephila, Zonaeginthus, Stizopt-*

era, *Lonchura, Amadina, Cardeuelis* and other genera.

Native habitat:	Found in most areas of the world
Coloration:	Varies with species
Length:	Body is 3 to 8 inches long; tail can be as long as 16 inches, such as seen in the giant whydah.
Life span:	About 5 years, depending on the variety
Age at maturity:	Over two months.
Sex determination:	Male is usually brighter colored or differently colored than female. In some varieties, however, no color differences exist.
Cage requirements:	The larger the cage the better. For a single pair, ideal size would be at least 36"L × 14"H × 10"W.
Nutritional requirements:	Food offered should be similar to that of other small birds.

These popular little birds are easy to maintain and are hardy. They do not demand a great deal of attention, but it's best to buy two birds, because they like company. Some do have a pleasing "melody," while other vocalize with a "beeping" call. There is a tremendous variety of colors, shapes and sizes. Each species has its own personality, and some can even become finger-trained.

Finch Varieties

Zebra finch: *(P. guttata)*	These birds are perky, hardy and pretentious. They make high-pitched spurts of noise. They are the most popular of all the finches. Description: The male has a white mask surrounded by a narrow black band below the eye; the tail is black-barred with white; the cheeks are a pale chestnut. The underparts are white with cinnamon flanks and white spots; the upper parts are ash gray, the beak orange, the feet salmon. The female is gray on the crown; plain buff below with a black and white barred rail, and is brown on the upper parts. Their length is 4 to 4½ inches long from head to tip of tail.
Society finch: *(P. domestica)*	They have a squeaky little "melody" and will socialize with other varieties because

they have a friendly nature. This variety is believed to have resulted from a cross between the striated and sharp-tailed finches bred by the Chinese centuries ago.

DESCRIPTION: The sexes are alike. They are found in varying shades of brown, some with white or cinnamon. Their length is 4 to 4½ inches long from head to tip of tail.

Lady Gouldian:
(C. gouldiae)

This finch is often called the most beautiful bird in the world. They can also be friendly. Since they come from a warm climate in Australia, it is important to keep them warm and dry during the winter months.

DESCRIPTION: The top and sides of the head are scarlet with a fine black band in both sexes; behind the band at the nape is a broader band of turquoise. Chin and throat are black; breast is a deep purple; underparts are golden. Back and wings are green, beak white with a red tip, and the feet are pink. The female has a lilac chest. Their length is 5 to 5½ inches long from head to tip of the tail.

Paradise whydah:
(S. paradisaea)

This graceful bird has a gentle disposition. It is hardy, lives long and gets along well with other finches. A larger cage is needed to accommodate its long tail.

DESCRIPTION: During the breeding season, the male's underparts are white; the head is black; the chest is chestnut, and this color extends out to the nape, wings and tail. The beak is black and the long tail, which is seen only in males, is 6 to 14 inches long. The female is buff on the underparts and brown-streaked along the lower back, and a black line extends along the side of the crown and behind the eye. When not in breeding plumage, the male usually resembles the female. The body length is 6 inches.

I would like to thank Rosemary Low, Tony Silva, Wayne Schulenburg, Mary and Joe Lannom and especially my birds, who have taught me to respect their intelligence, beauty and unpredictability.

Appendix B

Bird Breeding

Before Getting Started . . .

by Betty Byers Schmidt

Quick PROFITS AND MINIMAL TIME—these are two of the most common misconceptions many people have about breeding birds. If this was as easy as breeding dogs and cats, birds would be considerably less expensive and more people would be in the bird breeding business. Successful breeding requires hard work. There is much to learn, a lot of time required and many obstacles to overcome before successes begin to outweigh the failures. It should be thought of as a labor of love.

Before jumping in and spending a lot of money, first take the time and learn about birds and how to breed them. Most importantly, remember that simply placing a "boy" and "girl" bird together will *not* mean they will produce offspring. The more knowledge a breeder has about the breeding requirements of the particular birds, the more likely chicks will be produced. It is recommended that you learn from successful bird breeders and join local and national bird organizations.

Two excellent books to include in a library for those interested in bird breeding are Rosemary Low's *Parrots, Their Care and Breeding—Revised and Enlarged Edition* (Blandford Press, 1986) and Tony Silva's *Psittaculture—The Breeding, Rearing & Management of Parrots* (Silvio Mattacchione & Co., 1991).

There are many factors to consider before beginning a breeding program. The following discussion is only a short overview of some of the more important elements.

Basic **Supplies Needed to Begin a Breeding Program:**

TYPE OF BIRDS	COCKATIELS	AMAZONS
NUMBER OF BIRDS	2 (male and female)	2 (male and female)
SEX DETERMINATION	color variations	no obvious characteristics
CAGING	24″L × 24″H × 18″W	6′L × 3′H × 3′W
ACCESSORIES	nest box, etc	nest box, etc.
INCUBATOR	usually not needed (parents should sit on eggs)	may be needed (parents may or may not sit on eggs)
BROODER	may be needed	may be needed
FOOD	parents and chick(s)	parents and chick(s)
MINIMUM "START-UP" COSTS:	$550 & up	$2,100 & up

Eye appeal	Personality
Popularity of species	Breeding tendencies
Feeding requirements	Housing requirements
Cost of birds	Time and attention required

In addition, there will be recurring monthly expenses. These include food, electricity/gas, repairs, maintenance and possible veterinary bills.

CHOICE OF SPECIES

Finches, budgerigars and cockatiels make excellent choices for the beginning breeder. The reasons for this include:

- They breed readily in captivity.
- The sexes are usually distinguishable by their coloration.
- They have minimal feeding and housing requirements.
- They provide a good "springboard" for larger and more valuable species.
- Most importantly, whether or not bird breeding is enjoyable can be determined *without* investing large sums of money.

Although the larger birds, such as macaws and cockatoos, are more beautiful and are a greater status symbol, they are considerably more difficult to breed. The breeder of these birds must be more experienced and more dedicated to achieve success. There will also be additional expenses.

296

SITE SELECTION AND HOUSING

Some factors to consider:

Neighbors and noise	Weather
Ability to expand	Space availability
Security and safety of birds	Number and species of birds
Hobby versus occupation	Zoning laws
Indoors vs. outdoors	

MANAGEMENT

Regardless of the size of the breeding operation, there will always be plenty of chores. Many of these must be performed daily, so developing a regular routine is essential. Good management of the birds is the only way to ensure success in the future.

Caring for birds is time-consuming. The temptation to buy more birds is always present. However, do not own more birds than can be adequately cared for.

Many of these responsibilities are listed below:

Social Contact: It is important for the birds to get to know their caretaker. Every day, consider offering each bird a treat from the hand. It will reduce their stress and help them to better adjust to their home environment.

Inspection and Observation: Every day, each bird should be looked at and observed for any problems.

Record Keeping: Like any business, good records are essential. Each bird should have its own record, consisting of age, sex, weight, band number, health history, breeding success, number of babies produced, etc. Newborn chicks need a record, too. This will include hatch date, daily weight, parent-fed vs. hand-raised, food requirements, general observations, weaning date, etc. This information is important because it will help determine what's working and what's not, detect problems early and provide useful data to share with other breeders. Good financial records must also be kept for tax purposes.

Feeding and Watering: This daily routine should be done at about the same time each day. Uneaten fruits and vegetables should also be removed at this time.

Environmental Temperature: Be concerned about extreme weather changes. Healthy birds generally adapt well to cold; however, dampness and cold together can cause sickness.

Seasonal Management: In cold climates, outdoor flights should be enclosed; also, consider feeding warm foods and be sure the water does not freeze. Removable, inexpensive plastic polyethylene sheeting can be used to cover the outside walls. During hot weather make sure the birds are protected from the sun and have good ventilation. A sprinkler system for misting the birds could be installed.

Cleaning Cages and Flights: Cages and concrete floors should be cleaned daily. Flights should be cleaned every few days. The entire enclosure should be disinfected periodically. Wooden nest boxes should be replaced after each clutch.

Rodent Control: Rodents can carry disease, eat the food and disturb nesting birds.

Nest Box Inspection: During the breeding season, carefully examine the nest boxes twice daily. Look for eggs and any problems such as cracked eggs or an egg-bound hen. During the rest of the year, check the boxes for rodents and other pests.

Sick Birds: All sick birds *must* be kept isolated from other birds. Treatment should be provided as needed.

Vacations: Birds cannot be left alone for even short periods of time. The ability to just "pack up and go" is seriously limited. A qualified caretaker must be found to care for the birds during any absence, short or long.

APPENDIX C

Environmentally Friendly Bird Keeping

PLANET EARTH NEEDS HELP. Since our birds share space on this planet too, here are some ideas for bird owners to help preserve "mother earth." In the process a healthier environment will be created for both our birds and ourselves.

THE CAGE

- Use newspapers, computer paper or paper bags to line the cage. Besides being inexpensive, they are recyclable.
- Select wooden or leather toys made from materials *not* from the rain forests. Also, these materials should not have been treated with any chemicals.
- Branches from willows, maples and fruit trees make great chew toys or perches. Use only branches that have *not* been chemically treated. Remove the leaves. Wash and air-dry the branches before putting them in the cage.
- If the cage cover has been made from a sheet or other linen, wash it several times before using it. It may have been treated with chemicals.

THE DIET

Organic foods—fruits, vegetables and grains—are chemical free. There are also commercially formulated organic bird diets available. The leftover crumbs and small pieces of uneaten food can be recycled as compost, and seed hulls can be added to mulch.

THE HOME

Since birds have a unique and specialized breathing apparatus, they are particularly sensitive to any type of air pollution. Maintaining good air quality in the home is important. Here are only a few of the many suggestions to consider:

- Use nontoxic cleaning solutions. There are many available, and some can even be formulated at home. For example, lemon juice mixed with mineral oil makes a safe and effective furniture polish.
- Use a plunger to unclog sinks and toilets rather than chemicals. Clean the drains regularly by first pouring baking soda down the pipes and then adding white vinegar. This solution will bubble and foam without toxic fumes being emitted.
- Eliminate the use of aerosols, and substitute pump sprays instead.
- Replace nonstick cookware with plain, stainless-steel pots and pans. The fumes emitted by this cookware when overheated are fatal to birds. Also, all cooking fumes should be exhausted from the home.
- Tobacco smoke can cause serious problems in birds. Smoking in bird-occupied homes is *not* recommended. However, if this is not possible, keep the smoke away from birds. Good ventilation and air filters are suggested.
- When purchasing new carpet, have it "aired out" for a few days before delivery. Birds should still be removed from the area for a few days after installation.
- Indoor plants are an excellent method of reducing air pollution. They help to absorb pollutants while producing oxygen.
- For fresh air, leave a window open in the house for a few minutes each day.

THE YARD

This section is most important for birds kept in outdoor aviaries. However, even fumes from outside can "drift" to the inside of homes. The following are a few of the many alternatives:

- Eliminate the use of chemical pesticides and herbicides whenever possible.
- Attract insect-eating birds to the yard with wild bird seed and bird baths.
- Purchase "beneficial" insects, such as ladybugs, earthworms and praying mantises, to keep the "harmful" pest population down. Check with a local nursery for advice.

- Use old fashioned "sticky" fly paper. It has no chemicals and minimal environmental impact. Just make sure *not* to use use it in an area accessible to birds.
- Electronic "bug zappers" are effective, but do not allow birds to get too close to them. Unfortunately, these will also eliminate beneficial insects.
- Plant petunias and marigolds around the yard. The sticky petunia leaves will entrap gnats and other bothersome insects. Marigolds will repel fleas all summer long without any damage to the environment. These will add beauty to the home at the same time.
- If pesticides must be used, select those containing pyrethrin products. Prior to spraying, remove all animals from the area. Do not allow food or water to be exposed.

In addition to these few suggestions there is a wealth of other information available through many various sources. A good book is *Nontoxic Home*, by Debra Lynn Dadd (J. P. Tarcher), as is *The Inside Story: A Guide to Indoor Air Quality*, published by the U.S. Consumer Product Safety Commission, Washington DC 20207.

APPENDIX D

Bird Organizations and Publications

NATIONAL BIRD ORGANIZATIONS

The American Federation of Aviculture (AFA) promotes and encourages aviculture as a means of conserving bird wildlife through captive breeding. It is involved in the preservation of endangered species of bird wildlife. To assist in these tasks it monitors legislation, sponsors veterinary and public educational seminars and also publishes a bimonthly magazine, *The Watchbird*.

The AFA
Suite 713
3118 W. Thomas Road
Phoenix, AZ 85017
Phone: (602) 484-0931

The Aviculture Society of America (ASA) is concerned with the preservation of birds threatened with extinction. They publish a monthly journal, *The ASA Bulletin*, on the care, feeding and breeding of birds in captivity.

Aviculture Society of America
c/o Joe Krader
24692 Paseo de Toronto
Yorba Linda, CA 92687-5115
Phone: (714) 996-5538

The African Lovebird Society is an international organization concerned with the improvement and standardization of all species of Lovebirds. They publish a bimonthly journal, *Agapornis World*, and an annual roster.

African Lovebird Society
P.O. Box 142
San Marcos, CA 92079-0142
Phone: (619) 727-1486

The American Cockatiel Society is instrumental in establishing show standards for cockatiels. They also publish a bimonthly bulletin on the care, breeding and exhibiting of cockatiels.

American Cockatiel Society
613 Diane Drive
Melbourne, FL 32935
Phone: (407) 254-8319

The International Avicultural Society (IAS) is an international organization beneficial to all aviculturists.

The IAS
102 White Court
Williamsburg, VA 23188

There are also numerous local clubs throughout the United States. For information on these, contact local pet bird stores, avian veterinarians or the club information section of Bird World Magazine and American Cage Bird Magazine.

FOREIGN BIRD ORGANIZATIONS

The Hon. Secretary
The Avicultural Society of
  England
Warren Hill Hulford's Lane
Hartley Wintney
Hants RG27 8AG
England

Australian Aviculture
52 Harris Road
Elliminyt
Victoria 3249
Australia

Australian Birdkeeper
PO 6288
South Tweed Heads
New South Wales 2486
Australia

Parrot Society
108b Fenlake Road
Bedford MK 42 OEU
England

Papageien	Singapore Avicultural Society
Brueckenseldstr. 30	1 Gold Hill Plaza
7518 Bretten	Podium Block 03 43
Germany	Singapore

PUBLICATIONS

Bird Talk is published monthly. It contains informational articles on all aspects of bird keeping from cage care to parrot psychology.

Bird Talk
Subscription Department
P.O. Box 57347
Boulder, CO 80323-7347

Bird World is published bimonthly. Its articles on bird care are usually more scientific in nature.

Bird World
P.O. Box 3098
Salinas, CA 93912

American Cage Bird Magazine is published monthly. This magazine focuses on providing information to breeders on the care, feeding and breeding of parrots, canaries, finches and other cage bird species.

American Cage Bird Magazine
1 Glamore Court
Smithtown, NY 11787

APPENDIX E

Avian Research: The Pet Bird Owner's Role

IN JUST the past decade alone, tremendous advances have been made in the fields of avian nutrition, disease treatment and prevention, behavior, reproduction and conservation. These gains are the result of many years of research by some very dedicated individuals and organizations. Much of the new information contained in this book has resulted directly from research relating to pet birds. Since we receive so much joy from our feathered friends, why not give something back and help them live longer, healthier lives?

There are many dedicated, hard-working people doing the best they can on minimal research grants. Contributing to research can be a great source of personal satisfaction knowing you have helped make a difference.

There are a number of ways contributions can be made. These include writing a check, and budgeting a regular contribution. For breeders, consider donating a portion of sales. For bird clubs, consider setting up a donation program as part of the by-laws. In addition, as a tribute to a beloved pet, make a donation in its name or memory.

Excellent research programs are now under way in several universities across the country as well as through several national bird organizations. A list of universities may be available from bird clubs and periodically appear in bird magazines. For information on the research currently in progress and for donation inquiries, the university should be helpful and can be contacted directly.

Two national organizations, the Association of Avian Veterinarians and the American Federation of Aviculture, have set up programs to receive and distribute monies to various research groups.

The Association of Avian Veterinarians' Research Fund's stated goal is to fund research projects directly related to diseases of pet birds. They also support bird conservation projects and provide scholarships for veterinary students with special interests in avian medicine.

Make checks payable to: AAV Research Fund
c/o AAV
P.O. Box 811720
Boca Raton, FL 33481

The stated goal of the American Federation of Aviculture Research Program is to fund research projects directly related to breeding birds.

Make checks payable to: AFA Research Program
P.O. Box 56218
Phoenix, AZ 85079-6218
Phone: (800) BIRD CALL

The stated goal of the American Federation of Aviculture Conservation Fund is to promote conservation of avian species. This includes propagation of endangered avian species and other avian conservation related projects.

Make checks payable to: AFA Conservation Fund
P.O. Box 56218
Phoenix, AZ 85079-6218
Phone: (800) BIRD CALL

The International Avian Research Foundation is a private, nonprofit foundation organized to fund research in areas related to avian health.

Make checks payable to: IARF
P.O. Box 532
Athens, GA 30601

APPENDIX F

Weights and Measures

METRIC CONVERSION TABLE

Abbreviations

oz. = ounce	tbs. = tablespoon	cc. = cubic centimeter
lb. = pound	qt. = quart	ml. = milliliter
fl. = fluid	g. = gram	L. = liter/litre
tsp. = teaspoon	kg. = kilogram	

Volume

---

1 cc. = 1 ml.	1 tsp. = 5 cc.
1000 cc. = 1 L.	3 tsps. = 1 tbs. = 15 cc. = ½ oz.
8 fl. oz. = 1 cup	2 tbs. = 30 cc. = 1 oz.
4 cups = 1 qt.	1 qt. = 946 cc. = 0.946 L.
4 qt. = 1 gal.	1 gal. = 3785 cc. = 3.785 L.

Weight

---

16 oz. = 1 lb.	1 kg. = 2.2 lb.	1 lb. = 454 g.
1000 g. = 1 kg.	1 oz. = 28 g.	

Bibliography

The following references are listed by category as a helpful guide for additional reading.

Bird Anatomy and Physiology

Harrison, Greg J., D.V.M., and Harrison, Linda R., B.S. *Clinical Avian Medicine and Surgery Including Aviculture*, Philadelphia: W. B. Saunders, 1986.

King, A.S., and McLelland, J., *Birds Their Structure and Function*. 2nd. ed. London: Bailiere Tindall, 1984

McDonald, Scott E., D.V.M. "Anatomical and Physiological Characteristics of Birds and How They Differ From Mammals," *Proceedings AAV—Basic Avian Symposium*, 1990, pp 372–89.

Bird Diseases

Axelson, R. Dean, D.V.M. "Avian Dermatology," *Dermatology for the Small Animal Practitioner*. Veterinary Learning Systems Co., Inc., 1991, pp 183–204.

Burr, Elisha W., ed. *Companion Bird Medicine*. Ames: Iowa State University Press, 1987

Doane, Bonnie Munro, *The Parrot in Health and Illness: An Owner's Guide*, New York: Howell Book House, 1991.

Gaskin, Jack M., D.V.M., Ph.D. "Psittacine Viral Diseases: A Perspective," *Bird World*, Sept./Oct. 1990, pp. 34–44.

Harrison, Greg J., D.V.M., and Harrison, Linda R., B.S. *Clinical Avian Medicine and Surgery Including Aviculture*, Philadelphia: W. B. Saunders Company, 1986.

Johnson-Delaney, Cathy, D.V.M. "Feather Picking: Diagnosis and Treatment," *Journal of the Association of Avian Veterinarians*, 1992, vol.6, no. 2, pp 82–83.

Bibliography

Oglesbee, Barbara L., D.V.M., "Hypothyroidism in a Scarlet Macaw," *Journal of the American Veterinary Medical Association*, Nov. 15, 1992, vol. 201, no. 10, pp 1599–1601.

Phalen, David N., D.V.M., Wilson, Van G., Ph.D., and Graham, David L., D.V.M., Ph.D. "Avian Polyomavirus Infection and Disease: A Complex Phenomenon," *Proceedings of the Annual Conference of the Association of Avian Veterinarians, 1992*, pp. 5–10.

Ritchie, Branson W., D.V.M., Latimer, Kenneth S., D.V.M., Ph.D., and Campagnoli, Raymond, M.S. "A Polyomavirus Overview and Evaluation of an Experimental Polyomavirus Vaccine," *Proceedings of the Annual Conference of the Association of Avian Veterinarians, 1992*, pp. 1–4.

Ritchie, Branson W., D.V.M., M.S.; Niagro, Frank D., Ph.D.; Lukert, Phil D., D.V.M., Ph.D.; et al. "A Review of Psittacine Beak and Feather Disease: Characteristics of the PBFD Virus," *Journal of the Association of Avian Veterinarians*, 1989, vol. 3, no. 3, pp 143–48.

Bird Emergencies

Association of Northwest Avian Veterinarians. *Avian Emergency Care: A Manual for Emergency Clinics*. 2nd ed. Lynnwood, Wash: 1991. Multiple authors.

Doane, Bonnie Munro. *The Parrot in Health and Illness: An Owner's Guide*. New York: Howell Book House, 1991.

Harrison, Greg, D.V.M., and Harrison, Linda R., B.S., *Clinical Avian Medicine and Surgery Including Aviculture*. Philadelphia: W. B. Saunders, 1986.

Joyner, Kim L., D.V.M. "Avian Reproductive Emergency," *Veterinary Medicine Report*, Summer 1990, vol. 2, no. 3, pp. 246–49.

Martin, Howard D., D.V.M. "Avian Reproductive Emergency," *Veterinary Medicine Report*, Summer 1990, vol. 2, no. 3, pp. 250–53.

Ritchie, Branson W., D.V.M., M.S. "Emergency Care of Avian Patients," *Veterinary Medicine Report*, Summer 1990, vol. 2, no. 3, pp. 230–44.

Sakas, Peter S., D.V.M. "Safe at Home," *Bird Talk*, Apr. 1991, pp. 39–45

Speer, Brian L., D.V.M. "Lead Poisoning," *Bird Talk*, Dec. 1990, pp. 39–44.

Bird Home Physicals

Association of Avian Veterinarians. "IME 551—Polydipsia, Polyuria and Diarrhea in Birds: A Diagnostic Approach (Abstracted from 1985 A.A.H.A. Annual Meeting)," *Association of Avian Veterinarians Newsletter*, spring 1985, vol. 6, no. 1, pp. 223–25.

Rich, Gregory A., D.V.M., B.S.M.T. "Basic History Taking and the Avian Physical Examination," *Veterinary Clinics of North America: Small Animal Practice Pet Avian Medicine*. Philadelphia: W. B. Saunders, Nov. 1991, vol. 21, no. 6, pp. 1135–45.

Smith, Jeanne. "Use of Droppings for Diagnosis," *Exotic Bird Report*, Avian Sciences, UC Davis, summer 1991, pp. 4–5.

Nutrition

Roudybush, Tom "Nutrition" and "Nutritional Disease." In Rosskopf, W. J., and Woerpel, R. W., eds., *Diseases of Cage and Aviary Birds*. Philadelphia: Lea & Febiger, in press.

Worell, Amy B., D.V.M., "Iron Content in Diets for Softbills," personal communication, West Hills, California.

Bereavement

Anderson, Moira K. *Coping with Sorrow on the Loss of Your Pet*. Peregrine Press, 1987.

Brown, Judith Gwyn. *Companion Animal Loss and Pet Owner Grief*. ALPO Pet Center, ALPO Pet Foods, 1986.

Kübler-Ross, Elisabeth. *On Death and Dying*. New York. Macmillan Publishing Co, 1969.

Lemieux, Christina M. *Coping with the Loss of a Pet: A Gentle Guide for All Who Love a Pet*. Wallace R. Clark, 1988.

Nieburg, Herbert A., and Fischer, Arlene. *Pet Loss: A Thoughtful Guide for Adults and Children*. New York: Harper & Row, 1982.

Quachenbush, Jamie, and Graveline, Denise. *When Your Pet Dies: How to Cope With Your Feelings*. New York: Simon & Schuster, 1985.

Sife, Wallace, Ph.D. *The Loss of a Pet*. New York: Howell Book House, 1993.

Bereavement for Children

Rogers, Fred. *When a Pet Dies*. Family Communications, Inc., 1988.

Viorst, Judith. *The Tenth Good Thing About Barney*. New York: Macmillan Publishing Co., 1971.

Wilhelm, Hans. *I'll Always Love You*. Hans Wilhelm, Inc., 1985.

Miscellaneous

Burek, Deborah M., ed. *Encyclopedia of Associations*. 27th ed. Detroit, London: Gale Research Inc., 1993.

Dorland's Illustrated Medical Dictionary, 21st ed. Philadelphia: W. B. Saunders, 1968.

Forster, Susan. "The Environmentally Correct Birdkeeper," *Bird Talk,* Apr. 1991, pp. 86–91.

———. "Environmentally Sound Birdkeeping," *Bird Talk,* Apr. 1992, pp. 17–22.

Orosz, Susan E., Ph.D., D.V.M.; Ensley, Philip K., D.V.M.; Haynes, Carol J., M.S. *Avian Surgical Anatomy Thoracic and Pelvic Limbs,* Philadelphia: W. B. Saunders, 1992

Schroeder, Dick. "Softbill Diets," personal communication, Fallbrook, Calif.

Parrot Training

Athan, Pattie-Sue, *Guide to a Well-Behaved Parrot*. Hauppauge, N.Y.: Barron's, no date.

Warshaw, Jennifer. *The Parrot Training Handbook*. Fremont, Calif.: Parrot Press, no date.

General Index